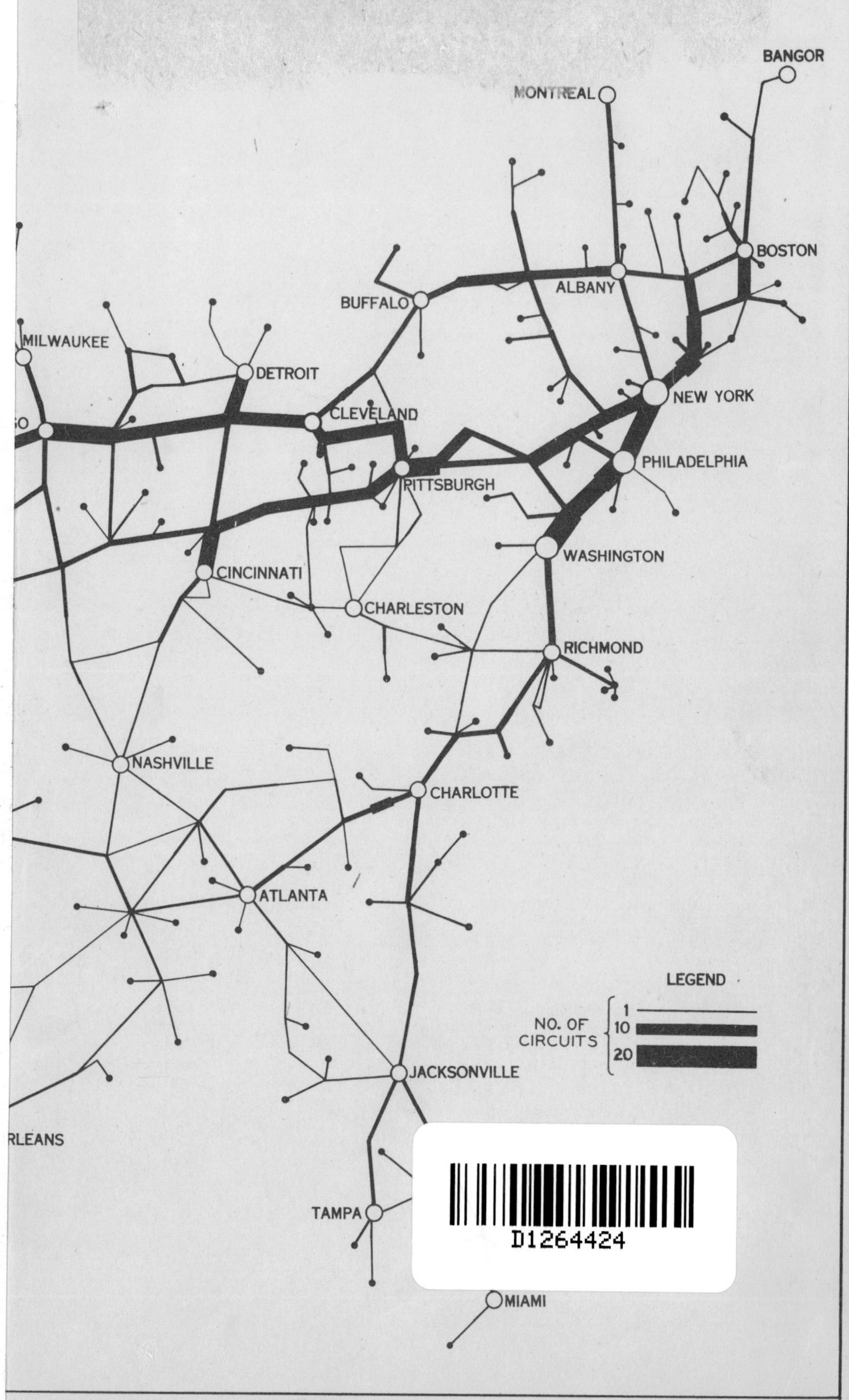
BANGOR
MONTREAL
BOSTON
ALBANY
BUFFALO
MILWAUKEE
DETROIT
NEW YORK
CLEVELAND
PHILADELPHIA
PITTSBURGH
WASHINGTON
CINCINNATI
CHARLESTON
RICHMOND
NASHVILLE
CHARLOTTE
ATLANTA
LEGEND
NO. OF CIRCUITS
1
10
20
JACKSONVILLE
TAMPA
MIAMI

PUBLICATION

OF

THE BUSINESS HISTORICAL SOCIETY

LONDON : GEOFFREY CUMBERLEGE
OXFORD UNIVERSITY PRESS

The cover sheet of a song published in 1877, "The Wondrous Telephone," Balmer & Weber, publishers, St. Louis.

COMMERCIAL BROADCASTING PIONEER

THE WEAF EXPERIMENT

1922–1926

by WILLIAM PECK BANNING

FORMERLY ASSISTANT VICE-PRESIDENT

AMERICAN TELEPHONE AND TELEGRAPH COMPANY

1946

HARVARD UNIVERSITY PRESS

CAMBRIDGE · MASSACHUSETTS

PRINTED IN THE UNITED STATES OF AMERICA

BUSINESS HISTORICAL SOCIETY

INCORPORATED 1925
BAKER LIBRARY, SOLDIERS FIELD
BOSTON 63, MASSACHUSETTS

The Business Historical Society, Inc., was organized by a group of business men and scholars who realized that a determined effort should be made, in the best interests of both private business and the general public, to promote the study of business enterprise from an historical point of view.

The purposes of the Society are to discover and preserve the original records of business operations of the past years; to place these data in suitable depositories; to supply such facilities and information as may be necessary for the study of the history of business; and to encourage the publication of the results of research.

CONTENTS

CHAPTER IV—THE "TOLL BROADCASTING" IDEA

PART II. THE BIRTH OF WEAF, 1922

CHAPTER V—THE ESTABLISHMENT OF WBAY

CHAPTER VI—WBAY BECOMES WEAF

CHAPTER VII—PROGRAM EXPERIMENTS AT WALKER STREET

PART IV. MILESTONES ALONG THE WAY, 1924

CHAPTER XIII—EARLY EPISODES OF 1924

CHAPTER XIV—RESOLVING THE PATENT SITUATION

CHAPTER XV—NETWORK BROADCASTING MADE PRACTICAL

CHAPTER XVI—THE ARMY TESTS THE BELL SYSTEM

PART V. THE TRAIL IS BLAZED, 1925-1926

CHAPTER XVII—NETWORK EXPANSION

CHAPTER XVIII—ANOTHER DEFENSE TEST DAY

CHAPTER XIX—THE SALE OF WEAF

ILLUSTRATIONS

All illustrations have been supplied by the American Telephone and Telegraph Company.

TABLES AND CHARTS

TABLES

CHARTS

EDITORIAL INTRODUCTION

THE RADIO INDUSTRY has become a giant both economically and culturally. From the standpoint of public acceptance, it began only in 1920; but into the brief stretch of years which have followed have been packed many developments of first-rate importance and many contributions by companies and individuals that we must remember, if we are to know whence we have come and whither we are going.

When the early history of the radio in America is fully written, the work of many concerns will be recorded, notably Westinghouse, General Electric, the Radio Corporation of America, and the American Telephone and Telegraph Company. It is to the little-known work of the last-named company that this book is devoted.

It early appeared to the executives in the American Telephone and Telegraph Company that there were good prospects of providing telephone subscribers and users with fresh services, for example, radio telephony across the ocean, from ship to shore, and to and from moving vehicles. This interest was primarily in private conversation that flowed both ways.

The broadcasting of programs was a one-way performance. Although radio broadcasting was thus different from telephony, the American Telephone and Telegraph Company kept on with its experimental work during the period 1922-26. Apart from providing the interconnecting channels for network broadcasting, it made at least three contributions. It greatly added to technical knowledge and experience in radio. It experimented with programs that would appeal to and serve the public. It learned how these programs could be financed. How nearly unique the contributions of the American Company were is not for us to say.

From the standpoint of business one of the great challenges of radio broadcasting was how to pay for the service rendered. There were at least three principal methods of doing this. One was to license the users of radio sets. This method has been adopted abroad, notably in Britain, where the licensed user pays a tax to the government and the government provides the financial support for the programs, recently far beyond the yield of the tax. The second method was to have the manufacturers of radio sets finance the programs so that people would buy and use their sets. No one knows just how well this would have succeeded. The third method was to have advertisers pay for time on the air and thus finance programs without direct cost to the listening audience. This commercial broadcasting, the American way, is the chief of several contributions of the American Telephone and Telegraph Company, according to the thesis of this book. To the reader it seems logical that toll broadcasting should be a contribution of the company and the industry which was already using that method in its own business—charging for the time used. Perhaps we owe this contribution to President Walter S. Gifford more than to any other one official of the Company.

Apparently it was in 1942 that President Gifford conceived the idea of having recorded the story of what the American Telephone and Telegraph Company had done for radio, centering the story particularly in the station WEAF, which once belonged to the American Company and in which the experiments were carried out. The history was to be written "for the Library;" that is, it was to be made part of the record of the American Company and deposited in the Company's historical museum. Mr. Banning, who was chosen to do the writing, has stated that he prepared the manuscript "for the information of Bell System personnel."

It was to be expected that Mr. Arthur W. Page, Vice-president in Charge of Public Relations, would see the value of such a piece of work for the public. On reading the manuscript he became convinced that the public would be interested and referred it to this committee for an opinion of its historical merit.

The American Telephone and Telegraph Company is proud of its many services to the public and apparently sees in the story of WEAF just one more example of its contribution to the American scene. It does not alter the situation that the radio is now one of the best customers of the American Company through the use of telephone wires to connect radio stations: much or most service in life is probably rooted in intelligent self-interest. The important facts are that the intelligent efforts of the American Company were successful and that they were of public service.

The American Company felt that Mr. Banning was the best man in its organization to write the history of WEAF during its experimental years because he was an interested and observant contemporary of the events, because he could consult those who were directly concerned, and because he had access to the Company's records. The American Company has been anxious to hold aloof from the actual authorship of the book. Indeed, in no way can this book be regarded as an official history. Nevertheless, the American Company has facilitated the publication of the book by meeting the costs of editorial preparation and by purchasing a substantial number of copies primarily for distribution among the employees, many of whom participated in the experiments recorded. Thus, the outsider is inclined to see an undertaking which was originally designed for internal consumption come to be used also to further public relations. Such a combination comes close to the highest form of current business policy.

The author of this book was born in 1880 in New York City. In 1902 he was graduated from New York University. After 18 years of experience in editorial and newspaper work and in the advertising departments of two large business concerns, he entered the employ of the American Telephone and Telegraph Company. In 1920 he was publicity assistant, in 1922 assistant publicity manager, in 1924 publicity manager, and from 1927 to his retirement in 1944 assistant vice-president in the field of public relations.

When we were permitted to read Mr. Banning's manuscript, we at once saw that the story was important, that it was interestingly written, and that the treatment was an honest effort to unfold the truth. While an insider is likely to be over-enthusiastic about the facts, an outsider is likely to be ignorant of the facts. Perhaps the ideal would be joint authorship combining the insider's first-hand knowledge and the outsider's critical detachment.

Publication by the Business Historical Society does not involve a guarantee of facts or generalizations. The Society is happy to present to the public an opportunity to read a story written by an insider to commemorate the work of his company and the accomplishments of his fellow-employees. It happens that the events herein described are of obvious importance to modern business and to society as a whole. It is also true that the mode of presentation and the rich documentation help the reader to appraise the record.

At times we have thought of suggesting to the author that the complimentary passages and fine enthusiasms be eliminated because they might be objectionable to realistic readers. Then, in passage after passage, we realized that the author was expressing true feeling and that this feeling has been and is a germinating and dynamic force in the whole Bell System. Moreover, it is of great importance to business history to have examples of employee attitudes in large corporations. Since the book was written for inside use rather than for public consumption, indeed, the expression of enthusiasms, mutually shared by other employees and participants, becomes a vital part of the flavor of the book and of the essence of the record.

Furthermore, for the future of business it is very promising that a large company should sponsor the publication of a record of the work done by the human beings in it. It has long been a fiction that a business concern is one and indivisible; that the company does everything and the employees nothing notable. Here is evidence that employees planned, worked, sacrificed themselves, and attained success.

The fear that we are advertising a business must be banished. In developing the subject of business history we must make facts known, and the facts have to do with firms and companies; this promises to be the almost exclusive task till we have a large body of information, when we can begin to write about whole industries. And then, some day in the not too distant future, we may safely generalize about business history as a whole. In the process of building up a fund of information, we shall be furthering the cause of the public relations of business, than which there is no more important social problem in our time. To participate in the breaking down of anonymity and secrecy, ignorance and misrepresentation, would be the good fortune of any individual or institution, unless it is to be assumed that we must live in the past where the dead are so comfortably buried.

* * *

The Business Historical Society has continued to enjoy the hospitality and assistance of the Harvard Graduate School of Business Administration. Within the framework of the School the Society is able to encourage research in business history. Its own special contribution lies more particularly in the publication of the results of research and in the distribution of the articles and books published. The Society welcomes this opportunity of coöperation with both the School and the American Telephone and Telegraph Company in the publication of the present volume.

In preparing the manuscript for the press, after the author's retirement from the Company, there came the tasks of verifying quotations, obtaining releases for reprinting extracts from newspapers and magazines, and checking printer's proofs. In these and similar matters we have had the efficient assistance of the author's former official staff. At the Harvard School of Business Miss Josepha M. Perry has made many suggestions for which the Committee is grateful. Mrs. Elsie H. Bishop, Assistant Executive Secretary of the Business Historical Society, has been responsible for those many final editorial jobs so thankless but so important; she has also compiled the index.

N. S. B. Gras

14 March, 1946 For the Committee on Program and Publication
Business Historical Society, Inc.

AUTHOR'S PREFACE

THE FOLLOWING PAGES, prepared for the information of Bell System personnel, constitute the first record to be compiled to trace the genesis and development of an almost forgotten experimental undertaking—the establishment and operation by the American Telephone and Telegraph Company of Station WEAF, in New York City, for a test of "toll broadcasting."

Bell System experimentation, as generally understood, relates to scientific or technological exploration, and details of its progress are usually sought in the records of accomplishments of engineers and laboratory workers. Such records, of course, disclose the research and development effort that brought about radio telephony itself, just as they reveal the birth and development of other transmission systems, the evolution of complex communications instrumentalities, the improvement of apparatus and equipment in thousands of categories.

The progress and the result of the WEAF experiment are not to be traced from technical data alone, however. The exploration involved far more than the technique of broadcasting or the functional efficiency of broadcasting apparatus and connecting wire lines. It was primarily a social and economic experiment, undertaken to find an answer to a question of vital concern to America because of broadcasting's sudden emergence upon the communications scene—the question of radio's economic development as a public communications service. The laboratory for the investigation was society, and the history of the venture is therefore to be gleaned from the record of society's adjustment to it.

The company's conception of the radio telephone, in the form of broadcasting, as an instrumentality for public use, was born in a period of acute "growing pains" for the newcomer in the communications field, and was fathered by an obligation of ownership—an obligation to protect institutional accomplishments in the development of the communications art and an obligation to ensure their application for the common good.

Some of these accomplishments were represented by patent rights relating to broadcasting equipment for which there was a persistent and mounting demand on the part of many wishing to utilize the radio approach to a public excited over the novelty of this approach. Such a demand could have been satisfied by the manufacture and sale of the equipment being sought, but obviously an unrestricted sale of broadcasting equipment soon would have resulted in so many stations, competing for attention on the same wave length or on a comparatively few wave lengths, that their usefulness to their owners could not possibly be commensurate with the expense of purchase and operation.

Another obligation of ownership, engendering an effort to give stability and direction to broadcasting developments, was inherent in the exclusive possession of a wire network. A third institutional resource was the availability of a personnel with unusual knowledge and skill in radio telephone techniques that had been gained through the experimentation of years. And motivating the command of such resources was the business philosophy which had brought about the growth of telephone service as a public utility, to wit, that the cost of transmitting a communication should be borne by the one originating the communication.

Thus the impulsion to bring economic stability, if possible, to an unorganized and inchoate communications development was compounded of many elements. It crystallized in the idea of exploring broadcasting's service potential by making broadcasting facilities *available to anyone desiring to employ them to talk to the public.* The facilities provided to test this idea, at a time when the transmitting end of broadcasting was the exclusive privilege of station owners and hence was employed only in their own immediate interest, were those of station WEAF, America's first broadcasting "pay station."

Like the company's pioneer transcontinental line, the pioneer facilities of WEAF were to be in commercial demand more and more as the fields of business, entertainment, education, and politics recognized and adjusted themselves to the new medium, and as the listening public reacted to their use of it. It was this action and reaction that progressively revealed the direction in which broadcasting should move in order to become a useful and stable institution in the American scheme of living.

The experiment, as it expanded, took the telephone institution far afield from its normal responsibility, exposing the company to misunderstanding and criticism, to jealousy and attack. It not only involved a substantial financial risk but it inevitably generated situations of unpleasantness, and even danger, for an enterprise that required harmonious public relations as a foundation for its service and its growth.

The experiment was continued, nevertheless, until its animating idea had been proved. Its pioneering was historic. When it was over, and station WEAF passed to new ownership, public hospitality to broadcasts of every type had been tested, network broadcasting had been established, and the economic basis upon which nationwide broadcasting now rests had been founded. A trail had been blazed that thereafter could be followed without hesitation. A self-imposed service of investigation had answered the question, "Quo vadis, radio?"

Thus can be summarized the broadcasting operations that were begun in 1922, that were concluded in 1926, and that are registered in broad outline in the following pages. What the reader will find is a factual continuity based on documents obtained from many separate files, on current publications, on the recollections of early WEAF personnel, and on the writer's own personal memories.

The record was begun a few months before the author's retirement from the American Telephone and Telegraph Company and completed shortly afterward. The selection of material has been arbitrary, and his comment unsupervised and unrestricted. The purpose has not been to prepare a formal history. The endeavor rather has been to link together reports and episodes so as to afford a backward look at the conditions under which the challenge of a social need was met by a social-minded organization. The result, it is hoped, will refresh the memories of veterans in that organization and will serve to introduce new members to an unfamiliar chapter in Bell System history.

In the preparation of this record the secretarial assistance of Mrs. M. E. Roe has been invaluable. Grateful acknowledgment is also extended to associates at Bell System headquarters, in its Long Lines organization, and in the Bell Telephone Laboratories for their coöperation. Because of this coöperation the task of compilation has been a most congenial one with which to conclude a quarter-century of Bell System service.

W. P. B.

New York, April 15, 1945

A CONDENSED WEAF CHRONOLOGY

1922		
March		Antenna construction is begun on roof of Long Lines building, 24 Walker St., New York.
July	25	First program (recorded music) broadcast from WBAY.
August	3	First evening program from WBAY.
	15	Long Lines organization is canvassed for entertainment talent.
	16	WBAY becomes WEAF.
	24	WEAF program has its first instrumental soloist: Nathan Glantz, saxophonist.
	28	WEAF's first "commercial" broadcast.
October	2	WEAF becomes Class B station, with the following schedule: 4:30- 5:30 P.M. Daily except Sunday 8:10-10:00 " Mon., Wed., Thurs., Sat. Sunday programs as desired.
	28	The first football game broadcast: Princeton *vs.* University of Chicago, at Stagg Field, Chicago; long-distance lines used for broadcast from WEAF.
November	1	A. T. & T. Co.'s Radio Broadcasting Department established.
	5	WEAF's first Sunday program: Beth Israel Hospital.
	11	Broadcast of the opera "Aïda" from the Kingsbridge, N. Y., Armory: WEAF's first "remote-control" broadcast.
	19	WEAF's first Capitol Theatre broadcasts: the overture by the Capitol Grand Orchestra at 2:30 P.M. and 7:30 P.M.
	22	The first broadcast of New York's Philharmonic Orchestra.
	26	The first organ-recital broadcast: Organist Samuel Baldwin, at the College of the City of New York; first recital in a series of six.
December	5	WEAF's broadcasting schedule enlarged by adding 30 minutes daily (except Sunday) from 7:30 to 8:00 P.M.
1923		
January	4	The first simultaneous broadcasting from two stations: WEAF in New York and WNAC in Boston.
February	4	First combined stage and studio broadcast from the Capitol Theatre, New York.

February 11 WEAF's first regular Sunday program featuring Dr. Newell Dwight Hillis in WEAF's studio, the Men's Conference of the Bedford Branch, Brooklyn YMCA, and Capitol Theatre stage and studio broadcasts.

24 First of series of broadcasts from Gimbel Brothers' department store "Radio Show."

25 First program from the Skinner Organ Studio.

28 WEAF's broadcasting schedule further extended by adding "11:00 A.M. to 2:00 P.M. as needed."

March 3 Broadcast of Seventh Annual Inter-Collegiate Glee Club Contest from Carnegie Hall, New York.

April 2 Lord Robert Cecil broadcasts from WEAF's studios.

4 Broadcast of concert by Oratorio Society of New York, from Carnegie Hall, New York.

10 Broadcasting begins from WEAF's new studios at 195 Broadway, New York.

11 WEAF broadcasts the musical show "Wildflower" from stage of Casino Theatre.

18 WEAF's first broadcast of a debate: subject: The Volstead Act.

30 WEAF's studios at 195 Broadway formally dedicated.

May 6 First studio broadcast of Inter-denominational services under the direction of Dr. W. B. Miller, Secretary, New York Federation of Churches.

15 WEAF's first broadcast on wave length of 492 meters.

June 1 Broadcast from Pennsylvania Hotel, New York, of banquet tendered to British visitors, by the Associated Advertising Clubs of the World.

7 Long-distance lines used, following weeks of testing, for broadcasting of program from Carnegie Hall, New York, of National Electric Light Association, through four major stations: WEAF, KDKA, KYW, WGY.

21 Long-distance lines used for first Presidential broadcast: President Harding's St. Louis, Mo., speech on the World Court.

July 1 Long-distance lines used for beginning of three months' WEAF program service to WMAF, South Dartmouth, Mass.

4 A. T. & T. Co.'s second experimental station, WCAP, in Washington, D. C., opened with a program transmitted from WEAF over long-distance lines.

12 First broadcast of heavyweight championship prize fight: Willard *vs.* Firpo.

August 5 Broadcast from Calvary Baptist Church, Washington, D. C., of memorial services for President Harding.

31 Broadcast of Wilson-Greb prize fight from the Polo Grounds, New York.

October 10-15 Broadcasts from New York's Yankee Stadium and Polo Grounds of World Series Baseball Games.

14 First program transmitted from WEAF over long-distance lines to WJAR, Providence, R. I.

November 2 Broadcast of ceremonies in connection with an address by David Lloyd George.

10 Address by ex-President Woodrow Wilson broadcast from three stations: WEAF, New York; WCAP, Washington; WJAR, Providence.

12 First broadcast of a series of ten Philharmonic concerts from Carnegie Hall, New York; conductor, Van Hoogstraten.

28 First broadcast from St. Paul's Chapel, Columbia University, New York.

December 6 Long-distance lines used to broadcast President Coolidge's message to Congress from six stations: WCAP, Washington; WEAF, New York; WJAR, Providence; KSD, St. Louis; WFFA, Dallas; WDAF, Kansas City.

10 Harding memorial address by President Coolidge from the White House broadcast from WEAF, New York; WCAP, Washington; WJAR, Providence.

31 WEAF's first experimental broadcast with 5-KW transmitter.

1924

February 6 Funeral ceremonies for ex-President Woodrow Wilson broadcast from WEAF, New York, and WJAR, Providence.

8 First broadcast involving transcontinental telephone circuits and also the first to include a Havana station: demonstration of the telephone art for the Bond Men's Club in Chicago.

April 22 Broadcast of President Coolidge's address to the Associated Press at the Waldorf-Astoria Hotel, New York, from 11 stations, involving the use of 7,000 miles of long-distance circuits: WEAF, New York; WNAC, Boston; WJAR, Providence; WCAP, Washington; WFI, Philadelphia; WCAE, Pittsburgh; WWJ, Detroit; WMAQ, Chicago; KSD, St. Louis; WDAF, Kansas City; WBAP, Fort Worth.

May 19 First concert of dinner music from the Hotel Waldorf-Astoria, New York.

21 Broadcast of National Electric Light Association meeting from Atlantic City, N. J., by WEAF, New York; WJAR, Providence; WCAP, Washington; WGY, Schenectady; KDKA, Pittsburgh; KYW, Chicago; a broadcast remembered because of special repeater installation on long lines to ensure satisfactory transmission of music by Paul Whiteman's orchestra and two violin solos by Zimbalist.

June 10-12 Activities of Republican National Convention at Cleveland,

		Ohio, transmitted by long-distance lines to 12 cities for broadcasting.
June 24-July 9		Activities of Democratic National Convention in New York City, transmitted by long-distance lines to 12 cities for broadcasting.
August	11	Notification program for Democratic Presidential candidate John W. Davis, broadcast from WEAF and 12 other stations.
	14	Notification ceremonies for Republican Presidential candidate, Calvin Coolidge, broadcast from Washington over 14 stations.
September	12	Defense Test Day Program, broadcast from WEAF and 17 other stations employing 19,000 miles of long-distance circuits. President Coolidge's address in DAR Continental Memorial Hall, Washington, D. C., accepting Republican Presidential nomination, broadcast from WEAF and 13 other stations.
October	4-10	World Series baseball games in American League Park, Washington, and Polo Grounds, New York, broadcast by 8 stations.
	14	Network service started on the "Red Network" from WEAF to WJAR, Providence; WEEI, Boston; WGR, Buffalo; WCAP, Washington; WCAE, Pittsburgh.
	23	President Coolidge's address at the dedication of the U. S. Chamber of Commerce building in Washington, broadcast by WEAF and 19 other stations; the first time that Los Angeles, Portland, and Seattle were connected by long-distance lines for broadcasting.
1925		
January	1	First of series of broadcasts by "Victor Artists."
	31	Broadcasting service furnished from the United States to Canada for the first time by the addition of CNRO, Ottawa, to the Red Network.
March	4	Broadcast of inaugural ceremonies for President Coolidge from WEAF and 20 other stations.
July	4	The first major nationwide network broadcast; Defense Test Day, broadcast from 28 stations utilizing 70,000 miles of wire.
1926		
May	11	Announcement of WEAF's incorporation as the Broadcasting Company of America.
July	7	Radio Corporation of America receives option to buy Broadcasting Company of America in conclusion of negotiations with A. T. & T. Co.
September	1	Red Network service from WEAF to WFI, Philadelphia, and WCAP, Washington, put on permanent basis for 16 hours' daily service.
	13	Announcement of formation of the National Broadcasting Company.

October	13	WTIC, Hartford; WTAG, Worcester; WJAR, Providence; WEEI, Boston; added to Red Network on permanent basis.
	29	Radio Corporation of America conveys to National Broadcasting Company its right to the purchase of WEAF.
November	1	Sale of WEAF to NBC formally consummated.
December	15	National Broadcasting Company's "christening;" Red Network broadcast from 19 stations.
1927		
January	1	Service on permanent basis is begun for National Broadcasting Company's initial "Blue Network" connecting WJZ, Bound Brook; WBZ, Springfield; and WBZA, Boston; with temporary service to Pittsburgh and Chicago.

PART I

THE GENESIS OF BROADCASTING

1915-1921

CHAPTER I

EARLY BELL SYSTEM EXPERIMENTATION

The Beginning of the Record

THE first problem of the writer who attempts to trace the beginnings of broadcasting in the United States is to select a starting point for his narrative. If he wants to register the time when the idea of distributing entertainment and news was first associated with electric communication, he must, to be consistent, start with the birth of telephony itself. The so-called "speaking" telephone was, in fact, born from earlier experiments in the transmission of musical tones, and the entertainment idea is distinguishable in Alexander Graham Bell's early demonstrations of it. An interesting handbill of 1877 invites the citizens of Lawrence, Massachusetts, to an exhibition of his "wonderful and miraculous discovery," and promises that "vocal and instrumental music and conversation will be transmitted a distance of 27 miles and be received by the audience in the City Hall."

Another contemporary reference to the telephone's utility for purposes of entertainment is in a song published only a few months after Bell's invention and called "The Wondrous Telephone." On the cover of this musical tribute are sketches picturing groups listening to lectures and concerts carried by wires to homes and auditoriums. "You stay at home and listen," is the assurance of the composer, "to the lecture in the hall, or hear the strains of music from a fashionable ball!" Such conceptions, however, are not intended to be prophetic of chain broadcasting or public-address systems, for "The Wondrous Telephone" was published as "a humorous song," and its final verse was evidently considered by its author as a climax of comicality:

> There surely is no knowing what things may happen soon,
> We may perhaps be talking with the old man in the moon!
> And everybody's secrets then to us will all be known;
> The whole world be united through this Wondrous Telephone.

For a while, according to the cartoons of the day, there was humor in the mere thought of distributing entertainment telephonically, since the notion was deemed to be an extravagantly absurd one. Quite naturally it was the technical press that first began to consider such a result seriously. It is historically interesting that an electrical periodical observed in 1890, when commenting on an exhibit of the long-distance aspect of telephony at New York's Lenox Lyceum, "It seems strange, indeed, that up to the present time, the telephone companies have not done more towards exploiting a field which could certainly be made a source of considerable revenue by the furnishing of musical and other entertainments by wire at the fireside."[1]

When this opinion was expressed there was, of course, little or no appreciation of the fact that the telephone technique of the time was not physically capable of delivering the volume and the frequency range that were required if listeners were to be impressed with something more than the novelty of entertainment originating at and transmitted from a distant point.

Critical comment on the limitations of this technique cannot be expected in the accounts of demonstrations that were currently being given by the American Telephone and Telegraph Company in order to arouse popular interest in its service. The company itself, founded for long-distance service, was only five years old in 1890, and only fourteen years had elapsed since the Emperor Dom Pedro II had exclaimed in wonderment, "It talks!" when Bell's crude instrument was shown to him at Philadelphia's Centennial Exposition.

[1] *Electrical Engineer*, vol. ix, no. 103 (Apr. 23, 1890), p. 258, in an editorial on "Possibilities of the Telephone."

One such report, appearing in September, 1890,[2] merits partial quotation at the outset of this review because of its historical details. Referring to "really notable musical and vocal entertainment" that was "given from New York to a very large audience assembled at the Grand Union Hotel, Saratoga," the description runs in part as follows:

. . . . As our readers will conjecture, the audience, which numbered at times no less than 800 people, was brought *en rapport* with the performers by means of a "Long Distance" telephone circuit running a distance of 180 miles from 18 Cortlandt street, New York, to Saratoga. From Cortlandt street a circuit had been run to the Madison Square Garden and the concert being given by the Strauss Orchestra was taken in alternation with the other numbers of the programme which comprised selections by the Long Distance orchestra, flute and cornet solos, a whistling song and glees by members of the technical staff, one of whom also recited Tennyson's "Charge of the Light Brigade." The orchestral music was listened to at Saratoga by means of sets of hand telephones, and every note was heard distinctly, even to the applause of the audience gathered at Madison Square. Some of the songs and solos and the recitation were heard all over the room at Saratoga by means of a single loud speaking receiver provided with a large funnel-shaped resonator to magnify the sound. Great delight was expressed by the audience at Saratoga with the evening's entertainment, and the exhibition was considered one of the best and most successful that has yet been given over the Long Distance Company's system.

The account further tells how a telephone official caused a circuit between his home in New Jersey and the Cortlandt Street exchange to be connected with the circuit running to Madison Square Garden, with the result that "the strains of the famous orchestra were heard so plainly . . . that dancing was carried on with perfect ease and comfort by the guests there assembled. . . . We believe this is the first instance recorded of the transmission of music by telephone with sufficient volume and clearness for dancing to be indulged in by the listeners."

Thus it can be said that in 1890 there were "entertainments by wire" of a sort. As a matter of fact, the idea was tried in some

[2] *Ibid.*, vol. x, no. 123 (Sept. 10, 1890), p. 269, in an editorial headed "Dancing to Music from Afar Off,"

European capitals where wire distributing systems were in actual operation. Their transmission limitations were admitted, however, before the turn of the century. "Music by telephone," reports the *Electrical Review*,[3] in a 1901 article that describes the distribution of news to some 6,000 subscribers by Budapest's *Telefon-Hirmondo* (telephonic news teller) ". . . still leaves something to be desired. The telephone timbre must be got rid of before music can be transmitted satisfactorily."

Vacuum-Tube Radio Telephony

The American story of transmitting entertainment to be enjoyed "at the fireside," which was the *Electrical Engineer's* vision in 1890, properly begins with the development of de Forest's audion into a reliable and serviceable amplifier for telephony, dating from 1913. An account of this development in the telephone laboratories would therefore be a fitting introduction to the record of WEAF's pioneer broadcasting activities which these pages will present, yet a long technical preface seems superfluous for a review of an experimental venture that was preponderantly social and economic in character.[4] This record will therefore start from the time when the vacuum amplifier had been made a practical instrumentality, when transcontinental telephony thereby became an accomplished fact, and when Bell System engineers felt certain that, from the scientific point of view, there were no longer insurmountable technical obstacles in reaching their goal of universal telephone service in the United States.

There remained, however, the challenge of extending this service over bodies of water, and the telephone technicians believed that, in their tube development, they had the agency with which the technique for this might be obtained. Since their activities to this end had historic consequences with respect to broadcasting they must be

[3] Vol. xxxviii, no. 17 (Apr. 27, 1901), p. 516.

[4] The reader interested in technical details is referred to the indexes to the publications of the American Institute of Electrical Engineers and the Institute of Radio Engineers, to the *Physical Review* and to the *Bell System Technical Journal,* which list a host of articles by Carty, Jewett, Arnold, Colpitts, Carson, Vanderbijl, Campbell, Espenschied, Nichols, Martin, Fletcher, Nelson, Blackwell, Wilson, Heising, Bown, Mills, and other Bell System scientists who played notable parts in the transmission developments upon which both the wire and wireless arts are based. See also *Radio's 100 Men of Science,* by Orrin E. Dunlap, Jr. (N. Y., 1944).

Amagansett, N.Y.
Apl. 21 /15.

Montauk Wireless Co.

Gentlemen:-

We have a little amateur Wireless Telegraph Station here, and on Monday evening we heard rather indestinctly, conversation and whistling and perhaps a cornet. We are quite curious to know if it could come from Montauk. Would you kindly tell me in the enclosed envelope if it is probable that it might have come from your wireless telephone Co. at Montauk. Thanking you for your courtesy in advance,

I am Yours truly Nathaniel Leek

A letter from an amateur experimenter, April 21, 1915, the envelope being addressed to Wireless Telephone Experimental Station, Montauk, L. I. It may be the first evidence of an amateur experimenter's picking up vacuum-tube radio telephone transmission.

High-vacuum tubes at Arlington, Virginia, 1915. Some of the 500 tubes used in the first transmission of the human voice across the Atlantic.

briefly traced here, in order to provide some background for this WEAF story.

Experiments with the radio telephone were begun in real earnest by Bell System investigators in 1915, after the original transcontinental line had been demonstrated in dramatic ways and had then been dedicated to public service. In order to take vacuum-tube radio telephony out of the laboratory for a field trial, a vacuum-tube transmitter of a few watts' output was developed and installed at Montauk Point, Long Island, and was tested with a laboratory-designed amplifying receiver located some 200 miles away.[5]

The experimenters were then granted the use of the large antenna of the Naval Station at Arlington, Virginia, and a new vacuum-tube radio telephone transmitter was developed and installed, employing hundreds of tubes with a capacity of some 15 watts each. For reception during the tests the Navy Department made available its stations at the Canal Zone, on the Pacific Coast, and in Hawaii. It was speech experimentally transmitted from Arlington in the fall of 1915 that was heard by Bell System engineers stationed at all these distant points, and in the Eiffel Tower at Paris, to signalize the first transoceanic accomplishment of telephony.[6]

Radio activities at this period were both professional and amateur in nature and consisted almost entirely of telegraphic communication. The professional activities related to marine radio telegraphy and to the international radio telegraph service which commercial wireless telegraph companies were beginning to offer.

Activities of Amateur Experimenters

The amateur activities should have more than a passing reference here because they have a direct connection with this review.

[5] See "Pioneering in Radio Telephony," *Bell Telephone Magazine,* vol. xx, no. 1 (Feb., 1941), pp. 21-37.

[6] The engineers stationed at the various points were:

Arlington: R. A. Heising, B. B. Webb, and H. W. Everitt, Western Electric Company
Paris: H. E. Shreeve and A. M. Curtis, Western Electric Company
Honolulu: Lloyd Espenschied, Engineering Dept., American Telephone and Telegraph Company
Darien, Canal Zone: R. H. Wilson, Western Electric Company
Mare Island, Calif.: R. V. L. Hartley and William Wilson, Western Electric Company
San Diego, Calif.: William Wilson, Western Electric Company

The novelty of radio and its initial use as a means of communication between ships, and between ships and the shore, naturally stimulated amateur experimentation among those having an interest in electrical phenomena and an inclination to explore them for personal pleasure and satisfaction. Such experimentation was a hobby that was easy to acquire, for a home station could be built at little cost, and the fascination of operating it grew with every success in detecting the coded telegraph messages being launched on the air waves, and in establishing contacts with other experimenters gripped by the same fascination.

All that was needed to search for signals was a simple apparatus comprising a crystal detector, a condenser, one or two coils of wire, and a telephone receiver. All that was needed to enable the enthusiast to broadcast his own signals was a source of power—usually the home electric-light circuit—and transmitting equipment which in primitive but adequate form could be assembled and made to function without much difficulty.

To guide anyone embarking on such a venture there were suggestions presented in popular scientific publications together with the advice of neighborhood addicts. To equip him with transmitter units, such as transformers to produce high voltage power and coils, condensers, and spark gaps to produce and regulate radio frequencies, there were local dealers in electrical supplies as well as mail-order concerns.

With an antenna erected to conform with his premises and a telegraph key for coding his signal, the amateur experimenter was ready for the practice of radio telegraphy, just as previous generations of amateurs, simply by connecting instruments and batteries to a circuit that was half wire and half ground, had enjoyed the thrill and gained the skill of sending the fundamental code designed by the telegraph's inventor.

And so the beguiling adventure of radio exploration bred amateur practitioners in ever increasing numbers. Because of their mutual interests clubs were formed for the interchange of experiences in building, improving, and operating their home apparatus, for there were at first practically no books dealing with radio transmission. The increasing number of such clubs naturally led to a national organization, which was called the American Radio Relay League (1915), and then to the appearance of one of America's first radio publications, *Q S T,* which reported league activities, circulated the news of amateur experience and accomplishments, and served as a medium for the announcements of radio-equipment manufacturers.

So great was the lure of radio that by 1912, when some five hundred commercial ships were equipped with the apparatus required by the Ship Act[7] passed two years earlier, several times that many radio telegraph stations in the United States were being operated under a license granted by the government. Their amateur owners were skilled in radio technique, well informed on new developments, alert and anxious to test and report on improvements and new equipment. That they should embrace with special enthusiasm the opportunity to experiment with radio telephony, when vacuum tubes became available in electrical stores, was the natural result of the amateur spirit when challenged by scientific advance. In the postwar period, when the ranks of beginners were swelled by men made expert and knowing by war training, these radio enthusiasts eagerly listened to and coöperated with the professional radio telephone experimenters, such as those of the Bell System, and thus they constituted, as will be indicated on a later page, the first radio "audience" to the pioneer form of "broadcasting."

Still using the Navy's Arlington antenna for their transmitter, the engineers of the Bell System gave a test for the Navy in 1916 which was probably the first successful unification of radio and wire

[7] This act, passed June 24, 1910, required all vessels leaving ocean or lake ports to be equipped with an efficient apparatus for radio communication capable of transmitting and receiving messages over a distance of at least 100 miles. The Radio Communications Act of August 13, 1912, required all transmitting stations to obtain licenses from the Department of Commerce. The later licensing of broadcasting stations was based on provisions of this act. A few days prior to its passage Congress had vested the Interstate Commerce Commission with authority over "telegraph, telephone and cable companies (whether wire or wireless) engaged in sending messages in interstate or foreign commerce." Its provisions concerning the licensing of transmitting stations were very ambiguous. After the war, court decisions held that the Secretary of Commerce had no discretionary authority to deny a license but that he could allocate wave lengths. Later he set aside 360 meters (later, also, 400) as the wave length for broadcasting, but a multiplicity of applications led to the abandonment of these limitations. Licensing under the Act of 1912 became a mere matter of registration. Chaotic conditions resulted which President Coolidge reported to Congress, and the Radio Act of 1927 was enacted, creating the Federal Radio Commission, which functioned as the radio regulatory body until the Federal Communications Commission was created in 1934.

lines for through two-way telephony. Conversation during this test was carried on by the Secretary of the Navy, at his desk in Washington, and the Commanding Officer of the *S. S. New Hampshire,* which was at sea off the Chesapeake Capes.

This successful experiment accented the possibilities of radio as a means of extending the System's point-to-point service across bodies of water—of linking local telephone systems on islands, for example, with the millions of instruments on the American mainland. It was an encouraging event to scientists and technicians whose institutional objective was "universal service."

War's Impact on Telephone Research

But the entry of the United States into the first World War made it necessary to postpone the complete exploration of this idea. Then, as during World War II,[8] the System's entire scientific resources were called upon for the development and production of new communications instrumentalities for the Nation's government.

Immediately upon the outbreak of World War I the company was asked by the Signal Corps of the Army to study the problem of operating wireless telephone systems between an airplane and the ground and between two airplanes. Similar requests were received from the Navy Department with reference to wireless equipment for hydro-airplanes and for submarine chasers.[9]

It is interesting to note from the record the speed with which the Bell System scientists and engineers, building upon their previous fundamental radio work, accomplished these emergency assignments. It was late in May, 1917, that the Army's Chief Signal Officer

[8] The *Annual Report of the American Telephone and Telegraph Company for 1944* states: "Bell Telephone Laboratories has continued to devote its efforts almost wholly to the needs of the fighting services. It now employs about 8,000 persons and has nearly 500 active military projects. About 55 per cent of its war work has been for the Army, about 35 per cent for the Navy, and about 10 per cent for the Office of Scientific Research and Development. Not only has the Laboratories developed war communication equipment, both wire and radio, but it has also made notable contributions in radar, submarine warfare, rocket design, electrical computers, electronic tube development and in other fields which cannot be divulged at present."

[9] *Radio Communication Theory and Methods,* by John Mills (1917), perhaps the first authoritative book on the vacuum tube, was based on a course of lectures given by Mills and other telephone scientists to Signal Corps personnel.

The beginning of two-way telephony with aircraft, in World War I. Scene at Camp Alfred Vail, Little Silver, N. J. (now known as Fort Monmouth), 1918. Telephone Laboratory Engineers: E. B. Craft, Ralph Bown, Nathan Levison, N. H. Slaughter. Photo by Rosenfeld.

President Wilson directs airplane maneuvers, White House Lawn, 1918. A demonstration of the development of radio telephony in World War I. Photo by U. S. Army Signal Corps.

called a conference to consider the feasibility of radio communication for planes in flight. As a result of the conclusions reached, the telephone laboratories were asked to develop radio telephone apparatus for airplane service. Within six weeks experimental apparatus was ready and tests were carried on at Langley Field, Virginia, from June 20 to July 5. On July 2, speech was successfully transmitted from plane to ground. On July 5, good transmission was obtained from ground to plane. Further tests, using modified apparatus, were made the following month and on August 18, successful two-way transmission was attained between plane and ground. Two days later there was conversation between plane and plane.

In addition to these accomplishments in the realm of radio telephony, there were others in the production of radio telegraph equipment, especially apparatus for the reception and amplification of signals and the development of small portable transmitting and receiving sets for field use. Work on the problem of submarine detection reached large proportions and hundreds of Bell System engineers were engaged in it. Thus it came about that the research groups whose development of the vacuum tube had made possible transcontinental speech by wire, and then transoceanic speech by radio, were mobilized for government development projects. There was at the same time a similar mobilization of the research groups of other industrial organizations, such as the General Electric Company, whose tube developments had improved the practice of radio telegraphy.

The fact to note particularly in connection with this backward look at Bell System broadcasting activities is that, in developing new uses of the tube for the war emergency, patent rights were ignored by the various institutional scientific groups that were called upon for speedy help, uninhibited by patent considerations, in furthering the nation's war effort.

Among the gratifying testimonials to the Bell System war contribution was that of the Secretary of War, Newton D. Baker, who complimented the American Company's President, Theodore N. Vail,[10] on "the splendid spirit of coöperation and helpfulness which

[10] Mr. Vail died on April 16, 1920, and was succeeded by Mr. Harry B. Thayer.

has been evinced during the war by the wonderful engineering organization of the American Telephone and Telegraph Company." Mr. Baker's letter referred particularly to

> the Airplane Radio Telephone Set,[11] which has proved so satisfactory to the Air Service and which has brought about entirely new methods of military use of airplanes. The evolution and development of this and other important apparatus was made possible only because your engineering staff freely furnished the highly technical knowledge and skill necessary in the development, design and manufacture of the sets.

It is pleasant to recall, also, that the services of the entire Bell System during World War I were recognized by the War Department in a Certificate of Merit which was awarded to the American Telephone and Telegraph Company:

> For especially meritorious service in the prompt and patriotic action of its organization and its associated companies, in placing its personnel, equipment and facilities at the disposal of the War Department. Through its hearty co-operation, the Signal Corps of the Army was enabled to organize, with the splendid personnel contributed, sufficient battalions of signal troops to meet the early demands of the emergency. Its loyal support and the technical ability, intelligence and superb qualities of the personnel furnished, aided in a high degree in the phenomenal results obtained by the Signal Corps in the part it performed in the World War. And, for the efficient and satisfactory manner in which it assisted in providing and maintaining the communication service at home, notwithstanding adverse conditions such as had never before existed in the history of our country and the depletion of its technical force for service in the Army.

The System's wartime radio activities had indeed been noteworthy. By diverting research activity to a considerable degree from the development of wire instrumentalities to those related to wireless, and by organizing to acquire new manufacturing techniques, it had been possible to make a substantial contribution in the communications equipment of all branches of the service. Among other things, thousands of radio sets and hundreds of thousands of vacuum tubes had been produced by the System's manufacturing unit, the

[11] This is described in the paper "Radio Telephony," by E. B. Craft and E. H. Colpitts, published in the *Transactions of the American Institute of Electrical Engineers,* vol. xxxviii, part 1 (Jan. to June 24, 1919), pp. 305-343.

Western Electric Company. It was in recognition of highly important contributions to the war effort that the American Company's John J. Carty and Western Electric's Frank B. Jewett were presented, in 1919, with the U. S. Distinguished Service Medal.

The entire telephone organization was proud of these varied scientific and manufacturing accomplishments, just as it was proud of the war service, at home and abroad, of telephone executives, technicians, linemen, installers, and women operators. The demands of World War II on the System's laboratory and production resources, and on its operating personnel, together with the complimentary references to the System's war contributions by officials and commanders, are reminders that the previous generation in the telephone organization had a similar challenge and an outstanding record of accomplishment.[12]

The Bell Telephone Laboratories

With the Bell System's pre-Armistice radio activities now briefly sketched, it is necessary, in order to provide an institutional background for the postwar radio developments, to particularize regarding the headquarters units that were concerned. To make clear the organization structure, these units must be registered to some extent, even though it seems unjustly discriminating to name but a few individuals.

In the Engineering Department of the Western Electric Company were the specialist groups occupied with fundamental scientific research and experimentation, the design and improvement of telephone apparatus and equipment, and the development of communication systems. Because of the size and equipment of the company's laboratories (reorganized in 1924 as Bell Telephone Laboratories, Inc.), and because of the total personnel engaged in research and development, the Bell System had a scientific and experimental organization that could not be matched by any government administration or by any corporation engaged in similar work.

Directing the postwar radio activities of the Western's engineers was Chief Engineer Frank B. Jewett. He had been head of the

[12] For an extended summary of the varied activities of the telephone organization in World War I, see *Circuits of Victory*, by A. Lincoln Lavine (Garden City, N. Y., 1921).

"transmission development" group in the American Company's Engineering Department when he was transferred to the Western's engineering laboratories to accelerate the transcontinental project, and he later returned to the American Company as Vice-president in Charge of Development and Research and also became President of the Bell Telephone Laboratories.[13]

Dr. Jewett's Engineering Department was divided into two main divisions, each headed by an Assistant Chief Engineer. One division was devoted to development and research under Mr. E. H. Colpitts. The other, under Mr. E. B. Craft, was charged with the development of apparatus and the design thereof for production.

Mr. Colpitts had formerly been a member of the American Company's Engineering Staff in Boston and had joined the Western's organization when the headquarters staff moved from Boston to New York in 1907. He functioned under Dr. Jewett as Director of Research, with groups of scientists and experimenters assigned to the many ramifications of the research responsibility. One of these scientists was Dr. H. D. Arnold (famous for having converted de Forest's audion into the high vacuum tube), who later himself became Director of Research.

Mr. Craft had long been associated with the Western's "apparatus-development" responsibility, and during World War I his department had produced the final designs for the radio telephone sets which the company manufactured, as has already been stated, for submarine chasers and for aircraft.

Both divisions headed by these chief lieutenants of the Western's Chief Engineer were concerned with radio matters when, following the war, the usefulness of radio telephony for peacetime purposes could again be studied. The organization charts of the period show some shifting of personnel from time to time, but the main spheres of activity can be registered as follows: (1) a group in the research

[13] Dr. Jewett's eminence in the scientific world was recognized by the award of many scientific and academic honors, including the Edison Medal which was bestowed in 1928, by election to the presidency of the National Academy of Sciences in 1939, and by reëlection in 1943. His distinguished telephone career covered 40 years, and upon his retirement in 1944 the company established in his honor a trust fund permitting five "Frank B. Jewett Fellowships" to be awarded annually, to provide for the continuation of academic research by their holders.

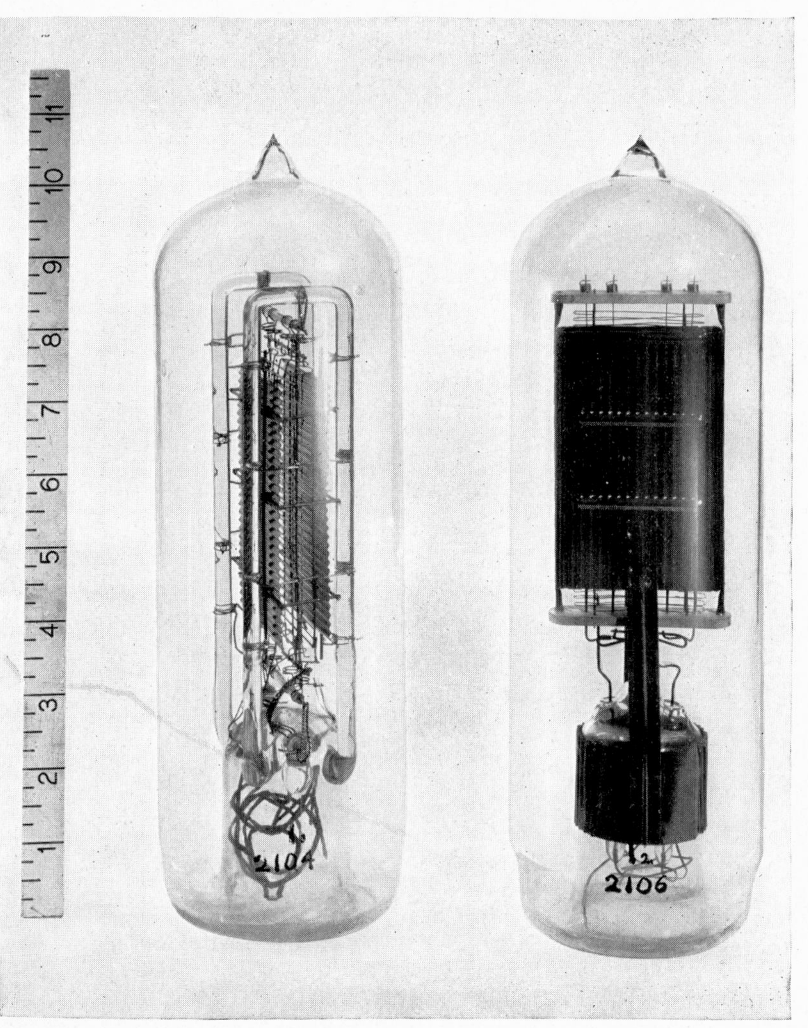

Power tubes (types 11 and 12) developed in 1919; basis of the radio transmitters built by Western Electric for ship-to-shore radio telephone experiments and for broadcasting (1920-1922).

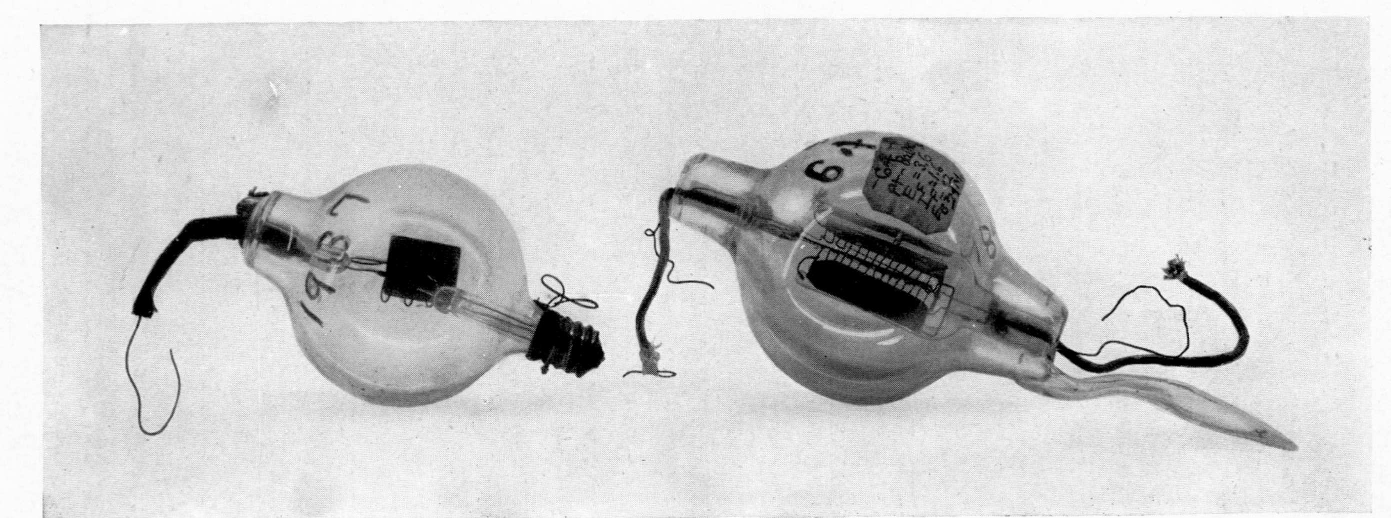

These two tubes, on exhibit in the Bell System Historical Museum at Bell Telephone Laboratories Headquarters, illustrate the transition from the de Forest audion to the Arnold high-vacuum tube. On the left is the audion of 1908. The other tube was actually used in long-distance service in the fall of 1913.

division, headed by Mr. H. W. Nichols, that addressed itself to the more fundamental investigations of radio and its usefulness in extending the System's telephone service; (2) a group in the "Apparatus Development" under Mr. J. J. Lyng, that concerned itself with practical designs for the production of radio apparatus to be sold by the Western to outside users. With respect to radio transmitting equipment, the records show that certain research engineers joined with apparatus-development specialists for the study of problems relating to mechanical and circuit design, and then transferred to the latter group.

Organization at Telephone Headquarters

At the headquarters of the American Telephone and Telegraph Company there was also an Engineering Department that was giving a "general staff" service to Bell regional telephone companies, and to the company's long-distance operating unit known as "Long Lines."

This division had many groups of plant, traffic, commercial, and other specialists who were charged with the responsibility of studying and advising on construction and operating matters. It also had a large staff of scientists and engineers whose broad activity was to survey all developments relating to the communications art, and to analyze the service considerations created by the unfolding of that art through invention and laboratory research.

When postwar telephone growth compelled, in 1920, an expansion and further subdivision of the company's general staff service, the first-mentioned groups became the Department of Operation and Engineering. It was headed by Vice-president Bancroft Gherardi and was known throughout the System as "O&E."

The other groups of the headquarters Engineering Department, namely those engaged at home, and in the field, in studying loading problems, electrical interference, signalling systems, switchboard, cable and sub-station development, telegraph and telephone systems in general, electronics,[14] and a multitude of other matters related to the art and practice of communications, were organized, in 1920, as

[14] See "The Role of Electronics in Telephone Service," by Austin Bailey, *Bell Telephone Magazine*, vol. xxiii, no. 3 (Autumn, 1944), pp. 172-181.

the Department of Development and Research. Its head was General John J. Carty, then returned from his distinguished war service, who had formerly been the company's Chief Engineer.[15] Its usual headquarters designation was "D&R."

The ship-to-shore project was in large part an enterprise of the American Company's Engineering staff, and when D&R was organized, the project was supervised by that department's Transmission Development Engineer, Mr. O. B. Blackwell. Although his subdivision of the D&R responsibility was especially concerned at the time with wire telephony, including the study of multiplex or "carrier" systems, some of its members were specifically assigned to radio investigations.[16] The organization charts of the day show Mr. H. S. Osborne and then Mr. Lloyd Espenschied heading this special radio group.[17] It worked in close relation with the laboratory radio research mentioned above, and thus telephone headquarters was enabled to weigh all technical developments as it considered the usefulness of radio in extending the wire telephone service.[18]

The Tube a Factor in Many Activities

As will be seen from the skeleton outline of the organization just given, there were two broad and continuing activities following the war that were involved in radio progress—the over-all effort to develop radio telephony to supplement the wire service, and the over-all effort to be ready for radio-apparatus sales opportunities if such should develop. Both activities, of course, rested on progress in developing the radio and vacuum-tube arts and consequently were affected by the confused situation as to patent rights that had been unheeded during the war emergency.

In this connection the reader is reminded that the tube's impor-

[15] An extended account of the career of this world-famous figure in the development of telephone service is given in *John J. Carty: An Appreciation,* by Frederick L. Rhodes (privately printed, 1932).

[16] The names of some of this D&R radio group will appear later in this narrative. In 1922 it comprised Engineers Ralph Bown, M. E. Strieby, D. K. Martin, Austin Bailey, C. H. Fetter, G. D. Gillett, and O. A. Long. Mr. Bown is today director of radio and television research of Bell Telephone Laboratories.

[17] See Lloyd Espenschied's "Origin and Development of Radiotelephony," *Proceedings of the Institute of Radio Engineers,* vol. xxv, no. 9 (Sept., 1937), pp. 1101-1123.

[18] When the company's broadcasting experiment was launched later, other D&R subdivisions were of course concerned with the venture.

tance in telephone development projects was not only because of its adaptation for purposes of amplification. In addition to its rôle as an amplifying agent in the functioning, for example, of public-address and "carrier" systems,[19] and other wire applications, it had other vital rôles in the expanding communications art. Radio broadcasting itself relies on the tube's function as an oscillator for generating the high-frequency currents required for radio transmission, and on its function as a modulator, a device for enabling sound wave currents to be imposed on such high-frequency oscillations and thus transmitted to a distance. Telephone research contributed notably to the development of each of these functions and to the technical literature describing them.[20]

These matters are mentioned now in order to suggest the backlog of invention on the part of telephone scientists which existed in the technique surrounding vacuum-tube uses at the time, and to show that when controversies over tube patent rights later developed with manufacturers of radio apparatus, the telephone management had to be mindful of its service responsibilities, as well as of its opportunities for manufacturing and marketing equipment.

Bell System Experimental Radio Stations

To further the development of radio apparatus, the Engineering Department of the Western Electric Company operated two experimental radio stations, 2XB[21] located at the headquarters building at 463 West Street, New York City, and 2XF[22] at Cliffwood, New Jersey. In order to study the application of radio to the specific prob-

[19] It is interesting to recall, as "carrier" systems during the copper shortage of World War II provided circuits needed for the war emergency, that the Bell System's first commercial installation of multiplex telephony was in 1918, when World War I similarly brought emergency circuit needs.

[20] Mr. Colpitts and Mr. Hartley, of the telephone laboratories, were among the pioneering workers in the use of the tube as an oscillator; Messrs. Colpitts, Vanderbijl, and Heising made important contributions to the art of modulation; the modulating method used in early transoceanic experiments was devised by Mr. Vanderbijl and Mr. Arnold. Mr. Heising's "constant current" method was employed in the Bell System's ship-to-shore experiments, in its broadcasting transmitters, and solved the government's problem of obtaining transmitting sets in World War I. For technical expositions see indexes to *Proceedings of the Institute of Radio Engineers, Journal of the American Institute of Electrical Engineers,* and *Physical Review.*

[21] Licensed on Oct. 28, 1919.

[22] Licensed on Oct. 29, 1920.

lem of extending service to ships at sea, another experimental station, having the call letters 2XJ, was established at Deal Beach, New Jersey, with a companion receiving station situated a few miles away at Elberon.[23]

The ship-to-shore experiments at the Deal Beach site were carried on in the main by Mr. E. L. Nelson and Mr. A. A. Oswald and their staffs. These engineers had to start, as it were, from scratch. While vacuum-tube improvement proceeded at the laboratories, particularly that which resulted in the 50-watt "G" tube (Western Electric 211 type) and the 250-watt "I" tube (Western Electric 212 type), they had their station to build, equip, and connect with land wires, and they had an operating technique to acquire. The 2XJ log book shows that as a part of this program the Deal Beach group undertook transmission tests in the spring of 1920 which involved the broadcasting of speech and music directed toward other engineers and the amateur listeners, just as another group of engineers was doing at the West Street station.

Generating one kilowatt, the Deal Beach station had as high a power in its wave band as any in the area, and its tests were awaited by listeners with great interest. One flattering indication of this interest, and of radio's novelty, was a report reaching the station engineers that at the seaside resort of Asbury Park, N. J., an enterprising gentleman had installed a receiver in a wheelchair which he pushed up and down the boardwalk so that strollers, for a small fee, might listen through headphones to the Deal Beach signals.

The Radio Audience of 1920

Pages of the Deal Beach (2XJ) log book show how amateur experimenters over a wide area were receiving actual entertainment through the Deal Beach tests to stimulate them to communicate with the station.[24] Range tests, for example, for May 8, 1920, began

[23] Later, when measurements disclosed the full value of locating marine stations actually at the water's edge, the sending station for commercial ship-to-shore service was located at Ocean Gate and the receiving station at Forked River.

[24] "Note Book No. 340, 2XJ," in the laboratory files, is a complete log. It is an exceptionally interesting record because its details show the character and scope of the experimentation which founded the transmission technique later so successfully applied both in ship-to-shore telephone service and in broadcasting.

at 11:42 P.M. with a general radio telegraph call to amateurs followed by regular test schedules involving the transmission of both speech and music. The record shows that the telephone engineers on duty at the time, as a pioneering venture, used a "phonograph with magnetic reproducer" for the transmission of music. Another log detail refers to a telegram from a South Carolina amateur reporting the station's signals "very loud and plain."

The record for the following day, May 9, also suggests how the station was functioning at the time. A few minutes after the general call to amateurs at 9.53 P.M. there was a direct call from a ship, KFY, and later the station itself individually called two amateur stations, 8DI and 8DR. In these two direct calls is the evidence of the informality and spirit of camaraderie that prevailed in the ranks of all radio students.

During the war period the amateur enthusiasts had been denied the use of the air by an order issued in April, 1917, by the chief radio inspector of the Department of Commerce. This order directed that "the antennae and all aerial wires be immediately lowered to the ground, and that all radio apparatus both for transmitting and receiving be disconnected from both the antennae and ground circuits and that it otherwise be rendered inoperative both for transmitting and receiving any radio messages or signals and that it so remain until this order is revoked."[25]

It was two years later that the ban on amateur receiving was removed. Restrictions on amateur transmission remained in force until the end of September, 1920. Despite the transmitting restrictions, however, thousands of former amateur experimenters resumed their hobby of building and testing home receiving stations, and the interest of many new enthusiasts was kindled by contacts and experiences with radio during war service.

And so there was a sizable "radio audience" for the test transmissions from 2XJ at Deal Beach and 2XB at the laboratories, an audience that included every walk of life from boys to bank presidents, as well as professional radio operators on many vessels. The keen interest of these listeners in the developing art of radio telephony is

[25] Immediately after the attack on Pearl Harbor, Dec. 7, 1941, similar restrictions were imposed on the operation of amateur radio stations.

evident in the special collection of their letters, preserved in the files of the Bell Telephone laboratories, reporting on radio transmission tests from Station 2XB during March, 1920.

Because these letters so well disclose the current appeal of the novelty of radio, a number of them are quoted below. As the reader notes the enthusiasm of their writers he may be interested in the fact that many of the circuit arrangements employed in the apparatus under test were built into the 500-watt and 100-watt transmitters which were later used for broadcasting. Similar equipment was used for the Catalina Island radio telephone system that is referred to in another section of this book. And the 500-watt transmitter was used by the American Company in inaugurating its broadcasting experiment in 1922 at station WBAY, the predecessor of WEAF.

As a further matter of interest it can be recorded here that the 500-watt transmitters installed for point-to-point communication in Pekin and Tsientsin, China,[26] were of this same fundamental design, as was the first installation in the United States for broadcasting purposes. This was for the Detroit *News* Station WBL (later WWJ), the interest of the newspaper in Western Electric transmitting equipment having been aroused by listening to the experimental transmission from the company's 2XB station.[27]

The 2XB Transmitter Tests

Mr. L. M. Clement,[28] who headed the group of engineers responsible for the electrical design of the China and Catalina equipment—Mr. A. W. Kishpaugh being responsible for circuit design—was in charge of the 2XB tests of 1920 during which the coöperation of listeners was specifically requested. Invitations to participate were given during periods of actual transmission or by personal letters to important experimenters in the radio field. For example, one such

[26] Installed by Mr. F. R. Lack, of the Western Electric Company.

[27] The final design information for both 500- and 100-watt transmitters, in the form in which they were first used for broadcasting, was prepared under the direction of Mr. E. L. Nelson in 1921, the mechanical design being under the supervision of Mr. J. O. Gargan and the electrical design under Mr. A. W. Kishpaugh. The installation of the transmitter in Detroit, that went into service in January, 1922, was under the supervision of Mr. F. M. Ryan, now the American Company's Radio Engineer.

[28] Mr. Clement is now Vice-president of the Crossley Radio Company in charge of engineering.

letter in the files is the following invitation to the head of the Naval Aircraft Radio Laboratory in the District of Columbia:

In connection with some tests we are making on a new experimental model of a medium power radio telephone tube set, we hope to carry on conversation with one of our experimental stations along the coast, according to the attached schedule.

For the present all the transmitting will be done from our New York laboratory on a wave-length of 1200 meters.

The set in question is capable of an output of 500 watts into an antenna of 1500 m.m.f. equivalent capacity and 4 to 10 ohms resistance. The actual antenna current during the preliminary tests has been approximately 14 amperes with an oscillator plate input of 850 watts at 1100 volts, the total filament power consumption for the set being 360 watts.

The antenna being used is of the T flat top type mounted on the roof of our laboratory, which is a steel structure.

We thought that as you have been doing considerable experimental work during the evening on various receiving arrangements you might be interested in listening-in on some of our tests.

If you should find it convenient to listen-in we would greatly appreciate criticisms or suggestions of the signals, or schedule, etc.

Such personal requests, of course, stimulated most helpful coöperation from fellow-investigators, as is shown by the reply received from the chief engineer of a radio laboratory in the Midwest:

I am in receipt of your letter of the 10th and am very much interested in your radio telephone tests. We have made a note of your schedule and will have our operators listen for you and call you back on our 375 meter 2 K.W. spark set with which you should have no difficulty in hearing us as we work many other New York stations with it.

Our call as you may know is 9ZN. We should have no difficulty in hearing you as we have been able to carry on regular communication with Mr. Gowen of the De Forest Company, who has been using considerable less power than you will have. We will advise you immediately after each of these schedules as to results obtained, and will be very glad to receive any further information which you may have on subsequent tests.

It is in the voluntary response of radio amateurs, however, that one senses their spirit and notes the eager interest in the novelty of radio entertainment which was to become the basis of broadcasting's growth. There are scores of communications in the collection to be found in the binder in the Laboratories' file labeled "Case 287," and the temptation to quote from all of them is strong, because they reveal so naïvely every symptom of "radio-itis." Here are a few (with signatures omitted) which 2XB received from coöperative listeners:

Stamford, Conn., March 6, 1920.

Last night, March 5, 1920, at about twenty minutes to twelve and again at twelve I received your wireless telephone signals from the laboratory. I heard your arc set first and then the voice followed. The voice was as clear as a whistle and it seemed as if you were right in my room. I heard you say that if anyone heard you, would they kindly let you know, so I thought maybe you would like to know what distance you were covering.

I also heard you say that you were going to make some more tests on Monday night at ten fifteen, using a wavelength of 1200 meters. I will listen in for you at that time. If it is possible would you please call me. I would like to hear what it would sound like to listen to someone calling me by wireless telephone. I am an amateur operator and at present I have only a large receiving set. Hope to hear you Monday night.

* * * * * *

West Haven, Conn., March 8, 1920.

This is to advise you that I very successfully picked up your wireless phone tests at each of the fifteen minute periods on Friday evening March 5th.

The speech was very clear and pure, it being possible to understand every word, even to those not accustomed to wireless. It was possible to understand every word approximately one foot from the receivers.

The apparatus used at my station consists of the following:

Receiving transformer, 800 meters, primary #22, secondary #30; loader #22 wire; straight audion hookup used; auditron detector; B-battery 30 volts; variable condenser shunt across secondary; 600 ohm phones; aerial thirty feet high, approximately 85 ft. in length, two-wires; water pipe ground.

* * * * * *

Locust Valley, N. Y., March 8, 1920.

I am an amateur experimenting to some extent with wireless, and while listening in this evening at 11:45 P.M. I overheard your conversation. Then you asked that anyone hearing you would write to the Western Electric Co. Room 721 and owing to interference I could not catch your name.

Perhaps this would be of interest to you. I was using a crystal detector (Radiocite), Murdock Loose Coupler, Variable condenser (.0004M) Murdock Phones (3000 ohms).

If this does not concern the party who first opens this letter, I wish they would please pass it on to the party concerned.

I shall be very glad to give any other information desired in regards to the conversation or my set.

* * * * * *

Cattaraungus, N. Y., March 9, 1920.

Last night (March 8) while listening to NSS, I moved my secondary condenser and heard your Wireless Telephone—also heard you send by code. So I am sending Diagram of my set so you can see what I heard you with. My outfit is all of my own make. Coupler—primary 4 inch long 3 in dia. wound with No. 24 Enamel wire. Secondary No. 30 wire, B-battery five No. 703 Flash light. Bulb straight tubular. 54 feet from ground. I used about one half of primary winding Used oscillator so you see for NSS. I was using a sort of false process, but is the only way I have of hearing Arc stations. I am 445 miles from New York City and I heard you as though you were just through the partition; don't know as this will interest you but thought as you were experimenting you might like to know this. If there is anything further I can do let me know and will do so.

* * * * * *

New York City, March 11, 1920.

At the above address, using a most rudimentary wireless set, namely, 2,000 ohm Brandes' phones, 1500 meter loose coupler, silicon detector, and small fixed condenser, I heard your radiophonograms (how does that word sound) with a little bit stronger intensity than an ordinary telephone, but much clearer and plainer, and with no rasping sounds. Your last message, however, the one about 11:40 and 11:45 last night was poor. Voice was not distinct, and there was a loud rasping noise. The second test, about 10:30 last night, I thought the best of all.

When you are making your acknowledgements and thanking people tomorrow night for writing to you, etc., I wonder (since all of my amateur friends will be listening) if you will boost my radio standing in the community by including in your acknowledgements "Mr. ——— of East 42nd St." Don't refuse now; have a heart; remember you were an amateur once, too.

* * * * * *

Bridgeport, Conn., March 11, 1920.

This letter is to let you know that your 'phone tests last night with 2XB were very clearly received at my station. Although this is not "a considerable distance from New York" as your telephone operator stated, I am writing nevertheless. The receiver consisted of a single Roome tube made regenerative by tuning the plate circuit although this did not seem to be necessary in receiving you. Your wave was literally "all over." I should judge your wave length was about 2300 but I could get you easily 300 meters each side of that.

With the exception of the last two sentences, the transmission was far clearer than a land line to New York from here. The last two sentences seemed to come on two waves which were interfering.

Could you notify me when these tests take place and I will try and be on for some more of them. Also where is 2XB?

* * * * * *

Lawrenceville, N. J., March 12, 1920.

On Wednesday night March 10 I heard your experiments being carried on with the wireless telephone from your place in New York. I also heard you ask that anyone hearing the experiments were asked to make a little report to you. I have a little station at my house here with a two wire aerial about 100 feet long and about 45 feet high. I am using Galena, Silicon and Audion. I heard the signals very clearly with the Galena and Silicon. I also used the Audion and could not see much difference in the strength of the signals. The words spoken were so clear and clean cut that there was no mistaking what you were saying. It came in so loud and strong that it was hard for me to believe and have not yet gotten over the wonder of it.

This station is about 60 miles from New York. Lawrenceville is six miles northeast of Trenton, N. J. I should say that the wave length of your station is just a little longer than NAH.

I would appreciate it very much if you would let me know when and what time you are going to make more of these experiments (what day and what time of the day).

* * * * * *

Shelton, Conn., March 13, 1920.

Hello! Hello! Hell——o!, Mr. Plummer. Is that your name? I'm not quite sure. Hello, Mr. Clement. I heard your gentle voice talking last night. The signals came in very loud and clear.

I'm not quite one hundred miles from New York, but I thought I would drop you a line just to let you know that I am still on the job. My mother says that she likes to hear you talk, but she don't like to listen to the buzzer because she can't understand it. I can't get all you say as I am just starting in the wireless game and haven't got old Morse down pat yet.

You said something about wanting to know the kind of set us fellows use. Mine is a cabinet set, made by the Universal people of Elmira, N. Y., a UME3 Tuner and ET-1 Detector.

So you send on a wave length of 1200 meters, do you? I thought that it was high, but it is hard to tell just what wave lengths are used with this set. I'm not able to figure up wave lengths yet. Pardon these mistakes because I am writing this in a hurry.

I don't know anything about wireless telephony so I guess I can't send you in any valuable facts about receiving it. You came in last night loud enough to hear about 3 inches from the ears. The buzzer I could hear with the phones laid upon the desk.

Albany, N. Y., March 13, 1920.

I have been much interested lately in your radio telephone messages, and am glad to inform you, that your voice comes in here *very* clear and distinct. In fact, on last night and last Wednesday night, it was not always necessary to have the receivers to one's ears to hear you. We are located about 7 miles northeast of Albany.

We are getting you on an ultra-audion circuit and a pair of Baldwin "fones," connected to a two wire aerial ½ mile long.

* * * * * *

New Haven, Conn., March 13, 1920.

Although not a hundred miles from N. Y. I must write to tell how I heard your signals last night. I happened to catch a part of the 10:45 period. At 11:15 when I found you were on a longer wave length than I expected, heard every word *Beautifully.*

Monday night we are having a little company to listen to you and if you can acknowledge by a word or two to me, will be more than delighted.

Received you on a tuning coil only 1¼ inch diameter and 3 inches long, 9 taps on primary and 8 on secondary (tunes from 300 to 2500 meters). Used one and an Audiotron 40 volt "Hi Volt" Storage Battery with self-contained rectifier, which I manufacture. These batteries are for sale by the C. D. Tuska Co. of Hartford, Conn. My aerial is mostly under the roof of an ordinary two family house. No. 22 cotton covered wire four strands the length of the house.

I worked with Prof. Fessenden on Roanoke Island and Cape Hatteras in 1901 and 1902, old coherer days; then did nothing more with wireless until about three years ago, since which time I have been more or less associated with Mr. Tuska. All this history just to show you why I am such a bug on wireless.

* * * * * *

South Lyme, Conn., March 16, 1920.

I enjoyed another very pleasant evening listening to your radiophone conversation last night, and I wish to thank Mr. Ward for so kindly informing me (via radiophone) in regard to your schedules.

Signals did not come in quite so clear on the crystal as they did last Friday night, owing to considerable of local QRM and possibly atmospheric conditions, so after the first period I improvised an "A" battery for my Audiotron, from several partly run down dry cells, and while the "A" juice lasted, signals and voice were much louder than on the crystal, in fact louder than a wire phone, but after a few minutes the juice would run down so low that I could not get the bulb up to the oscillating point, and then it was N.G.

I could not hear Schenectady or Washington answer you at all, but thought I did hear Camden, once, very faint. Did you get replies by radio from any of them?

I shall be right on deck Wednesday evening, and will write you again how things come in. It only costs me a stamp and if you don't care to read my chatter, why you probably have a good big waste basket around there somewhere.

I intend to stick out that all night session, Friday night if I can, and in the "wee sma' hours" of the morning I might be tempted to whisper to you by wire phone, so if you are too busy to be bothered with me, just spit it out OM.

* * * * * *

Lakewood, N. J., March 16, 1920.

At 10:15 P.M. on March 15, I was listening to the telephonic messages coming from your laboratory. I listened to all the talking until the end at 12 P.M. I heard you call Mr. Johnson at Schenectady, N. Y. Also reading from newspaper, subject on Democratic and Republican politics. You called Commander Taylor at Washington, requesting him to call you on the land line. You also stated you were using a 500 watt transmitter on 14 to 15 amperes. Mr. Warren read news of Civil warfare in Berlin. Called up Camden and requested an answer. You stated interference was great in your section, but I had absolutely no interference the whole evening. Voice was very clear. Later you called up Mr. Bowman, Mr. Packman, Mr. J. Carter, Mr. Insell of 117 North 16th St., Mr. Lloyd and Mr. C. Stevens. Mr. Ward was speaking. On Wed. you will send part of time on 1700 meters. Hoping you the best of success.

* * * * * *

Boston, Mass., March 17, 1920.

It would perhaps be of interest to you to know that your radiophone was heard last Monday night at my station in Auburndale. I used a single tube regenerative receiver on a two wire antenna 120 feet high and 250 feet long. The observed audibility of the voice signals was between 1100 and 1200. All of the conversations were wonderfully clear and distinct,—the conversation of persons in the room being easily understood.

I put in a long distance call, in the hope of establishing a two-way conversation, but was unable to reach you before everyone had left for the night.

If at any time I can be of service to you by acting as an intercept station, please let me know.

* * * * * *

Brooklyn, N. Y., March 27, 1920.

Conforming to your request of last night on the Wireless Telephone, if anyone of long distance heard you, I cannot resist the temptation, although I was only in Brooklyn, of congratulating you upon your experiment. I enjoyed the music very much, especially "Hindustani." I was somewhat surprised that one of you fellows could not read Italian on that record, but neither can I.

I was listening in on the Wireless of Mr. Hill of the Brooklyn Eastern District Y.M.C.A. who is a cripple, and would appreciate it very much if you would call him out the next time you work after 10 o'clock as you can be assured he will be with you.

Kindly acknowledge this letter and accept the best wishes of a number of the boys here at the "Y" who are very interested in your experiments.

* * * * * *

Passaic, N. J., March 28, 1920.

On Friday last I had the pleasure of listening in on my wireless to your talking and musical experiments; and must say I thoroughly enjoyed it.

The talking was clearer than when heard over the ordinary telephone and the music sounded as though it was in the room. I could hear every word plainly, especially the one of Harry Lauder's. And the jazz pieces made my feet move in rhythm.

I would greatly appreciate your advising me, if possible, when these tests are going to be made and how often; as I would like to listen in, and enclose addressed envelope for your reply.

* * * * * *

To help further in indicating the contemporary interest in the 2XB transmitter tests, here are a few of the letters that the experimenters received from professional radio operators and ships' officers, including one from the captain of the *Mauretania:*

On Board the R-M-S-"Mauretania"
Pier 54, New York—March 23, 1920.

I was very interested indeed listening in to your wireless Telephone Experiments given the evening of Friday the 19th of March.

Mr. Brown (our senior operator) would no doubt tell you how interested we are in the subject having listened in two weeks previously when at Southampton to a similar experiment at Marconi's station at his experimental place in Esser, England, 85 miles away.

Your voice was far more distinct than the ordinary telephone with one receiver; using both receivers it was a "shout."

Best of luck to you and I understand you intend experimenting during the next few nights so hope to hear you at sea.

* * * * * *

S. S. "Hatteras"—New York, March 25, 1920

My object in writing at this time is because on the night of March 19, 1920 (I think that is right) I happened to be tuning my receiver to long wave lengths to see if anybody was working, when I heard 2XB calling 1XB and 9XD so I listened in just to hear what was going on.

I was certainly surprised when the person speaking said, "Hello Mr. Packman. Mr. Clement is here and wants to talk to you." Then a new voice breaks in and says, "Oh, Mr. Packman, we had an awful calamity. I leaned up against the soldering iron and broke a condenser," (or words to that effect). I am sure I appreciated the music very much indeed.

We were off of Sandy Hook at the time and the voices and music were very loud indeed and we also could hear others in the room, there, at the time and also other noises such as persons walking on the floor. I just had a Marconi 106 with Carborundum crystal. I heard the invitation for anyone hearing the phone over 100 miles away to drop a line, but I am taking the liberty of writing you anyway. I am at present on the S. S. Hatteras running between Marseille, Barcelona, Valencia, Gibraltar and New York.

* * * * * *

S. S. "Concord"
Pier 39, New York—March 27, 1920.

Might a stranger be permitted to state how much he enjoyed your Radio Telephone test shortly after four o'clock this morning? We were just passing Stamford, Connecticut, at the time and your signals came in very loud and clear. The music was fine and my shipmates and myself certainly enjoyed every note of it. I am going to be "Johnny-on-the-spot" Sunday evening at 11:30 and hope to be able to hear you then.

* * * * * *

S. S. "Mahopac"
Atlantic Transport Line
Philadelphia—April 3, 1920.

Many thanks for your entertainment by Wireless Telephone of the 3rd of April, 2 A.M.-4:30 A.M.

We were steaming up the Delaware River bound for Philadelphia at the time of reception, our distance being about 80 miles from Philadelphia.

The interference of ships stations prevented us from getting your conversation distinctly, but it was very clear at times.

You were most distinct on 400 meters, but could be heard on 600 meters.

I must say: your entertainment was thoroughly enjoyed by us on board the "S.S. Mahopac."

Let's know when your next programme is taking place. May hear you at sea.

* * * * * *

S. S. "Haverford"
Pier 53, Philadelphia
April 3, 1920

Your wireless phone signals were received very clearly on board S. S. Haverford at 11:35 and 11:45 P.M. New York time on April 2nd. Although not a great distance (only 120 miles S.E.) from New York signals were quite strong even on a crystal receiver and I have no doubt that if a valve was used they would be heard a considerable distance. Your wave was somewhere in the neighborhood of 1000 meters but signals were quite strong enough to be heard on 600.

We sail from Philadelphia to Liverpool on April 10th and if I can be of any service to you by listening in at a stated time each night, I would be pleased to do so and advise you distance signals received, if you would let me know what time you start up.

Best of luck.

* * * * * *

For a final exhibit this recorder has selected the following from far-off Panama:

Colon, Panama, March 9th, 1920.

I am pleased to report your telephone conversation as clear and understandable at Colon. This was on March 8th, 11 P. M. New York City time. Tuning for Key West Press I heard you sending the following:

"Hello *Green Harbor,* Hello, this is 2XB talking, 1,2,3,4,3,2,1. Let me know how this is. Is it clear? Anyone else hearing these signals please let me know. That's all now, good night."

I believe this is a record for your station and I am very pleased to report such.

L.E.D.
(Care Ship Owner's Radio Service,
Honolulu, H.I.)

A Radio Treat for Amateur Listeners

According to the Deal Beach and Elberon log books, the scientific appetite of the amateur audience must have been particularly stimulated by the technical "hors d'oeuvres" on the radio menu for May 24, 1920. These resulted from a demonstration of progress in ship-to-shore telephony which was given by Vice-president Carty of the American Company for Bell operating company officials who were meeting with headquarters officials at Yama Farms, near Ellenville, New York.

With telephone circuits connecting the conference room with the two radio stations, there was throughout the day and evening a unique series of tests of combined wire and wireless telephony. As the members of the conference listened, calls passed by wire and radio between American Company officials and engineers and a ship —"KQO"—as it steamed north along the Atlantic Coast from the neighborhood of Atlantic City to the tip of Long Island. The ship was equipped with special transmitting and receiving apparatus that had been developed in the telephone laboratories and that was being operated by laboratory engineers.

Listening amateurs must indeed have been impressed with the technical developments in radio telephony which were revealed by these conversations passing through the air. And there can be little doubt that such demonstrations, together with the earlier transmissions from the Western Electric stations, served to whet the appetite for radio entertainment which broadcasting, in the following year, would begin to satisfy.

Amateurs who heard the Deal Beach range tests steadily deluged the station with reports of reception and with other evidence of their close attention to and unusual interest in the operations. These reports were most welcome, for the engineers were helped by all technical comment, especially that which would assist their exploration of the phenomenon of fading, about which little was then known. The experimenters remember even today their intense disappointment when they were asked by headquarters to cease the sending of test schedules to the amateurs; programs had been announced, a response from listeners had been invited, and an abundance of valuable data had been expected from near and far.

There was good reason, however, for the headquarters' decision which occasioned this disappointment. An agreement was about to be reached between the American Company and General Electric that was intended to chart broad highways of progress by removing restrictions on the contracting parties from proceeding with developments in their respective fields, and at the same time it appeared that the American Company was not to obtain the right to use some important inventions of others in the amateur field.

For this reason the enthusiastic Deal Beach experimenters were instructed to abandon transmission which was directed specifically toward amateur listeners. Thereafter they concentrated on the ship-to-shore experimentation that soon was distinguished by notable results. During its progress many remarkable technical achievements were recorded, among them the operation in the same room of three radio transmitters working into separate but commonly supported

May 8-1920.

Range Test - amateur stations

ON	OFF	f	I	MOD	SIGS FROM	REMARKS <D.C.>
PM 11:42	11:53	750	13	Tgh	T	Msg 2XB QST amateur stations.
12:00	12:15			Sp Music		Regular schedule. SBR
12:18	12:30			Sp		Regular schedule SBR
1:00	1:15			Sp Music		Regular schedule SBR
1:18	1:30			Sp Music		Regular schedule Test completed.

Engineers:- Oswald, Corson, Knittles, Merriam, DeLong, Bach, Nilson, Bentley

(PM) Oswald, Knittles, Corson, Carpenter Nilson.

Trans. Set:- Arrangements made for range test. V.T. oscillator (1000~) connected to input through key. Phonograph with magnetic reproducer set up and J-tube amplifier constructed. Connections such that no control of amplification is necessary in passing from microphone to either phonograph or buzzer. On grounding filament of amplifier when operating on the antenna, amplification was reduced almost to zero. Necessary to move both phonograph and amplifier into screen cage. There is already evidence that it would be advantageous to more or less completely screen all parts of the trans. set, particularly the speech amplifiers. Under three channel operation, cross talk due to R.F. currents being rectified in the speech circuits may be a serious matter unless all telephone circuits are adequately protected.

Telegram rec'd from H.C. Wheat, Gaffney, S.C. Signals "very loud and plain ... static very heavy"

Approx distance -

Log of an early broadcast of speech and music during tests of 2XJ's transmitting equipment.

103

Demonstration for J.J. Carty & Presidents' Conference.

May 24th, 1920. (See preceding page).

On	Off	f Kilo-Cy.	I	Mod.	Sigs. From	Remarks
10:58	11:16	750.	12.0	Sp.	R & El.	Talk from Ellenville. Carty & Thayer to Mills. KQO 9 miles N.E. Barnegat. 23 miles from Asbury Park at 11:10. Mills & a female voice. Mills & male voice.
PM						
12:33	12:41			"	Ellen.	Crossing N.Y. Bay Should be off Fire Island by 2:00 pm. Hart & Ellen. Mills & Ellen.
12:47	1:55			"	Ellen.	Carty & Mills talking. Espenschied, Boyd, DeVoe, & Mills.
2:34½	2:49			"	N.Y.	Fire Is. at 2 pm. Colpitts talks from W.E. Colpitts says Mills' quality is not good.
3:33	3:53			"	R & N.Y.	Elberon calls KQO. Bowen talks from N.Y. Elb. spoke too loud. Farrington talks to Melrose 8010 ext. 258 Amplification on line boosted at end of talk as ship came into N.Y. a little weak. General conversation between Hart, Farrington, & Bowen.
5:35	5:56	750	12.0	Sp.	N.Y. & El.	N.Y. talks to KQO. Both come in good. KQO 25 mi. E ½ NE of Fire Is. Ellenville — Carty & Espenschied talk to Mills. 5:45 making changes in N.Y. switch board.
6:03	6:18			"	R & NY	Calling KQO from Elberon. N.Y. begins talking to KQO at 6:06. Talk between NY-Elb. & KQO. KQO reads so network can be adjusted for balance. Ship talk does not go out at Foxhurst at 6:10
6:22	6:27			"	R	KQO still talking for balancing network at NY. Due to too much modulation, #4 Mod. Pw. tube blows up, also modulation meter burns out, Mod. condenser breaks down. Two condensers put in, and a new tube at #4.
6:49	7:06			"	R & N.Y.	KQO talks for test. Two way KQO & N.Y. Call again at 6:35 EST
7:38	7:58			"	N.Y. & Ell.	Mills & Bowen talking. KQO between Shinnecock Light & Montauk Light. Read, Mills talk, from Ellenville. All were talking too loud at start and at times later.
8:35	8:43			"	R & N.Y.	Nelson and Hart, Bowen and Mills, talking
9:04	9:30			"	Ellenv.	Mills talks to J.J. Carty, Gerbert, Mrs. Conner, Mr. Seaman, Mrs. Peck. KQO changed to push button during talk as there was some difficulty in reception on the ship. After demonstration returned to duplex. KQO reports noise in their set. Reports making changes in set during talk. Again changed back to push button before signing off.

Engineers: Oswald, Krettles, Corson, DeLong, Merriam, Bentley.

Part of 2XJ's log of a ship-to-shore demonstration of radio telephony as an adjunct to land wires, May 24, 1920.

antennas, so that through a single station three simultaneous conversations could be carried on between different ships and telephone subscribers located anywhere on the wire network.[29]

[29] For an account recording the technical details of the Deal Beach experimentation the reader is referred to "Radio Extension of the Telephone System to Ships at Sea," by H. W. Nichols and Lloyd Espenschied, *Proceedings of the Institute of Radio Engineers,* vol. xi, no. 3 (June, 1923), pp. 193-240.

CHAPTER II

TUBE PATENT LICENSING ARRANGEMENTS

The Government's Request to Patent Owners

As HAS BEEN indicated in Chapter I, vacuum-tube rights were ignored during the war emergency. This meant that if, with the emergency at an end, patent-holders should resume tube developments for their own enterprises, there would be danger of infringement.

The patent situation constituted a threat to communications progress, as was emphasized by the Navy Department in January, 1920, in a letter as follows:

> . . . in connection with the radio patent situation and particularly that phase involving vacuum tubes, the Bureau[1] has consistently held the point of view that all interests will be best served through some agreement between the several holders of pertinent patents whereby the market can be freely supplied with tubes. . . . Now, the situation has become such that it is a public necessity that such arrangements be made without further delay, and this letter may be considered as an appeal for the good of the public, for a remedy to the situation. . . .

An Agreement to Cross-license

Stimulated by this appeal "for the good of the public," an historic agreement dated July 1, 1920, was entered into by the corporations involved, the purpose of which was to remove restrictions of patent ownership by an exchange of licenses. In other agreements the General Electric Company extended its privileges under the agree-

[1] The letter was signed by Mr. A. J. Hepburn, Acting Chief of the Bureau of Steam Engineering.

ment to the Radio Corporation of America,[2] and the American Company similarly extended its privileges to the Western Electric Company. Thus four large corporations became entitled to reciprocal patent rights in one another's patents, each in the field of its principal business activity.

Broadly, the cross-license agreement of 1920 extended to the General Electric Company licenses to use the inventions of the Telephone Company in making and selling radio telegraph equipment, radio telephone broadcasting receiving sets, and amateur radio telephone equipment; and extended to the Telephone Company a license to use the inventions of the General Electric Company in radio telephone equipment (as well as in wire telephone and telegraph equipment) for *public service uses.*

During the so-called "investigation" of the American Telephone and Telegraph Company by the Federal Communications Commission seventeen years later, these cross-licensing arrangements were succinctly explained in a statement prepared for the Commission by a representative of the non-telephone interests:[3]

During the pressure of war when producing apparatus for the United States Governmental services, manufacturers used the patents and inventions of others indiscriminately without remuneration to the owners of patents. Thus, by combining the various patented inventions, new devices were developed and out of these came the first practical radio telephone transmitters satisfactory for wartime purposes. Such terms as the Colpitts oscillator, Hartley circuit, Heising modulation circuit, Meisner circuit, became familiar terms in the radio industry.

Following the termination of the war these various companies found themselves with new devices which none of them could manufacture commercially without the use of one another's patents. The technical and commercial situation was in a hectic state and at a standstill. At this point, the companies whose

[2] R.C.A. was launched in October, 1919, as a subsidiary of General Electric to take over the American interests of the Marconi Company and thus provide American ownership for the facilities involved in international wireless telegraph communication. Through a cross-licensing agreement R.C.A. acquired rights to use and sell all radio equipment which General Electric was licensed to manufacture. Later it became the sales outlet for similar equipment manufactured by Westinghouse. Its gross sales jumped from not quite $1,500,000 in 1921 to over $5,000,000 in 1924.

[3] Statement by Mr. O. B. Hanson, Vice-president and Chief Engineer of the National Broadcasting Company. The first three inventors named by Mr. Hanson were members of the staff of the Western Electric Company's Engineering Laboratory.

patents were involved found it necessary to get together and discuss a method of procedure which would permit the orderly development of these new devices and to make satisfactory patent assignments in accordance with the patent laws.

That the agreement resulted from a spirit of coöperation in meeting the Government's request was made clear in the public announcement by the American Company which was issued on August 23, 1920, after newspapers had begun to inquire as to its significance. Here is the complete statement:

In response to a request from the press the following statement is made by H. B. Thayer, President of the American Telephone and Telegraph Company.

It is believed that the art of Electrical Communication by wire and radio transmission will be advanced, practically and beneficently, by a contract just entered into by the American Telephone and Telegraph Company and the General Electric Company, whereby such patents and scientific developments of both companies, through an exchange of licenses, are made available to each.

In January of this year both companies received letters from the Bureau of Steam Engineering of the U. S. Navy Department referring to the wireless situation and saying, "The Bureau has consistently held the point of view that all interests shall be best served by some agreement between the several holders of pertinent patents, whereby the market can be freely supplied." The letter also urges the necessity of some such arrangement so that ships at sea may get the benefit of the latest devices which would contribute to their safety and the safety of their passengers. The Bureau states further: "In the past the reasons for desiring some arrangement have been largely because of monetary considerations. Now, the situation has become such that it is a public necessity that such arrangement be made without further delay, and this letter may be considered as an appeal, for the good of the public, for a remedy to the situation."

Following this, negotiations were commenced between the two companies, with a view to the exchange of licenses so that the General Electric Company and the Radio Corporation of America, with which it had become interested, would be able to further the development of the art of radio transmission and especially of wireless telegraphy, and the American Telephone and Telegraph Company could employ in its present nation-wide system such radio apparatus as is adaptable to wire transmission and further, could supplement its wire system with wireless extensions where particularly adaptable, as between shore and ships at sea.

Much has been done in radio communication by all parties of interest which can be made fully effective in the public service only by this cooperation of the several companies.

The world-wide wireless system[4] of the Radio Corporation and the universal service of the Bell System are thus brought into a harmonious relation that will facilitate the use by the public of the present wireless telegraph facilities of the Radio Corporation and, as the art advances, will enable the American Telephone and Telegraph Company to extend its telephone service to ships at sea and to foreign countries.

The public interest lies in the fact that by exchange of licenses, as suggested by the Government, the patents of each company will be utilized to greater advantage and the progress of the art of electrical transmission and communication will be accelerated in America as in no other country.

Press Reports of the Agreement

An examination of the newspapers published the following day indicates that the news was considered important; some reporters and headline writers used the inaccurate terms "merger" and "patent pool" in their reports. Readers of the New York *Times,*[5] for example, were given the following introduction to President Thayer's official statement:

WIRELESS DEVICES PUT IN HUGE POOL

Bell Company, General Electric and Radio Corporation to Exchange Licenses
Would Develop Inventions

H. B. Thayer, Announcing Agreement, Foresees
Extensions of Public Phone Service to Ships at Sea

Some of the most important recent inventions, which make possible transcontinental telephoning, wireless telephoning at great distances, the transmission of words of command or public addresses by the loud-speaking telephone and the multiplex use of one wire, are pooled by an arrangement announced yesterday between the American Telephone and Telegraph Company, the General Electric Company and the Radio Corporation of America.

The arrangement was made at the suggestion of the Bureau of Steam Engineering of the United States Navy, which pointed out the commercial ad-

[4] In the American Company's Annual Report for 1920 (p. 17) there was further reference to the Radio Corporation's wireless system: "That corporation at the present time has a number of high-power radio telegraph stations engaged in long-distance radio telegraphy between the United States and foreign countries, and is erecting or providing for the erection of new and most powerful stations for this service in this and in foreign countries, with the end in view of providing to the American public adequate international and worldwide radio telegraph service." It was R.C.A. antennas at Rocky Point, L. I., that telephone engineers later utilized for experiments in transatlantic telephony.

[5] Aug. 24, 1920, p. 18.

vantages of the combined use of these patents and the improved field for invention and development which such an arrangement would create.

The unrestricted use of the various pooled inventions by the three great concerns involved is expected to speed the day of transcontinental and transoceanic conversation by wireless telephone and to make possible the maintenance of telephone systems with simpler plants and at lower costs than is possible today.

Another rather sensational report was that of the New York *Herald:*[6]

PHONE SERVICE TO EUROPE SEEN IN BIG MERGER
RADIO CORPORATION AND BELL SYSTEM AGREE TO LICENSE EXCHANGE, RESULTING IN MUTUAL USE OF PATENTS

U. S. Suggested the Idea
Plan Will Permit Several Conversations Over One Wire at the Same Time

An important contract that will revolutionize telephone and wireless telephone communication has been entered into by the American Telephone and Telegraph Company and the General Electric Company, according to a statement last night by H. B. Thayer, President of the former corporation.

Back of this contract lies the possibility of telephone communication with Europe and with ships at sea, by means of the ordinary desk telephone in the near future, according to radio experts.

The arrangement will also make it possible to conduct several conversations over one telephone wire simultaneously, without interference. It gives to the two concerns the mutual use of all patents and scientific developments made by each through an exchange of licenses.

Recent experiments by both companies have been successful in transmitting several conversations on a single wire simultaneously by employing the different types of vacuum tubes used in wireless telegraphy and telephony. These tubes and other apparatus are now placed at the disposal of the telephone company by the terms of the contract. It will mean that a tremendous sum will be saved annually in the cost of construction and maintenance of telephone wires, as well as increasing the efficiency of long distance and transcontinental telephony communication.

May Talk to Europe Soon

Other experiments have resulted in the development of the apparatus whereby the human voice can be automatically transferred from a land line telephone to a wireless telephone service at a "radio exchange." This has been made possible by the development of the amplifying valves that increase thousands of times the volume of sound from the original voice. Patents held by

[6] New York *Herald,* Aug. 24, 1920, p. 1.

both companies will now be merged. It is by means of such an exchange that it will eventually be possible to communicate with Europe over the ordinary desk telephone.

A similar account was given in the New York *Evening Journal*[7] under an equally arresting headline:

TELEPHONING TO EUROPE NOW BELIEVED NEAR, DUE TO MERGER. PATENTS ARE POOLED FOR LATEST OF WONDERS

Contract of Revolutionary Promise is Signed by Telephone and Radio Corporations Here

Perhaps the most understanding of all the announcements in New York newspapers was that appearing on the editorial page of the *Wall Street Journal*,[8] which is here quoted in full. It is based, as the present writer remembers, on interviews with American Company officials:

AMERICAN TELEPHONE BUYS INTEREST IN RADIO COMPANY EVIDENCE THAT COMPANY'S OFFICIALS SEE A GREAT FUTURE FOR WIRELESS TELEPHONING

Agreement with General Electric to Exchange Licenses, Patents and Scientific Discoveries a Long Step in Development—to Extend the Service to Foreign Countries and to Ships at Sea

American Telephone & Telegraph Co., in order to better carry out purposes of recent agreement with the General Electric Co. to co-operate in advancing the art of radio transmission and communication, has purchased a minority interest in the Radio Corporation of America.[9]

W. S. Gifford, vice-president of the American Tel. & Tel. Co., has been made a director in the Radio Corp. of America.[10]

[7] New York *Evening Journal*, Aug. 24, 1920, p. 3.

[8] *Wall Street Journal*, Aug. 25, 1920, p. 2.

[9] This stock was later sold, the Annual Report for 1922 stating, "The exchange of patent licenses between this and certain other companies, described in the report for 1920, has proved valuable. The cooperation in research and use of facilities which it provided has greatly facilitated our experiments in trans-oceanic wireless telephony. Ownership of stock in the Radio Corporation of America has not, however, proved to be necessary for co-operation. Therefore, in line with our general policy to hold permanently only the stocks and securities directly related to a national telephone service, we have disposed of all stock in the Radio Corporation, ..."

[10] Mr. F. A. Stevenson, Director of American Company's "Long Lines" Department, also served as a director later.

That the Bell System is going to leave no stone unturned in improving telephonic communication and that officials of that company believe in the future of wireless telephony within certain limited lines is emphasized by the agreement made between the company and the General Electric to exchange licenses and patents and scientific developments of both companies.

The late Theodore N. Vail not only believed in the wireless telephone but he Bell System has for years worked upon wireless telephone devices.

It was from the Bell Company's wireless at Arlington, Va., in 1915, that the longest distance through which speech was transmitted by wireless was made to the Hawaiian Islands in the Pacific Ocean. Since that time many new devices have been added.

That the time will soon come when a business man in New York will be able to talk to his representative in London and Paris is entirely likely, in the opinion of wireless experts, and the officials of the Bell Company do not deny that wireless telephony between the two continents may be nearer than many think.

The art is advancing rapidly and naturally the cooperation between the Bell System, the General Electric and the Radio Corporation will advance the art rapidly.

H. B. Thayer in his statement announcing the agreement pointed out that the contract between the companies will facilitate the use by the public of the present wireless telegraph facilities and as the art advances will enable the American Telephone & Telegraph Company to extend its telephone service to ships at sea and foreign countries.

It is interesting to note that the first wireless telephone transmission using the ether waves was accomplished by Alexander Graham Bell in 1882, employing short electromagnetic or light waves.

Of course there are important natural conditions which prevent radiography from usefulness for telephone purposes technically in crowded centers. It has been termed "the universal party line" because of its lack of privacy. Wireless telephone experiments have proved that all messages passing between Cuba and Key West, separated by 200 miles of water, could be heard by passing ships and other stations within hundreds of miles. On the other hand, the wireless telephone is invaluable for bridging desert lands and working from ship to ship.

As it develops, the next great step in communication will be when continent can speak to continent.

To illustrate the reception of the news in communications circles, the editorial comment of the *Telegraph and Telephone Age*[11] should be added to this record:

[11] Sept. 1, 1920, no. 17, p. 471.

Announcement has been made that an agreement has gone into effect between the American Telephone and Telegraph Company and the General Electric Company, for the purpose of advancing the art of radio transmission and communication. The Telephone Company has purchased a minority interest in the Radio Corporation of America, and Mr. W. S. Gifford, vice-president of the former company, has been made a director of the Radio Corporation.

This new development in the Communication world is of large significance. It may come as a surprise to some that the American Telephone and Telegraph Company discerns practical possibilities in radio telephony. The fact of the matter is, as early as the year 1915 the president of the company at that time—the late Theodore N. Vail—issued a formal statement outlining the company's relations with and obligations toward wireless communication, in which it was stated that: "As fast as conditions make it possible, or potential business makes present extensions of prospective value to the system and to the public, either directly or indirectly, the American Telephone and Telegraph Company will extend, enlarge and amplify its system in every way that scientific research and development make possible and social or business demands make desirable. To this end the American Telephone and Telegraph Company will, so soon as the necessary construction and equipment can be assembled, extend the universality of its system by wireless stations at selected points on the coast so located as to enable persons and places not able to be connected in any other way to maintain communication with the world through the Bell system."

The Executives now directing the affairs of the American Telephone and Telegraph Company are to be congratulated upon bringing to fruition at this early date the coordination of effort and of interest which will insure extension and progress of modern methods of long distance communication.

The ably managed Radio Corporation of America gains outstanding advantages in this pooling of resources; much wasteful litigation is, very likely, avoided; duplication of research and engineering effort is minimized, and it would seem that much may be expected in the way of promptly furthering the hook-up of wire and wireless methods of communication, where this is desirable.

Thus, in the summer of 1920, an agreement was reached that promised at the time to bring order and progress out of a confused and deadlocked situation.

Yet in a few months another deadlock was to come with the emergence of a new field of activity, lying between amateur experimentation and commercial communications service as known when the agreement was made—the broadcasting of entertainment and news to the public. This new field, created by broadcasting's phenomenal growth, did not then exist. Its growing commercial importance brought about a long and historic controversy over the agreement's interpretation, challenging both the wisdom and the patience of telephone management in the protection of telephone service and the fruits of telephone research. It was Vice-president Gifford who finally proposed arbitration proceedings in order to settle the dispute without litigation—proceedings which were suddenly upset by a startling legal development which will be referred to later on in these pages.

CHAPTER III

THE STAGE IS SET

Early Radio Supplements to Wires

LET US resume now the review of Bell System accomplishments in developing and applying radio telephony in order to extend the reach of the wire lines. In continuing this effort an experimental station was established near Plymouth, Mass., and telephone engineers stationed there joined with those at Deal Beach in effecting two-way conversations with ships experimentally equipped and sailing between Boston and other coastal ports.

From the experience and technique gained in all of this work there were some exceedingly practical results. One was the first use of radio telephony for public service. This was a radio link which went into service July 16, 1920, between the town of Avalon on Catalina Island in the Pacific Ocean, 30 miles away from the California mainland, and a land station at Long Beach where junction was made with the wires of the Bell System. The transmitters had a carrier output of about 100 watts, and two-way communication was obtained by using two frequencies—638 kc from California to Catalina, and 750 kc in the opposite direction.

This project was engineered by American Company and Western Electric Company engineers for operation by the Southern California Telephone Company, a subsidiary of the Pacific Telephone and Telegraph Company. A cable to carry the traffic from the island to the shore (owing to conditions growing out of the war) could not be manufactured as soon as required. Radio was therefore turned to because it could be made available promptly.

Service was given over this radio link for three years, when it was replaced by a cable which better met telephone needs. The radio circuit was in such demand that two operators at each end were needed to handle the calls between Catalina and the mainland. The project conclusively demonstrated that radio telephone links were eminently practicable and was the forerunner of the Bell System's present radio telephone services which, prior to World War II, reached some seventy countries.

The operation of this radio link stimulated the public interest that followed every radio activity of the time. Initially, there was no means of securing privacy, and conversations between Catalina and the mainland could be picked up by anyone in the vicinity having the necessary receiving equipment. There were reports of reception by ships hundreds of miles distant in the Pacific. Technically minded listeners wrote from many points in the West to report on the transmission efficiency of the two radio stations involved. The intimacy of the talk passing over the circuit became the subject of private gossip and even of public comment. This situation, so distressing to an organization engaged in the business of rendering a private telephone service, had much to do with accelerating the development of the "speech-scrambling" device later employed generally in the Bell System's overseas service and such a device was successfully employed on the Catalina circuit during the later period of its operation.

Late in 1920 there was another interesting demonstration of the technique of using radio to extend the reach of telephones. The occasion was a dinner for the Preliminary International Communications Conference given in New York in December. For the benefit of the members a circuit was set up between a steamship off the Atlantic Coast and Catalina Island in the Pacific. Conversations over this unique circuit, made up of a radio extension at each end of the transcontinental wire system, were clearly heard by the delegates.

Coast-to-Coast Transmission Demonstrations

In recalling this cross-country demonstration that so impressively combined the arts of wire and wireless telephony, it is interesting to note from the record that the American Company called a transmission conference in New York in the fall of 1920, and instituted a transmission school at which engineer representatives of all Bell companies might learn at first hand of new technical developments.

This headquarters service was of particular importance to the Bell System constituent on the West Coast, the Pacific Telephone and Telegraph Company, because of the communication needs of the vast area in which that company was responsible for service. This area extended all the way from the country's northern to its southern border and several hundred miles eastward.

The Pacific Company's network of intercity lines was, of course, extensive because of the rapid growth of Western Coast cities and their distance from one another. Many of these circuits were extremely long, and their usefulness was constantly being affected by progress in the telephone art, such as important improvements through telephone research in telephone repeater equipment and the "carrier" technique.

In other words, the West Coast telephone organization had many engineering problems of the long-distance variety. To meet these a specially trained engineering group was necessary and was carefully developed following the transmission conference of 1920. As a result, the Pacific Company's technical men were well prepared for the engineering teamwork required when its own circuits were combined with those of the American Company for the spectacular coast-to-coast demonstrations that are recorded in later pages of this review.

Prognostications of Broadcast Entertainment

All of this 1920 experimentation was in the well-established groove, marking the institutional effort to develop the radio telephone for use in rendering telephone service specifically.

As this effort was proceeding, however, other imaginations were conceiving other uses. Throughout the year there were reports and discussions which were, in fact, prognostications of radio's coming place in the world of entertainment. One example of this is the *Technical News Bulletin*[1] of the Bureau of Standards in Washington, which tells of the transmission of music by radio: ". . . . The

[1] June 4, 1920, no. 38, p. 18, paragraph 13.

possibilities in this direction are great and very interesting. By this means a concert given in one place may be available to those living at a distance. Experimental concerts are at present being sent out on Friday evening from 8:30 to 11:00 by the Radio Laboratory of the Bureau of Standards, using a wave length of 600 meters."

Similar evidence that the entertainment "possibilities" of radio were envisioned by many is the account given, in the *Scientific American* of May 22, 1920,[2] of an apparatus developed by the Bureau of Standards called the Portaphone. The account is headlined "A Wireless Set for Dance Music or the Day's News," and reads in part:

> The portaphone opens up many new possibilities. For instance, at 8:30 o'clock each evening a central station might send out dance music from its transmitting apparatus and those who cared to dance could set up their portaphones on a table, turn on the current and have the music furnished sufficiently loud to fill a small room. Or in the morning a summary of the day's news might be sent out to be received by a portaphone and digested by a family at breakfast, in which all could participate whether paterfamilias had the paper or not.
>
> Obviously there are a number of other applications of this simple device which serves to reproduce sound from the waves sent through space. A glance at the apparatus shows its simplicity. On the inside of the door of the case is shown a rectangle of wire forming the radio compass, direction coil, or "loops," which takes the place of the usual elevated aerial or antenna. The capacity can be adjusted so as to tune the apparatus to the required wave length. The receiving set makes use of a vacuum tube detector and a two-stage amplifier, all operated by dry cells. The signals are passed on to a special loud-speaking telephone to make the vibrations audible, while the large horn reinforces the sound waves until they completely fill a small room.
>
> The instrument as constructed at present has a range of about 15 miles, or well within the limits of an ordinary city. The impulses sent out can be of such a wave length as not to interfere with commercial wireless. The instrument is not sufficiently sensitive to respond to the ordinary long-distance signals coming from Government or marine or commercial stations. So far the only application of the portaphone has been purely experimental at the Bureau of Standards, but it presents interesting possibilities for more general and utilitarian applications. A similar device with a larger coil has been built there in the Radio Section, which develops sufficient power in connection with a trans-

[2] Vol. cxxii, no. 21, p. 571.

mission source to reproduce music loud enough to fill a very large room suitable for dancing.

Other significant prognostications of broadcast entertainment are to be found in contemporary D&R files. That there was imagination as well as "know-how" in this headquarters department is shown, for example, by the reports and opinions which originated with the group of engineers who were giving special study to developments in broadcasting by wire and wireless and to progress in multiplex telephony or "carrier." The technicians developing and improving transmission systems would naturally give thought to what such systems might distribute if fully utilized.

The memoranda and suggestions passing from this group to department heads and executives through organization channels show a marked sensitiveness to entertainment "possibilities." One suggestion in the files that is dated December 18, 1919, discusses a system of broadcasting comprising carrier transmission over the power-distributing network and remarks:

> By using channels of different frequencies, different classes of aural amusement would be simultaneously transmitted, permitting the subscriber to select at will his own type of amusement merely by pushing the proper button which controls the selective circuit employed . . . . The amusement might come from stored sources, as from phonograph devices, or might be given directly by a speaker, or by a concert.

Another memorandum dated May 7, 1920, refers to "the recent phenomenal expansion of the musical instrument and phonograph industries," and points out how a carrier system on telephone circuits might be used for the distribution of amusement.

There is a third review of conditions, written in July, 1920, that has the imaginative conclusion: "So large seem the opportunities for broadcast transmission of information and amusement, particularly in farming country, that one wonders as to whether radio may not be in this respect another phonograph or movie development."

The researcher in these D&R files notes still another report that is dated a few months later, on "Radio Transmission Engineering of the Broadcasting Program." In this is seen the shadow of coming events, for the author, after pointing out the transmission deficiencies of existing broadcasting stations, proposed development work in this field on the basis that "in any broadcasting enterprise of this company the transmission performance and standards must be the best obtainable."[3]

While the American Company's scientific men were thus studying and reporting on radio's entertainment possibilities, there were occasional rumors, which were quite unfounded scientifically, that radio might develop into a competitor of the telephone. This notion cannot be said to have been prevalent. But it was voiced often enough to indicate a confused state of mind as to radio's usefulness, and this served to alarm some holders of telephone securities.

An example of the publicity contributing to this alarm is a widely printed dispatch from Italy in March, 1920, attributing the following fantastic statement to Marconi, the wireless telegraph pioneer. In the newspaper clipping before the writer[4] the headline reads:

WIRELESS TELEPHONES TO SUPERSEDE PRESENT SYSTEM, MARCONI SAYS

Within this present year vocal communication without wires will begin to replace the cumbrous system of today.

Remarkable economic advantages will follow this, because it will dispense altogether with the cost involved in apparatus and the maintenance of lines. . . .

To stockholders made nervous by such statements the American Company's Annual Report for 1920 gave reassurance by pointing out:[5]

. . . the facilities of the ether for the simultaneous sending of numerous telephone messages are so limited that the ether itself can carry but a small

[3] The first three memoranda referred to are signed by Mr. Espenschied, and the fourth by Mr. Bown, of the special D&R group studying radio. Mr. Espenschied, the leader of this group, was perhaps the first to recognize broadcasting as a promising form of mass communication and to anticipate the company's part in its development.

[4] From the Atlanta (Ga.) *Georgian,* Mar. 4, 1920.

[5] The Secretary of Commerce, at his Radio Conference held in Washington in 1922, made the flat statement, "The use of the radio telephone for communication between single individuals, as in the case of the ordinary telephone, is a perfectly hopeless notion."

part of the enormous volume of the telephone traffic required by the entire world. The right of way, therefore, must be given to ships, to aircraft, to radio compass stations, and to all other radio stations so situated that wires cannot be employed.

The 1920 Report also contained two other references to radio developments. One described the December demonstration of conversations between a ship in the Atlantic and Catalina Island in the Pacific, as an exemplification of radio telephony's "special field," since it was "particularly adapted to use between ship and shore; between ship and ship; between airplanes in flight; between airplanes and ships; and from airplanes to the ground. For such purposes wires cannot be used."

The other reference was to the uses of the radio telephone for broadcasting:

For issuing storm warnings to mariners at sea, for broadcasting weather reports and frost warnings to agriculturalists, and for other similar purposes where it is desired to send information broadcast to be picked up simultaneously by any number of receiving stations, the radio telephone has special fields of future usefulness. For these purposes, and for the purpose of sending out calls for help from a ship or aircraft in distress, the fact that the telephone conversation or message can be heard by all who have proper receiving stations, is a decided advantage.

On the contrary, however, when the telephone message is intended to be received by only one station, this lack of privacy is a defect. . . .

This allusion to broadcasting, written several months after the patent agreement with General Electric, indicates the standpoint from which a service-minded telephone management naturally considered, at first, the newcomer among agencies of communication.

To executives responsible for developing and improving the telephone's point-to-point service, and who were pushing radio-telephone development for its extension, broadcasting *per se* did not meet the traditional Bell System concept of "service" which was point-to-point transmission of a private message. But coming events were to suggest that broadcasting through one-way and non-private telephony had a "service" potential and that the telephone organization had an institutional responsibility in exploring it. These events were those that marked the broadcasting boom which in a few months began to sweep the country like a prairie fire.

The Birth of Broadcasting

Popular acceptance of radio as a means of mass communication developed with amazing speed. What had been for years the beguiling hobby of amateur experimenters, fascinated by the details of technical exploration, began to grip the imagination of a vast non-technical public. For the thousands whose radio interest had a scientific basis there were soon to be millions whose interest was aroused solely by the novelty of a new source of entertainment and information.

Some radio historians have bestowed the title "Father of Broadcasting" upon Dr. Frank Conrad (1874-1941) of the Westinghouse Electric and Manufacturing Company in Pittsburgh, Pennsylvania, whose home experimental station 8XK was the predecessor of Westinghouse's KDKA, which is frequently referred to as the "pioneer broadcasting station of the world."

The paternity phrase just quoted is obviously of the "slogan" variety and therefore can be deemed somewhat exuberant, for no individual in reality "fathered" the fundamental idea of distributing entertainment and information by radio. As a matter of fact Dr. Lee de Forest, inventor of the audion which was the genesis of vacuum-tube radio telephony, was himself perhaps the first successful experimenter in this respect, having actually transmitted music by radio without the audion in 1907, and with the audion some ten years later.

Technically, of course, every active radio transmitter was "broadcasting" from its antenna. When its transmission was the coded language of the telegraph, its audience was naturally limited to those understanding the code. When an amateur station began to experiment with radio telephony, the code limitation ceased to exist. The station's potential audience at once, therefore, became larger, and its actual audience grew with the regularity of the broadcasts and their entertainment appeal. Thus, radio telephone "broadcasting" can be said to involve some station radiation for which there was a broadly distributed and expectant body of listeners.

According to this criterion, the Bell System's postwar experiments, already referred to, constituted "broadcasting," and they certainly were influential in creating an appetite for music and speech launched upon the air waves. On the east coast these experiments involved the use of the Deal Beach station and the two Western Electric experimental stations which have been named. This meant that amateur listeners in the country's most thickly populated area had varied and interesting tests of radio transmission for their antennas to pick up. From the flood of letters from amateur listeners commenting on these activities, and from the history of vacuum-tube development, the historians of the future may conclude that if there was any "father" of broadcasting, perhaps it was the telephone itself.

Or these future historians may decide to give the pioneering honor to the Detroit *News*. This newspaper was operating, in 1920, a low-powered installation of de Forest apparatus, the predecessor of WWJ. It was classified as an amateur station and had a transmitting radius of 20 to 30 miles. From reports by Detroit telephone engineers to D&R, covering radio activities in that city in the early fall of 1920, it is clear that there was "broadcasting" there at the time, according to the criterions of program regularity and popular expectation of entertainment. As for the latter, there were between 200 and 300 radio receivers in the neighborhood to provide a "radio audience." As for the program material, here is the description given by one of the engineers of the Michigan State Telephone Company:

> Several concerts have been given this fall with the above set, received mostly by Detroit amateurs. Some of the lake, ore, and passenger ships have heard the concerts also. Notice of the concert is usually given with the voice, then the title of the piece to be played is followed by a phonographic record played into the transmitter. Between phonographic records, late news items are given out. During the world baseball series the returns were sent out during the games describing the plays. It has been advertised that the coming election returns on November 2nd will be sent out via radio telephony.[6]
>
> The concerts referred to were given in the evening always between the hours of eight and nine. As a matter of interest the writer has heard these concerts very plainly using a crystal detector. When using a vacuum tube it has been possible to hear the music ten feet away from the receiving 'phones. Some of the amateurs in this city have held dances with the music transmitted

[6] Primary election reports had been broadcast in Detroit on the night of Sept. 1, 1920

from the News by using a one or two stage amplifier in conjunction with their rectifying VT tube.[7]

Such evidence of amateur "broadcasting" should not detract, however, from the very prominent part played by Dr. Conrad in what was later termed "organized" broadcasting.[8]

It is part of radio's romantic history that the Pittsburgh area was the scene of marked popular interest in radio when Dr. Conrad, after restrictions on amateur transmission had been lifted in the autumn of 1919, rebuilt and relicensed his home experimental station, and began to transmit music and speech instead of dots and dashes.

Such activity, conducted with special enthusiasm, was a welcome innovation to the other home-station operators in the neighborhood and, as it continued, new radio devotees were created. The electrical stores experienced a demand for crystal detectors, condensers, and other equipment items needed for home-made receiving apparatus. Finally a local department store took notice of the situation and advertised complete receiving sets for sale.

A glimpse of the radio interest in local collegiate circles is afforded by the story of a newspaper headline that is recalled with satisfaction by members of the Carnegie Institute of Technology's Radio Club of 1920.[9] This group of engineering students was working with some Western Electric radio equipment, including an "airplane type" microphone which, at the end of World War I, the institution had received from the Army Signal Corps, for experimental purposes.

Making ingenious use of this equipment in connection with experimental power circuits installed in one of the college buildings,

[7] Editor's note: With regard to the question of broadcasting pioneering, the National Association of Broadcasters in 1945 decided the question in favor of WWJ, saying that KDKA was ten and a half weeks younger.

[8] This term was used by General J. G. Harbord, President of RCA, in an article contributed to a supplement to the *Annals of the American Academy of Political and Social Science,* Mar., 1929.

[9] The member to whom the present writer is indebted for the reminiscence is Mr. Roy Corderman, of the Western Electric Company, who, as a matter of interest in this connection, became in Jan., 1921, KDKA's first regular transmitter operator.

the Radio Club broadcast every Saturday night over its station 8XC[10] the music of a college orchestra—an enterprising venture with "live talent" at a time when even the broadcasting of phonograph records was a novelty. That a group at the rival institution, the University of Pittsburgh, had depended on this music for holding a dance was news, both radio and collegiate, and the account was headed, "Pitt Dances to Tech Music." It can be suspected that a "Tech" reporter contributed both the item and its headline.

The mounting public interest in and around Pittsburgh, it is reported, gave a Westinghouse official the idea of erecting a company station in East Pittsburgh for the purpose of sending evening programs out on the air waves. As discussed later by one of his colleagues, the concept in general was, "If there is sufficient interest to justify a department store in advertising radio sets for sale on an uncertain plan of permanence, . . . there would be a sufficient interest to justify the expense of rendering a regular service—*looking to the sale of sets and the advertising of the Westinghouse Company for our returns.*"[11]

The result was the Westinghouse station KDKA, which inaugurated its venture on November 2, 1920, by broadcasting returns of the Harding-Cox Presidential election.

The event was naturally a local sensation, and national attention was focused on the station, and on the new medium, when KDKA broadcast an address by Secretary of Commerce Herbert Hoover at a Pittsburgh dinner a few weeks later.[12] Radio news was quickly spread by the press and by word-of-mouth report. More and more amateur experimenters adapted their transmitters to the technique of broadcasting music and speech. More and more people, in every part of the country, hurried to obtain apparatus wherewith to search the air waves for whatever words or music might be discovered. The demand grew to boom proportions. The market for manufac-

[10] These call letters indicate that the license was issued prior to Dr. Conrad's 8XK license.

[11] The italics are the present writer's. This statement is from a report printed in the *Proceedings of the Institute of Radio Engineers* for Dec., 1932 (vol. xx, no. 12, p. 1857) and is also quoted in G. L. Archer's *History of Radio* (N. Y., 1938), p. 202.

[12] Wires furnished by the Pittsburgh and Allegheny Telephone Company, a non-Bell operating unit, were used for the pickup.

tured receiving sets became enormous, and as this market increased, the demand for transmitting equipment became equally insistent. Popular enthusiasm for broadcasting in a few brief months created conditions that were entirely unforeseen when the patent agreement of 1920 was negotiated and signed.

CHAPTER IV

THE "TOLL BROADCASTING" IDEA

The A. T. & T. Company's Responsibility

As THE broadcasting boom was getting under way, early in 1921, the Bell System operating units were engrossed in the effort to meet the demand for additional toll and local service that followed the end of the war and the release of telephone properties from wartime government control. There had been a net increase of more than half a million telephones in 1920, the largest number ever added by construction in any one year up to that time—an especially gratifying record because of the prevailing shortages of material and trained personnel—and there were thousands of unfilled service orders.

Long Lines, too, was preparing for another year of unusual traffic growth, and of important construction to provide more long-distance circuits. A notable project was the interconnection of the telephones of the Cuban Telephone Company with those of the United States by means of cables between Cuba and Florida. These were dedicated to service in April, 1921, by President Harding.

Naturally the entire headquarters organization was in high gear, challenged by the forecasted service needs of the future as well as those of the immediate present—needs involving large construction, manufacturing, and financial operations. The functions of the American Company's General Staff in advising and assisting the operating units were being enormously stimulated by the postwar growth. The Development and Research projects under way numbered some 2,500; all were calculated to improve the System's service or make it more economical and were engaging the attention of more than a thousand physicists, chemists, and engineers. The five years to follow were to be marked by the building of two additional transcontinental lines and by an increase of the System's plant investment by more than a billion dollars. System telephones in service were to increase from 8,300,000 to 12,000,000; wire mileage from 25,000,000 to 50,000,000; telephone employees from 231,000 to 300,000; conversations handled daily from 33,000,000 to more than 52,000,000.

It was thus in a period of intense telephone activity that broadcasting developments arose to command attention and to create additional responsibilities for the executives at Bell System headquarters. Radio in general, which for so long had been the technical interest of D&R and Western Electric experts, was acquiring, in broadcasting, the character of a communications phenomenon which was posing over-all questions—how, when, and to what extent would developments involve the Bell Telephone System?

Vice-president Gifford, who was representing the American Company's investment in R.C.A. by serving on R.C.A.'s board of directors, sought an assistant to collate and report on these developments, and Mr. A. H. Griswold was detached from the Western Electric organization and appointed an Assistant Vice-president of the American Company. His first duties, which he assumed on March 1, 1921, were to serve as a specially delegated channel for the interchange of information with the operating units and to act as liaison with D&R and O&E.[1]

These duties were to expand rapidly with the growth of broadcasting activity, the mounting public interest in it, and the development of corporate relationships established by manufacturers who realized the commercial possibilities in the marketing of radio receiving sets. On July 1, 1921, a cross-licensing agreement was signed by General Electric and Westinghouse, who had been manufacturing rivals, thus completing the formation of what was to be known in later negotiations with the telephone organization as "the radio group." By October, 1921, there were two new Westinghouse stations on the air—WBZ in Springfield, Mass., and WJZ at Newark,

[1] See above, page 37.

N. J. *The Radio Service Bulletin* of the Department of Commerce issued in October showed a listing of twelve new commercial stations, the listing of new stations a month earlier having been nine. Business interests pressed the American Company to allow the sale of broadcasting apparatus manufactured under Bell System patents, a procedure which the company was unwilling to countenance until the direction of broadcasting developments should become better defined.

Broadcasting Facilities in Demand

The interest of business concerns in obtaining transmitting apparatus for broadcasting imposed an unusual responsibility upon the patent owners. Manufacturing operations could be carried on profitably by the Western Electric Company under the patent rights held by the American Company and according to the cross-licensing agreement of 1920. But it was increasingly apparent that many would-be purchasers of apparatus for broadcasting (as distinguished from those who might be interested in transmitters for other purposes) had little or no realization of the cost of operation and maintenance, and that their proposed ventures might easily result in disappointment and loss. Furthermore it was clear from the limited number of wave lengths available that a multitude of stations would create a condition of congestion which would certainly lessen and might possibly destroy the value of broadcasting to the public.[2]

The Telephone Point of View

One familiar with the specialized activities of the telephone headquarters organizations can readily realize how broadcasting trends were being watched by various groups of observers there.

In the first place there was the over-all concern—an entirely ob-

[2] In the statement prepared for the Federal Communications Commission by Mr. O. B. Hanson, quoted on page 33 of this volume, appears the following reference to this situation: "It would seem like good business for the Western Electric Co. to have accepted and filled these orders, but fortunately within the A. T. & T. there were those who looked beyond the immediate return of a handsome profit from the sale of transmitters to these prospective customers. If the orders received for transmitters had been filled and installed in the New York area, the history of broadcasting might be considerably different from that which I am relating."

jective one—as to the economics of broadcasting itself. The telephone mind would naturally weigh this question according to the philosophy which had developed through the experience of decades that had provided the basis for telephone growth, namely that a broadcast, like a telephone call, should be paid for by the one originating it. Current commercial broadcasting, on the other hand, was being conducted on the basis of an opposite philosophy—that the expense should be borne by the receivers, i.e., the radio listeners, who would in effect be paying for the communication through their purchase of receiving apparatus.

As for technical performances in current broadcasting operations, these were naturally observed with critical and professional interest by telephone technicians who were themselves extremely skilled in broadcasting technique. These were the groups whose transmission experiments at the Deal Beach and Western Electric stations had been in the same general band of frequencies that was being employed in broadcasting. Their professional knowledge, as well as that of their laboratory and D&R colleagues, was of course extensive, since the pickup and amplifying technique for broadcasting was based on the high-quality speech study which was a fundamental laboratory activity.

Other interested technical observers, including Long Lines engineers as well as laboratory specialists, were those occupied with the transmission problems involved in the development of loud-speaking telephone systems. Such a system had been publicly demonstrated for the first time in April, 1919, when long-distance wires brought talks by government officials, one of whom was Assistant Secretary of the Navy Franklin D. Roosevelt, to the great outdoor gatherings in New York, as part of the ceremonies promoting the Fifth "Liberty Loan." An improved laboratory loud-speaker model, installed at the Capitol in Washington, had enabled an audience of more than 100,000 persons gathered there to hear President Harding's inauguration ceremonies on March 4, 1921. On November 11 of the same year there was another impressive demonstration of this system's future usefulness when the apparatus was successfully applied to transcontinental circuits, following elaborate tests, en-

The Bell System's radio station at Deal Beach, 1921, and the small, temporary building used in 1920 for pioneering ship-to-shore experiments.

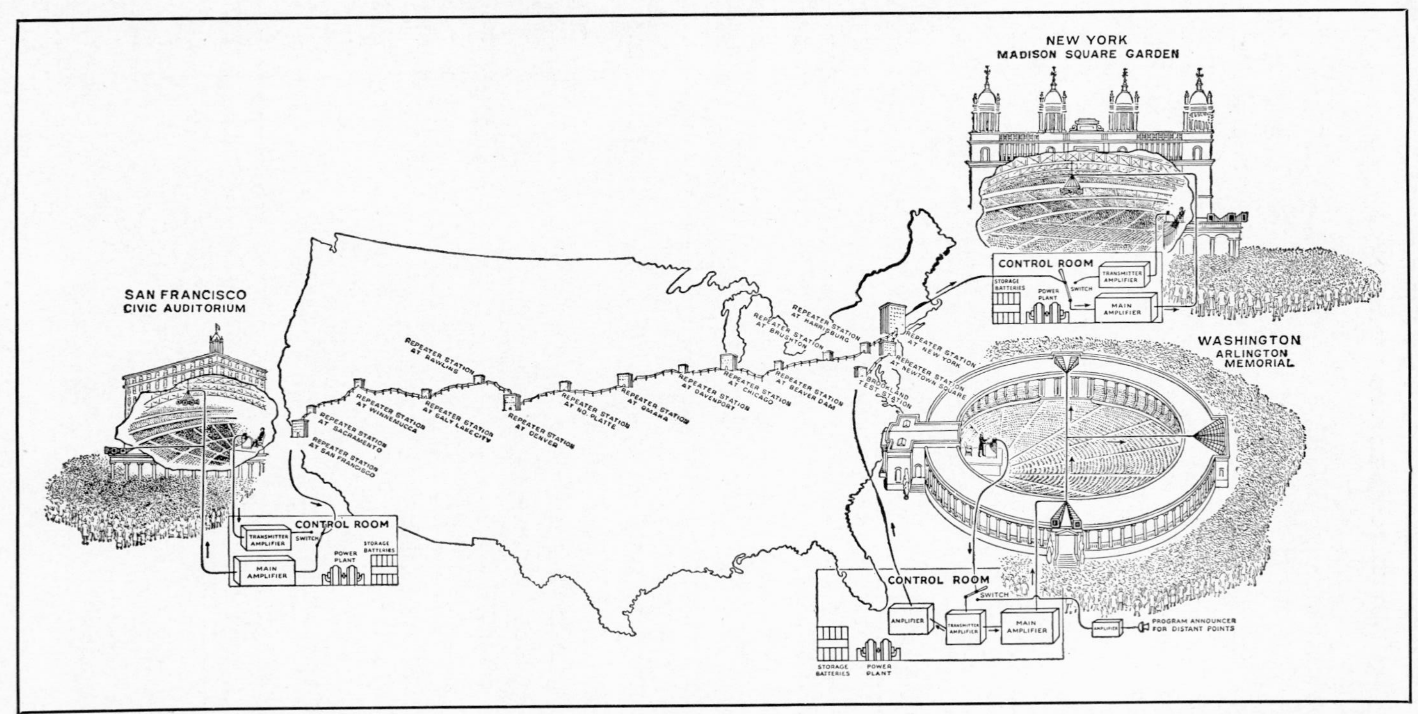

Telephone circuits and vacuum-tube amplifiers carried President Harding's Armistice Day address, in 1921, from the Tomb of the Unknown Soldier at Arlington to crowds in Washington, New York, and San Francisco. This contemporary diagram shows the course of the circuits.

abling large audiences in New York and San Francisco to hear the burial services for the Unknown Soldier in the National Cemetery at Arlington, Virginia. President Harding wrote to President Thayer,[3]

> I have not been quite able to realize even yet the marvel of having spoken on this occasion to vast audiences in New York and San Francisco as well as to the great concourse which was before me. The wonder of it has been magnified in my own mind by the reports which have come from those cities describing the attitude of the people; of how they followed the exercises in every detail, even to joining in the singing and in the words of prayer at the conclusion of the address.

The Challenging Demand for Wires

But those at Bell System headquarters who were most concerned over the symptoms of growing public interest in radio were the executives and their legal advisers, the reason being that, both technically and commercially, the wire network was needed for the development of broadcasting's public usefulness.

The need of wires for picking up programs was, of course, apparent from the very birth of "organized" broadcasting. Soon after regular broadcasting had begun at Westinghouse's Pittsburgh station KDKA in November, 1920, that station sought local telephone wires in order to broadcast church services. On January 15, 1921, telephone wires carried an address of President Harding from Pittsburgh's Duquesne Club to the station's transmitter.

Telephone officials realized, naturally, that in a demand for wires to be used in this way, a new consideration was developing with regard to the various corporate activities which were legally permitted under the cross-licensing agreement of 1920. This was emphasized, for example, by a request for wire connections by Westinghouse engineers whose specifications were:[4]

> We require the connection of a transmitter and speech amplifier connected to the telephone circuit. At the station's end we require connection from the telephone wire to the input circuit of a second speech amplifier or to the input

[3] The microphones used by President Harding on this occasion and at his inaugural are among the exhibits in the collection of historic transmitters in the Bell System Historical Museum at Bell Telephone Laboratories.

[4] Quoted from company files of Oct., 1921.

circuit of our radio transmitter. We have found it desirable to connect around the distributing frame at telephone centrals rather than to go through the switchboard equipment. . . . The telephone company will want to know what current and voltage will be applied to their standard telephone circuits. . . . We should be able to get along in all cases without exceeding 100 volts on the telephone circuit. The current should not exceed 100 milliamps. If the above figures are greater than the telephone company is willing to allow we wish to amplify up to what is allowable at the pick-up and finish the amplification at the station. For your information would say that we have had no trouble with this voltage and current while using the telephone circuit of the Independent Company in Pittsburgh.

Such a request did more than pose the general technical question of what the telephone company, with its time-honored policy of permitting no installations on its circuits other than its own in order to protect service from such hazards as cross-talk, should "be willing to allow." It indicated an assumption that the wire plant was available to the broadcaster, and this was not the case according to the company's interpretation of the 1920 cross-licensing agreement. It seemed both obvious and logical under this agreement that the rights of the "radio group" with respect to wireless broadcast transmission related only to transmission *from* stations and did not include transmission by wires *to* such stations.

This matter is mentioned here in order to prepare the reader for a later reference to the conflicting interpretations of the agreement that later proved to be irreconcilable. Incidentally, the request just quoted was not refused. The American Company's policy was to avoid any seeming arbitrariness while it waited for broadcasting trends to become more pronounced. Not till later did Vice-president Gifford decide to register the company's legal position by writing to this broadcaster:

It has come to our attention that the Westinghouse Company is using wires of both the Bell Telephone Company of Pennsylvania and the Independent Company of Pittsburgh in connection with your radio broadcasting station. I trust that you have not forgotten that the license agreement does not permit you to connect radio telephone equipment to the lines of any public service communication system. As you know, we have this matter under consideration at the present time. In the meantime, I am sure you will not wish to do anything in violation of our general agreement.

The "matter under consideration" was the extent of the company's obligation to the public because of its ownership of patents relating to broadcasting and because of its ownership of a nationwide network of wires. For it had already become apparent that involvement of some sort was a prospect. As Mr. Gifford recalled the changing situation to this compiler in the summer of 1944:[5]

> Nobody knew early in 1921 where radio was really headed. Everything about broadcasting was uncertain. For my own part I expected that since it was a form of telephony, and since we were in the business of furnishing wires for telephony, we were sure to be involved in broadcasting somehow. Our first vague idea, as broadcasting appeared, was that perhaps people would expect to be able to pick up a telephone and call some radio station, so that they could give radio talks to other people equipped to listen. It was impossible for a while even to guess what our service duty would be.

By the middle of the year broadcasting trends were more definite, and a D&R survey of the situation, dated July 14, contains one of the early references to a "service basis" in discussing the general question of wire connections to radio stations:

> Radio telephone "broadcasting" bids fair to become such an important matter in the communication world as to warrant a careful consideration of its possibilities from a business standpoint and a redetermination of what interest we may have in the field.
>
> The question uppermost from a business standpoint is: How shall collection be made for broadcast service rendered? It seems impracticable to collect regularly on a service basis. The only feasible way of obtaining returns is considered to be through the sale of apparatus. This has led to the conclusion, inasmuch as this company is not interested in the sale of apparatus outside the Bell System, that we are not interested in broadcasting.
>
> The exploitation of apparatus sales will be dependent, however, upon some news and amusement broadcasting service; and it would be well worth while for the companies interested in the field to underwrite such service in one way or another. The Government Departments may play an active part in

[5] It will be remembered by telephone personnel reading this account that Mr. Gifford used the same "pick up a telephone" phrase on October 20, 1927, when addressing the convention of the National Association of Railroad and Utility Commissioners: "The ideal and aim of the American Telephone and Telegraph Company and its Associated Companies is a telephone service for the nation, free, so far as humanly possible, from imperfections, errors or delays, and enabling anyone anywhere to pick up a telephone and talk to anyone else anywhere else, clearly, quickly and at a reasonable cost."

furnishing news. In any event, a successful service will require wire connections from the centers of information to the various broadcasting stations around the country and can best be conducted by through wire-radio telephone transmission. In other words, it seems reasonable to expect that we will be called upon for wire connections to these broadcasting stations—by Government Departments, for example, and also by commercial companies.

If we, ourselves, do not broadcast, we have to face such policy complications as the wire end of the service may involve, as well as the uncertainty of what effect such service may have upon our own service. . . . The fact that radio *supplements* wire service could in no way better be demonstrated continually to the public than by having this broadcasting conducted as a part of the Bell System. Certainly we are well prepared in both radio technique and in field setting to undertake it.

As the weeks went by, D&R continued to explore, under executive direction, the technical considerations involved in a wire "service" to broadcasting stations, and reported in October on the possibility of telephone lines serving as a "backbone" system for broadcasting.[6] The reference to loud-speakers instead of receiving sets rather significantly shows the institutional interest at the time only in the purely telephonic problem of transmission:

The technical possibilities of broadcasting from the Bell standpoint may be best indicated by picturing the setup for some national event, such as the Armistice Day ceremonies or the inauguration of the President.

Under such conditions we can imagine the President or other official speaking in Washington with or without the use of local loud speakers, and that his voice is then carried out over a network of wires extending to all the important centers of the country.

If each point on this network can be reached by two or more routes, the possibility of interruption to telephone service would be small. At the offices along the selected route connections are established through one-way repeaters to other circuits, to loud speakers and radio stations, without interfering at all with the main circuit. In each city and larger town there are halls equipped with loud speaking apparatus at which the people in the neighborhood are gathered and which are properly connected directly or indirectly to the backbone routes.

To properly do the above will require that we have available along all of our important routes one or more circuits which are constructed and maintained so as to give a somewhat better grade of transmission, and a somewhat higher degree of reliability.

[6] Joint D&R and O&E file.

The Concept of Broadcasting Service

There was still uncertainty as to the future, but there was no escaping the obligations of the present. By the end of 1921 the situation as to broadcasting was that hundreds wanted to broadcast, that millions wanted to listen, that no one was sure how broadcasting was to be supported, and that the rapidly growing industry was in an unwholesome and demoralized state.

This situation pressed for a solution and Vice-president Gifford, who had executive charge of the company's radio problems and was to become its President four years later, believed that the solution was to be found in the idea of sharing a broadcasting station among many program-makers. With the right of renting out broadcasting time inherent in the company's "public service" interest in radio agreed upon in the cross-licensing arrangements of 1920, with a system of wire lines, with technicians skilled in radio technique, there were institutional resources that could be used in an effort to stabilize the conditions which broadcasting enthusiasm had brought about. As the situation had been diagnosed there was a remedy that promised relief, and perhaps a cure, for conditions bordering on the chaotic. That remedy, in telephone parlance, was "toll broadcasting," and since there were no broadcasting facilities for public use, the company decided to furnish them itself.

In the announcement of this decision to stockholders, one simple phrase identifies the idea behind the decision to add a new responsibility to those involved in meeting the expanding communication needs of the hour. On page 20 of the company's report for 1921 was the statement:

> A field in which the radio telephone has possibilities is in the furnishing of broadcasting service, a one-way service which consists in sending out by radio telephone from a central station, news, music, speeches, and the like, which under favorable atmospheric conditions may be received by all who have receiving stations within the area served, and care to listen. The number of wave lengths available for this radio telephone service is limited, but we are preparing to furnish this broadcasting service to such an extent as may meet the commercial demands of the public, subject to that limitation.

It was this new concept of "broadcasting service" that was to be tested through the experience of the American people.

PART II

THE BIRTH OF WEAF, 1922

CHAPTER V

THE ESTABLISHMENT OF WBAY

Preliminary Investigations

THE unfolding of the "toll broadcasting" idea, which was to become the shining light on the highway of broadcasting progress, began when D&R transmission experts made preliminary reports on the apparatus, equipment, and wires that would be needed for a comprehensive system of radio broadcasting.

Company files show that there were preliminary estimates early in December, 1921. A nationwide system was the natural concept of an organization rendering nationwide telephone service, and 38 station locations on the Bell System's main long-distance routes were accordingly suggested as a basis for such a system. The approximate costs of establishing and operating them were supplied, as well as the costs involved in setting up "wire connections from the radio station to the point where a speaker or musician can be most conveniently reached."

Further accenting the function of wires in the proposed service, the early estimates discussed provisions for "connecting the broadcasting stations together . . . on those occasions of sectional or national importance requiring that all or a group of the stations be operated as one." Still another technical consideration was the possible need of the lines "for connecting together not only the broadcasting stations but also to connect to loudspeaker equipment in halls or outdoor gathering places," and the first D&R survey further assumes, "In the event that we should enter this field, I presume we would start out on a small scale in order to obtain a knowledge of the operating and business problems involved."[1]

Thus we see discussed at the very beginning the importance of long-distance circuits and the importance of a test "on a small scale."

According to the established practices of the business, the use of long-distance circuits would necessitate maintenance and operation by the Long Lines Department. Hence the proposed broadcasting service itself seemed a natural assignment for that department, which normally functioned as the supplier of telephone facilities for interconnecting Bell companies, and for the use of press associations and other "private-line" customers. It was therefore Long Lines that had the operating responsibility when the time came to test the scheme "on a small scale."

While D&R was investigating the technical implications of the broadcasting idea, other headquarters groups began to analyze the service functions of a toll broadcasting system from the standpoint of value to both user and listener. One of the most interesting documents of the period is a mid-December discussion of these values by O&E commercial development experts.[2] A few quotations from this survey will show how institutional habits of thought were shaping the fundamental idea into concrete "proposals" for study:

> Radio Telephone Broadcasting is now being carried on at eight different points throughout the country. . . . There is apparently considerable demand for this service and it would seem that, if properly conducted, it would be of considerable value to the public. The purpose of this memorandum is to discuss the various phases of radio telephone broadcasting, its potential value to the public . . . presupposing that the Bell System desires to enter the field.
>
> Broadcasting stations,[3] operated either by amateurs or by radio telephone apparatus manufacturers, are now located at Springfield, Mass.; Newark, N. J.; Pittsburgh, Pa.; Detroit, Mich.; Chicago, Ill.; Los Angeles, Cal.; San Francisco, Cal.; and Seattle, Wash.; . . . as to the number of receiving stations throughout the country at present more or less adequately equipped to receive the service, conservative estimates vary from 100,000 to 500,000 stations, probably one-half of which are along the East Coast. . . . The equipment at these

[1] Dec. 8, 1921, report of Mr. O. B. Blackwell, D&R Transmission Development Engineer.

[2] Prepared by Commercial Engineers J. F. Bratney and H. C. Lauderback.

[3] This refers to stations holding "limited commercial licenses" and engaged in the regular transmission of "news items, entertainment, lectures, sermons and similar matter" (see *Radio Service Bulletin* for Apr., 1922).

stations . . . is more or less capable of receiving radio telephone broadcasting in the event that broadcasting stations of sufficient power were established.

. . . . The present broadcasting is going forward at various wave lengths between 200 and 800 meters and, as yet, no definite regulations or standards have been effected . . . a chaotic condition[4] . . . .

Our proposed plans call for the installation of 38 broadcasting stations. . . . The radius of each of these stations will be from 100 miles upward. . . . It is proposed to give a very reliable service at reasonable cost. . . . Without straining our imagination we can appreciate the value of this broadcasting service particularly to the rural and outlying sections throughout the middle and far west.

This service would enable the national and local advertisers, industrial institutions of all kinds, and even individuals if they desire, to send forth information and advertising matter audibly to thousands. . . .

. . . . A first consideration is that the material broadcasted . . . be desirable to the receiver so that the demand for service will be stimulated.

. . . . Our present plans do not contemplate *our* providing talent for entertainment . . . . we propose to be responsible for the quality of the service in so far as the *broadcasting* is concerned.

Public Announcements of the Project

During the next four or five weeks plans were perfected for an initial broadcasting venture in New York. On January 26, 1922, Vice-president Gifford approved the expenditure necessary for installing broadcasting equipment at the building which housed the Long Lines operating organization at 24 Walker Street, about a mile distant from the American Company headquarters, and a formal announcement, issued to the press on February 11, outlined the broad and imaginative conception of broadcasting service that was being weighed at the time:

A permit has been granted for the erection of a wireless telephone broadcasting station by the American Telephone and Telegraph Company on the roof of the twenty-four story operating building between Walker and Lispenard Streets. This building is 350 feet high and rises conspicuously above any other building in the immediate neighborhood. The steel towers supporting the antenna will be 100 feet high.

[4] A few weeks after this memorandum had been written, broadcasting by amateur radio telephone stations was forbidden; all broadcasting stations were required to obtain limited commercial licenses, and were limited to 360 meters, with 485 meters reserved for crop reports and weather reports. This regulation considerably reduced interference with other services.

It is expected that the work will be started at once and that the station will be ready to begin operations in less than two months time.

This wireless broadcasting station will be unique in many respects. This important radio distributing station is to be equipped with the latest developments of the Bell System, including the use of electrical filters and new methods, whereby, as the business grows, several wave lengths can be sent out simultaneously from the same point, so that the receiving stations may listen at will to any one of the several services.

It will be unique in another respect, because it will be the first radio station for telephone broadcasting which will provide a means of distribution and will handle the distribution of news, music or other program on a commercial basis for such people as contract for this service.

The American Telephone and Telegraph Company will provide no program of its own, but provide the channels through which anyone with whom it makes a contract can send out their own programs. Just as the company leases its long distance wire facilities for the use of newspapers, banks and other concerns, so it will lease its radio telephone facilities and will not provide the matter which is sent out from this station. There have been many requests for such a service, not only from newspapers and entertainment agencies, but also from department stores and a great variety of business houses who wish to utilize this means of distribution.

The new station on the Walker-Lispenard Building is designed to cover a region from 100 to 150 miles surrounding New York City. However, under most favorable conditions, it might be heard for much greater distances, but even for its designed radius, it must be permitted to operate on a wave length free from other radio interference.

Within the area normally covered by this station there are now probably 35,000 receiving stations which would provide an audience for the lessees of the company's radio service. In this same area there are over 11,000,000 people, so that should such service prove popular, it can reasonably be expected that the number of receiving stations will be greatly increased.

This is a new undertaking in the commercial use of radio telephony and if there appears a real field for such service and it can be furnished sufficiently free from interference in the ether from other radio services, it will be followed as circumstances warrant by similar stations erected at important centers throughout the United States by the American Telephone and Telegraph Company. As these additional stations are erected, they can be connected by the toll and long distance wires of the Bell System so that from any central point, the same news, music or other program can be sent out simultaneously through all these stations by wire and wireless with the greatest possible economy and without interference.

While it is entirely possible, as has been demonstrated by the telephone company, to talk by wireless when all atmospheric conditions are favorable across the continent or even for much greater distances over water, such long distance radio telephone transmission is not dependable and is not to be compared from a standpoint of service or economy with the transmission which is provided over wire. However, for a broadcasting service, which involves only one-way transmission, where the same message is given simultaneously to a great number of people within reasonable distances of the transmitting station, radio telephony offers a promising field for development.

The new line of business to be handled by this radio telephone broadcasting station will be in charge of the Long Lines Department of the A. T. and T. Co. which is now engaged in solving the many problems both technical and commercial which arise in connection with this new kind of service.

This announcement naturally generated considerable press comment, and in some quarters there were references to "monopoly," the *Radio Dealer*[5] prophesying, in its April, 1922, issue: ". . . when it comes to monopolizing the air for mercenary advertising purposes, a real man sized vocal rebellion can be expected. . . . These wise would-be radio advertising monopolists are on the wrong end of a wonderful idea." The company's experimental motive was thus ignored or misunderstood at the very outset of the venture.

Of all the contemporary editorials preserved in the station files, one of the most interesting is that published in the *Electrical World*,[6] because it pictures the current amateur character of radio interest at the time, while speculating on the business trends and social benefits that were possible from broadcasting's growth:

FAR-REACHING INFLUENCE OF THE RADIO TELEPHONE

The American Telephone & Telegraph Company has announced that it will establish a radio-telephone broadcasting station in New York City that will be leased in much the same way that its wire service is leased. This is only another step in a remarkable development that has aroused intense public interest in the radio telephone during the past year. The manufacturing companies which have established similar stations, as well as the numerous private stations for broadcasting regular programs, have established a demand for the service that is recognized by the daily press, where full programs for the best-known stations are printed each day. The proposed station in New York will be the first commercial station that can be used by any one who is willing to pay the leasing charge. It is significant that the company announces that it will establish a chain of such stations in other important cities if the demand

[5] Vol. i, no. 1, p. 30.

[6] Vol. lxxix, no. 9 (Mar. 4, 1922), p. 419.

justifies, and that its long-distance facilities will be used to connect these stations together so that programs given in one section of the country can be heard in another section by any one having a receiving set.

The immediate result of the work of the past few months is shown in the creation of a new army of buyers. Radio-supply stores have sprung up by the hundreds all over the United States, and the manufacturers are finding it impossible to keep up with the demand for equipment. At the moment the retail dealer finds himself short of stock owing to the demand on him. To the disgusted buyer this seems to be a chronic condition, though the difficulty will soon be remedied by the further development of manufacturing facilities. More significant is the character of the customers. A large portion of them are youths ranging from ten to twenty-one. They are not technically trained, and yet even the youngest of them can talk inductance, capacity, impedance, resistance and the other technical terms with a pretty thorough grasp on their meaning and a good appreciation of their application in radio work. The observer is forced to speculate upon the far-reaching effect that this condition will have on the future citizens of the country. Fad though the movement may be styled at the present, the education that these young people are getting is of untold value. It may well prove to be one of the most effective aids in dispelling the mystery that has enveloped the electrical industry in the public mind. At the very least it is taking the minds of the younger generation from amusements that may be questionable and giving them something that will be of tremendous use in the future.

That the public-service aspect of the company's venture would not be generally recognized was, of course, inevitable under the circumstances surrounding broadcasting's swift blossoming. The current comment indicated that only a few observers detected that a public interest in the sending as well as in the receiving end of broadcasting was the *raison d'être* of the toll-broadcasting experiment. As the company succinctly explained its policy to one correspondent: "It seems to us that the maximum results from radio telephone broadcasting can only be obtained by some one agency establishing broadcasting as a commercial service on wave lengths exclusively set aside for such service, in this manner making the service available alike to everyone." [7]

Five days after this letter had been written, Vice-president Gifford formally requested of the United States Radio Inspector in New York that wave bands be specifically assigned to "commercial serv-

[7] Letter of Feb. 20, 1922, to the State Marketing Commissioner of Missouri.

ice." Following Secretary of Commerce Hoover's first Radio Conference, held at the end of the month, during which the Secretary commented on the remarkable growth of radio interest, broadcasting stations were grouped in four categories: (1) government, (2) public institutions, (3) private owners, (4) "toll broadcasting, signifying broadcasting by a public service radio telephone company as a paid service."

Another announcement should be quoted here to complete the record of contemporary institutional publicity regarding radio. It was the leading article[8] in the first issue of the *Bell Telephone Quarterly* (now the *Bell Telephone Magazine*) which was first issued by the company's Information Department in April, 1922, the present writer being one of its editors.

Vice-president Gifford's view for some time had been that a headquarters publication was needed to provide Bell System directors, officials, and department heads with background information on institutional developments. The result of his suggestion was the *Quarterly*, for which President Thayer wrote a dedicatory preface and supplied the masthead slogan that has guided the editors from the beginning, "A Medium of Suggestion, and a Record of Progress."

Thus it was "The Radio Telephone Situation" that launched a publication to report and interpret Bell System policies and responsibilities. The specific references to broadcasting were as follows:

> One of the most interesting applications of radio telephony is that of broadcasting, which is not intercommunication but a one-way service. It is in this field that radio, by virtue of its inherent nature, seems to have great possibilities. At the present time broadcasting is being done by various departments of the Government, by certain manufacturers or agents of radio apparatus, by experimenters, by newspapers, and until recently by amateurs. The existing broadcasting transmitting stations are operating in the particular interest of the owners of such stations and are not providing broadcasting transmitting service for the use of the public in general. The American Telephone and Telegraph Company controls the important patents on radio telephone broadcasting transmitting equipment for general public use and consequently is being besieged with requests to sell radio telephone broadcasting equipment or to provide radio telephone broadcasting service. We are selling the broadcast-

[8] "The Radio Telephone Situation," by A. H. Griswold, *Bell Telephone Quarterly*, vol. i, no. 1 (Apr., 1922), pp 8-12.

ing equipment and so many of these requests have been received that it has become apparent that if everyone who desires his own broadcasting equipment should purchase it, there will soon be so many broadcasting stations all operating on the same or a comparatively few number of wave lengths that real service from any of them will be impossible. Accordingly, we are now establishing in New York on the Walker-Lispenard building a broadcasting station of the latest and best type known to the art. It is not planned that we put on any program ourselves but rather provide the facilities over which others may broadcast at specified rates. We could doubtless provide and broadcast a splendid program, but by such a procedure we would be inviting the public to purchase receiving equipment in order to hear our program and we would be committed to the indefinite continuance of a service for which no revenues would be received. By providing facilities for the use of others it rests with those who broadcast to furnish a class of program to which the general public will desire to listen. It is thought that in this manner the true attitude of the public toward broadcasting may be determined, as it is realized that at present the public is in a more or less optimistic state of mind and that broadcasting must be placed on a much more sound basis if it is to remain as a valuable service.

If the experimental broadcasting station in New York is commercially successful, it is our plan to establish, as circumstances warrant, similar stations throughout the country, and not only may each station have available for use in connection with it all of the local lines in the zone served by that station but also at some future time it may be possible that all of such broadcasting stations throughout the country may, if conditions warrant, be tied together by the long line plant, so that any one, from practically any point, may use any number or all of these stations simultaneously if he so desires. It is our thought that only in this manner can the best, cheapest, and most extensive radio broadcasting service be given.

It should be understood that this service will not react to the exclusion of private or other broadcasting service and will not necessarily in any way directly displace such services. However, it is obvious that every one cannot own his own broadcasting equipment, and unless some provision for service such as we have outlined is made, only a limited number of people in the country will have broadcasting service available for their use.

. . . .

THE BELL SYSTEM AND RADIO

While we have important exclusive rights protected by patents, our interest in the extension of our field of service overshadows any interest in any patent or group of patents. Above all, we do not want to obstruct the work or play of scientists and amateurs. Progress follows experiment and use. In this new art we should experiment and encourage the experiments of others but without prejudice to later enforcement of our rights if and when such enforcement becomes necessary to the efficiency of a public service.

The question of most interest in the Bell System is naturally—"What do we propose to do with radio?" We propose to keep in mind our main purpose which is to furnish to the people of the United States as wide a range of communication facilities as possible. It may mean service with ships, railway trains and airplanes. It may mean a transatlantic service, but promises cannot now be made. It may mean broadcasting, the future of which cannot be determined as yet. It should be remembered that radio telephony, with its scope definitely limited by natural conditions, has only reached an elementary stage, even in its possible fields. Bearing in mind our fundamental policy of providing the best and most economical type of facilities to meet any given set of conditions, we shall continue our work of developing whatever possibilities there are for radio in the field of telephone communications.

Both of the company's published statements quoted above referred to the possible establishment by the company itself, "if circumstances warrant," of other stations, so that a national broadcasting service might eventuate. The vision from the beginning was that a need for service on a nationwide scale could be met by regional stations operating as parts of a telephonic system. Later pages of this record will relate the circumstances which led to the development of such a service with stations that were privately owned.

Centralized Analysis of Radio Problems

The reader should note, against the background of the various announcements just quoted, the establishment at American Company headquarters, in the spring of 1922, of a separate organization unit that was called "Department of Operation—B," to distinguish it from the main O&E Department. It was headed by Mr. E. S. Bloom, Vice-president, and radio matters were placed under his executive jurisdiction. Mr. Elam Miller of the D&R transmission group was assigned to act as Mr. A. H. Griswold's chief assistant, and was himself assisted by Mr. C. A. Buckard and Mr. P. W. Spence, who were joined in June, 1922, by Mr. R. G. Rich.

"Operation B" was a typical example of headquarters "General Staff" service, for in it was centralized the analysis, in behalf of all Bell System regional telephone companies, of the problems created for them by broadcasting's sudden coming and rapid growth. Its function was an all-important one—to carry on studies to serve as a basis for the formulation of Bell System policies and procedures in meeting the ever changing developments in the broadcasting field. In organizing the department for this function of analysis and service, Mr. Bloom at once asked each Bell operating company to appoint a representative with the special responsibility of keeping abreast of local radio matters, and of acting as a liaison with the headquarters company for the interchange of information.

Coincidentally, Operation B issued a preliminary bulletin, captioned "Radio Telephone Broadcasting,"[9] which provided information to enable System units to answer local inquiries, particularly with respect to radio telephone apparatus. Some of its references to this were:

> The Western Electric Company is not manufacturing radio telephone receiving sets for non-commercial uses. This equipment is now being furnished under our licenses by the Radio Corporation of America.[10] Accordingly you may suggest to your patrons that they direct their inquiries for such equipment to the nearest office of the Radio Corporation. . . .
>
> The Western Electric Company thus far is building only two sizes of radio telephone broadcasting transmitting sets, one delivering 100 watts to the antennae and the other delivering 500 watts. . . .
>
> With reference to the inquiries of your patrons for radio telephone broadcasting transmitting equipment, you should advise them that the Western Electric Company solely is licensed under our patents to make and sell such equipment. . . . The sales price of the Western Electric Company on the 100-watt set is about $8,500 and on the 500-watt set about $10,500. . . . For successful broadcasting it is also desirable to have a special transmitting room having proper acoustic qualities and generally some special equipment. All of this means that a broadcasting station completely equipped and ready for operation will probably cost somewhere between $10,000 and $15,000. The annual cost of operation of this equipment, not including any program features, will run at least one hundred per cent and may run two hundred per cent of the first cost. . . .
>
> In talking with such of your patrons as desire to purchase broadcasting transmitting equipment, we are very anxious that you give them as complete a picture of the situation as possible in order that no subsequent misunderstanding may arise. The Western Electric Company has sold to date sixteen

[9] This bulletin was the first of several and was dated Apr. 25, 1922.

[10] It is explained on a previous page that the Radio Corporation was the selling agent for both General Electric and Westinghouse.

broadcasting transmitting sets and has quotations outstanding for upwards of fifty more. . . . So many inquiries were received from New York and points nearby that it became evident to us that it was totally out of the question for every one who desired to broadcast to own and operate his own equipment. . . . Accordingly, we are now erecting an experimental broadcasting station. . . . We do not know what the outcome of this experiment will be. . . .

If there continues to be an insistent demand for broadcasting we feel rather sure that ultimately there will not be any particular advantage accruing to anyone by virtue of the fact that he owns a broadcasting station, but that facilities for broadcasting will be provided through some common agency and the public will be interested in the subject matter which is broadcasted and not whether the particular party broadcasting owns and operates his own equipment. . . .

You will doubtless receive inquiries with reference to broadcasting transmitting equipment other than that made by the Western Electric Company. Such transmitting equipments in practically every case constitute an infringement of our patent rights.

It will be seen from these excerpts how Operation B prepared Bell Companies at the outset to deal with local conditions. These generated more and more difficulties, with broadcasting's changing status, and consequently the department's general-staff function was of fundamental and continually growing importance.

This seems a proper place to refer specifically to the personal activities of Mr. Elam Miller and his associates in Operation B throughout the four-year period of the American Company's broadcasting experience. He, himself, had the responsibility of supervising the interchange of information and advice between telephone headquarters and the Bell System units, and of directing the investigations that were essential for the formation of decisions and procedures. He acted, in addition, as one of the company's representatives at radio conferences called by the Department of Commerce and by the Radio Inspector of the New York District. The files are filled with his careful analyses of ever changing and always challenging broadcasting developments.

The activities of Mr. Miller's assistants were similarly distinguished for their thoroughness in investigation and analysis. To Mr. P. W. Spence were assigned for study the conditions that specifically affected both the operating companies and the Western Electric Company; Mr. C. A. Buckard had a large variety of more general matters as a field of investigation; Mr. R. G. Rich became responsible for the statistical studies that encouraged advertisers to test the radio medium. The analysis of commercial problems which developed from broadcasting practice was the responsibility of Mr. J. A. Holman, who joined the department after serving as the Ohio Bell Company's radio representative. When he left the department late in 1923 to become WEAF's manager, his place in the group was taken by Mr. R. W. Armstrong.

A backward look upon the American Company's broadcasting activities and responsibilities brings into focus the importance to the experiment of the Operation B function. Its members had to deal with a multitude of exacting and changing conditions created by the challenge of broadcasting's wildfire and unstable growth. They were particularly successful in analyzing the new and peculiar problems which arose during the 1924 development of the idea of network broadcasting. Like the men of Long Lines they were behind the scenes, playing a part in developing the service of broadcasting that was best understood only by their associates.

Preparing for Operations

In the spring of 1922, with Mr. D. K. Martin of Mr. O. B. Blackwell's radio group in D&R serving as "project engineer," antenna wires nearly 500 feet above the street were spanning hundred-foot towers which topped the Long Lines Building on Walker Street in New York, and transmitting apparatus was being tested under an experimental license with call letters 2XY. When, on May 1, the limited commercial license was issued with call letters WBAY assigned, there were many business inquiries on file concerning the proposed toll broadcasting service. By the time the station was ready for "toll" business, nearly a hundred concerns and individuals, made curious by radio news and by the appearance of the tall antenna towers, had sought information as to the station's use. The company was unwilling, however, to start its experiment at once. This was because there were then some 15 stations in the vicinity using the wave length of 360 meters, which was the only one allotted to commercial stations by the Department of Commerce. The Department found itself unable under the law to grant a special wave length of 400 meters,[11] which was applied for in order to avoid interference, and a division of time with local stations had therefore to be arranged before operations were started.[12]

At a conference of station operators called by Mr. Arthur Batcheller, the U. S. Radio Inspector for the New York district, a broadcasting schedule was worked out, allocating day and night hours, to which all the local broadcasters agreed except the management of WJZ. The matter was thereupon referred to the Department of Commerce and it was not until July 24, 1922, that the proposed schedule was ordered to be put into effect. It assigned to WBAY the following hours:

Weekday mornings	10:00 A.M. to 12 noon.
Weekday afternoons	4:30 P.M. to 5:30 P.M.
Thursday nights	7:30 P.M. to midnight

WBAY Ready for Broadcasters

On the following day, July 25, WBAY began operations with a program of recorded music, with Mr. R. S. Fenimore of the Long Lines plant forces operating the transmitter, while an assistant anxiously listened on the 600-meter wave length which might be carrying some ship's SOS that would halt, according to the government regulations then in force, the station's debut.[13]

The authorization to start WBAY operations, sent from the headquarters building to the Long Lines organization on the morning of the 25th, stated:

[11] Later, in September, the Department of Commerce established a new classification of "Class B" stations, to include WBAY and WEAF, to which the 400-meter wave length was assigned.

[12] Since 5 of the 15 stations had very low power, only the following stations were affected:

WBAY—Amer. Tel. & Tel. Co., New York
WJZ—Westinghouse Elec. & Mfg. Co., Newark
WWZ—John Wanamaker, New York
WAAM—I. R. Nelson & Co., Newark
WHN—Ridgewood Times Pub. Co., Ridgewood, N. Y.
WOR—L. Bamberger & Co., Newark
WBAN—Wireless Phone Co., Paterson, N. J.
WBS—D. W. May & Co., Newark
WRW—Radio Research Lab., Tarrytown
WAAT—Jersey Review, Jersey City

[13] A receiving antenna and associated equipment was placed at Princeton, N. J., for the purpose of monitoring WBAY's signals, which were picked up and routed back to the station via the New York-Philadelphia cable line.

> . . . we should endeavor to fill up the morning and afternoon periods assigned to us as otherwise we may forfeit our right to the time. It is suggested that we utilize the player piano and phonograph for this purpose and perhaps supplement them by such features as can be obtained without incurring any considerable expense. This does not commit us to a policy of providing a program but is simply to fill up time and hold our place on the schedule until we can determine whether or not the general public desires to use our facilities.

It was a broadcasting station on the design of which, said the current issue of *Radio Broadcast,* "probably more thought and talent has been expended than on any other in existence;" a station which a later writer described as remarkable "for the clarity of its tone and its last-minute scientific equipment."[14] It was equipped with piano, piano-player, and phonograph, and was the first broadcasting studio in America to use a magnetic pickup for the reproduction of phonograph records.[15]

The scientific equipment thus referred to as "last-minute" not only included the standard Western Electric 500-watt transmitter but also expressed in many special ways the high-quality pickup experience of telephone engineers that was one of the technical resources available for the broadcasting experiment.

One concrete result of this experience was the condenser microphone which had been part of the public-address system demonstrated so successfully the preceding year and which was first used for broadcasting at WBAY. It created no noise through its own operation, was practically perfect in its reproduction, and was one of the reasons for the high quality of the company's broadcasts from the beginning. It also was the "mike" for the sound movies of early days and for electrically cut phonograph records.

Another instrumentality first used in broadcasting at WBAY was the "volume indicator," a fine example of results gained through the

[14] *History of Radio,* by Archer.

[15] The use of the phonograph and piano-player soon had to be discontinued because the station applied in September for a "Class B" license, which was a new classification announced in August by the Department of Commerce, to which a 400-meter wave length was assigned. The Department's original announcement specified that "mechanically operated musical instruments may be used only in an emergency and during intermission periods in regular programs." On September 26 the U. S. Radio Inspector reported an amendment to the specifications applying to "Class B" stations to the effect that "the use of mechanically operated instruments is prohibited."

WBAY's antenna on the American Telephone and Telegraph Company Long Lines Building, Walker Street, New York, 1922. The 24-story building, 350 feet high, rose conspicuously above those around it.

WBAY's radio broadcasting transmitter, 1922, at the American Telephone and Telegraph Company Long Lines Building, Walker Street, New York. Photo by Rosenfeld.

intimate and coöperative association of telephone engineers occupied with many different assignments in electronic research and development. This was a device which assisted the operator of a broadcasting transmitter in controlling the intensity or level of the audio frequency program currents about to be fed into his apparatus, in order to prevent the transmitter from becoming overloaded or the program from becoming undesirably weak. This vital tool for regulating sound input came out of the early ship-to-shore experiments at Deal Beach where the problem of transmitter "overloading" was first appreciated and acted upon, and its development involved not only radio engineers but also those occupied with wire and public-address transmission problems as well.

Another device, which was developed by the station's resourceful engineers and is now indispensable in broadcasting practice, is the so-called "mixer," an arrangement for blending the outputs of various microphones.

In early broadcasting there was but one microphone in each studio, and the need for accurate balance between voices or instruments as picked up by the microphone was not well understood. During rehearsals, of course, microphone locations could be changed until a balance had been obtained. During an actual broadcast, however, singers were inclined to shift their positions and instrumentalists often would play with varying degrees of volume, with a state of unbalance the result. As one of WBAY's engineers later described the situation, "Any attempt to restrain the artists in order to restore the balance usually confused them, and the result was worse than the unbalance itself."

To remedy the matter, WBAY and D&R engineers placed several microphones in the studio and brought the output of each to a variable potentiometer, so that the relative strength of each output could be adjusted in the control-room in accordance with the actions of the broadcasting artists. This "mixer" or "fader" permitted the output of one microphone to be faded out while the output of another microphone was being brought to a new level—one more telephone pioneering instrumentality which is now a commonplace in broadcasting technique both within and outside the studio.

And so WBAY was ready for use by anyone desiring a radio contact with owners of receiving sets, and notifications of its availability were sent to those who had already applied for information. The charge decided upon was $50 for a 15-minute period in the evening, and $40 for an afternoon period. The formal announcement to the local newspapers was as follows:

> A musical program will be given between 11:00 A.M. and 12:00 M and 4:30 P.M. and 5:30 P.M. weekdays over the new radio broadcasting station WBAY, which was recently erected on the Walker Street Building of the American Telephone and Telegraph Company. A program will also be given on Thursday evenings from 7:30 P.M. to midnight, to be announced later.
>
> Such a station, which is intended for commercial broadcasting, has been assigned, for the present, by the United States Department of Commerce, a wave length of 360 meters. This does not permit simultaneous operating with the other broadcasting stations operating on the same wave length in this area. As a consequence the available hours have been assigned to the different stations operating in the vicinity of New York by an agreement between the stations themselves and with the approval of the Department of Commerce. The above schedule of two hours in the daytime and four and one-half on Thursday evenings is the temporary schedule which has been assigned to WBAY.
>
> Mr. A. W. Drake, General Commercial Manager, in charge of this station, says that there have been close to 100 applicants for the use of this station and he has taken steps to arrange with these applicants for the programs which they will provide.
>
> While radio advertising has not as yet been prohibited by laws or regulation, it is considered, in the public interest, that applicants for the use of this station should provide programs of general interest.
>
> Until the details of the scheduling of private programs can be arranged, WBAY will continue to furnish a miscellaneous musical selection.

The reference to "programs which they will provide" expressed the original idea upon which the broadcasting venture was based, i.e., the simple provision of communication facilities, operated and maintained according to telephone service standards, to be used by others.

It seems a naïve expectation when read in retrospect, for a month was to pass before a toll broadcaster would engage these facilities.[16]

[16] In approaching prospective users it was discovered that the low charge made them think that broadcasting could not be of much value to them. Later the charge was $400 per evening hour and $200 per afternoon hour, and when shorter periods were found more

In the meanwhile the public attitude toward broadcasting made it clear that the provision of "sustaining" programs, to gain and hold public interest in the station, was fundamental to the broadcasting venture. This meant that the company had the alternative of abandoning the experiment entirely or of accepting an unanticipated rôle —that of entrepreneur of entertainment. Such a rôle, so foreign to the telephone responsibility, was of course both a startling and a disturbing prospect, but the executive decision was, in Vice-president Gifford's words, "There's no reason to do anything about broadcasting at all unless we do it right." The broadcasting experiment at once, therefore, took on a new aspect. The undertaking no longer merely involved the offer of "toll broadcasting" facilities. The challenge was to develop program policies that would establish and maintain a publicly acceptable station personality, and would accomplish this result without endangering institutional reputation.

An Investigation of Wave Radiation

Two days after the opening of the station for service the Radio Inspector, Mr. Batcheller, reported: "While listening in at our observation station my attention was particularly attracted by the splendid quality of the signal from WBAY. I expected this, however, since it characterizes the American Telephone and Telegraph service." This praise for quality was of course deserved, a tribute to the broadcasting equipment and technique that were born and bred from telephone experimentation.

It was at once noted by the engineers, however, that the signals being received from WBAY's antenna were "down," particularly in the north and south directions. This fact led to an exploration of such scientific importance that it should be referred to here in some detail.

The matter to be investigated was the radiation of waves from a tall building and across a great city area, and for this study there was adopted a special kind of receiving set that had been developed

desirable to offer clients, the charge became $100 for a 10-minute evening period, and $50 for an afternoon period. Considering the number of receiving-set owners within the Metropolitan area, which in 1922 was estimated to be 300,000 to 400,000, this new charge was very low in the opinion of various advertising authorities who were consulted.

for the ship-to-shore radio telephone experiments—a device which had been used in measuring the strength of signals received from ships as they proceeded along their courses.

The engineering survey which was entered into,[17] employing this device, marked the beginning of a practice which afterwards extended to broadcasting stations generally for the purpose of determining their effective range or "coverage."

The early tests involved the placing of engineers with the signal, or field strength, measuring set at some point of observation, and of varying the wave length radiated from the building. A few of these tests proved that WBAY's assigned wave length of 360 meters was just about the worst one possible from the standpoint of effective radiation. A longer or a shorter wave length would have been better. Under the existing conditions the building itself acted as an antenna because of its height; it partially neutralized the radiation from the antenna proper.

After discovering this fundamental reason for a restriction of WBAY's broadcasting range, the engineers discovered another by measuring the field strength all over the city area. These tests permitted a map to be drawn with contour lines of field strength comparable to elevation contour lines on a topographical map. The complete survey showed definitely that wave projection northward along the length of Manhattan Island was being rapidly absorbed by the forest of high buildings. The waves traveled well along the rivers bounding the island but were unable to persist in a due north or due south direction. Thus it was determined that the way to feed radio broadcast waves into New York City was not along the length of the island but from the side of it.

From these pioneer studies of "wave distribution" in broadcasting there arose the practice of making radio field-strength surveys, and the technical papers[18] reporting them became guides for the location of future broadcasting stations.

[17] Engineers Bown, Martin, and Gillett from D&R were particularly active in this survey.

[18] "Radio Transmission Measurements," by Ralph Bown, Carl R. Englund, and H. T. Friis, *Proceedings of the Institute of Radio Engineers,* vol. xi, no. 2 (Apr., 1923), pp. 115-152. "Distribution of Radio Waves from Broadcasting Stations over City Districts," by Ralph Bown and G. D. Gillett, *Proceedings of the Institute of Radio Engineers,* vol. xii, no. 4 (Aug., 1924), pp. 395-409. "Some Studies in Radio Broadcast Transmission," by Ralph

It might be mentioned in passing that another local case requiring the application of this newborn technique was that of the New York City Municipal Broadcasting Station, which the city was anxious to locate on the Municipal Building. Telephone engineers advised city officials of the difficulty to be expected and made broadcast transmission tests from the top of the Municipal Building, with results similar to those recorded for WBAY transmission. By obtaining a somewhat different wave length from that which previously had been available, the city operated the station with fair success but later abandoned it for a site on the Brooklyn side of the East River.

Program Problems

With the station's opening, the need for an experienced program director was accented, it being clear, as the radio press was asserting, that owners of receiving sets wanted definite and satisfying entertainment and were critically searching the air waves for it. The matter had, in fact, already received some attention, for at a conference before the station opened it was agreed, according to the record, that "there should be an expert in the broadcasting station with experience in broadcasting and phonograph work who would know how to obtain artists."

In searching for a director, Commercial Manager Drake dispatched Mr. W. F. Baker[19] to obtain the advice of Mr. E. C. Mills, the general manager of the Music Publishers Protective Association, an affiliate of the American Society of Composers, Authors and Publishers known as "ASCAP." It was Mr. Baker's second mission to Mr. Mills; he had previously been delegated to ascertain ASCAP's attitude toward the use of certain copyrighted music on WBAY's program.

It is worth recording at this point that permission to use such music was freely given at once, and that the company made no pro-

Bown, DeLoss K. Martin, and Ralph K. Potter, *Bell System Technical Journal,* vol. v, no. 1 (Jan., 1926), pp. 143-213, and *Proceedings of the Institute of Radio Engineers,* vol. xiv, no. 1 (Feb., 1926), pp. 57-131. "Radio Broadcast Coverage of City Areas," by Lloyd Espenschied, *Bell System Technical Journal,* vol. vi, no. 1 (Jan., 1927), pp. 117-141, and *Journal of the American Institute of Electrical Engineers,* vol. xlvi, no. 1 (Jan., 1927), pp. 25-32.

[19] Mr. W. F. Baker and Mr. H. C. Smith were the two members of the Long Lines Commercial staff who were assigned to arrange contracts for the use of the station for business announcements.

test later, as others did, when ASCAP required a fee before authorizing the broadcasting of copyrighted music. The editor of one radio publication[20] commented rather acidly on this situation:

When a station can be shown to be on a paying basis, then it seems proper for music writers to collect as their share of the proceeds as much as seems reasonable, but to insist on large royalties while the game is in the experimental stage seems very much like killing the goose which might, some day, lay golden eggs for them.

And in referring to the Telephone Company's attitude this editor wrote further that the company's

. . . . activities in the radio broadcasting field have proved so far a rather expensive proposition, yet they have come to some kind of an agreement with the Society of Composers, Authors, and Publishers, and tell their audience so every time they broadcast—tell it in phraseology which sounds as though it had been specified by counsel for the musicians. We think the public is rather "fed up" with this society and would enjoy some music without being informed of the copyrighters' existence.

Whether or not the public resented the company's announcements, the fact remained that a musical choice narrowed to non-copyrighted music would neither have satisfied radio listeners nor encouraged business concerns to "sponsor" programs of entertainment. To coöperate with ASCAP, therefore, was essential to the toll broadcasting experiment.

Upon the recommendation of Mr. Mills, a temporary post as program director was offered to Mr. Samuel L. Ross, who was prominent in musical and entertainment circles. Mr. Ross took up his new duties on August 1, 1922, and held the post with conspicuous success until three years later when he became Director of the station's "artist bureau," which was the first in the history of radio to be established.[21]

[20] *Radio Broadcast,* vol. iii, no. 3 (July, 1923), pp. 180-181. This publication will be frequently quoted in the pages that follow because it was particularly enterprising and alert in reporting and discussing contemporary broadcasting developments.

[21] Mr. Ross is still engaged in activities requiring extensive association with artists, being today an official of Broadcast Music, Inc.

The First Evening Program

The first evening program according to the schedule was to be given on Thursday, July 27, but WBAY stayed off the air out of courtesy to WJZ, which had announced a prize-fight broadcast. August 3, a week later, was the date of the station's first experimental evening broadcast. Mr. G. W. Peck, of the Long Lines Commercial Department, opened with a description of the station and the purpose for which it had been established, and the entertainment that followed consisted of vocal and instrumental solos rendered by amateur musicians among local telephone forces, most of them from the Long Lines organization. There was also a baseball talk by Mr. Frank Graham of the New York *Sun* and "Reminiscences of Minstrel Days" by the composer, Mr. Harry Armstrong. Because the program of the willing telephone amateurs is of historical interest, it deserves recording here in full:

PROGRAM

Station WBAY—24 Walker Street, New York—August 3, 1922

7:30–8:00	Victor records and player piano music
8:00–8:07	Announcement of opening of station—George W. Peck, Long Lines Commercial Department
8:08–8:22	Vocal selections, Miss Helen Graves, Long Lines Plant Department (a) "Just a Song at Twilight" (b) Selected (c) Selected Mrs. M. W. Swayze, accompanist, Long Lines Commercial Department
8:23–8:33	Talk: The value of effective speech in talking by wire and radio, followed by recitation of James Whitcomb Riley's "An Old Sweetheart of Mine" Miss Edna Cunningham, Long Lines Traffic Dept.
8:34–8:44	Violin selections, Mr. Joseph Koznick, A. T. & T. Drafting Department (a) Träumerei (b) Melody in F, Rubinstein Mr. William Schmidt, accompanist, New York Tel. Co.
8:45–8:59	Baseball Talk, Mr. Frank Graham, New York Sun

9:00–9:14 Vocal Selections, Miss Anna Hermann, Long Lines Commercial Department
(a) Selected
(b) Selected
Mrs. M. W. Swayze, accompanist, Long Lines Commercial Dept.

9:15–9:21 Piano solos, Mr. F. R. Marion, Long Lines Engineering Dept.

9:22–9:28 Report on weather and climate conditions throughout the United States as of 8:00 P.M., with reference to seashore and mountain resorts and to following points: Pittsburgh, Chicago, Denver, San Francisco, Miami, El Paso; information to be gathered and telegraphed to the studio by A. T. & T. Co. representatives. Mr. George Peck, Long Lines Commercial Dept.

9:29–9:49 Reminiscences of Minstrel Days; song and stories. Mr. Harry Armstrong, composer

9:50–9:55 Repetition of opening announcement—Mr. George Peck, Long Lines Commercial Department

9:56–10:06 Vocal Selections, Miss Edith F. Mills, Long Lines Traffic Dept.

10:07–10:13 Piano solo, Mr. F. R. Marion, Long Lines Engineering Department

10:14–10:24 Violin selections, Mr. Joseph Koznick, A. T. & T. Drafting Department
(a) "The Secret of Home Sweet Home"
(b) "For the Sake of Auld Lang Syne"
Accompanied by Mr. F. R. Marion, Long Lines Engineering Department

10:25–10:26 Final announcement to include "thank you" and "good night" by Mr. Peck

10:27–10:31 "Home Sweet Home" by Mr. F. R. Marion

CHAPTER VI

WBAY BECOMES WEAF

The Change to WEAF's Transmitter

WBAY'S first evening program, of August 3, 1922, must have been a somewhat disappointing event for the American Company's president, Mr. Harry B. Thayer. He had invited a group of friends to his home in New Canaan, Connecticut, to listen, and his chagrined report to D&R on the following day was that throughout the evening WBAY's signals were noticeably weaker than those from WJZ in New Jersey. But there was improvement in signal strength a few days later when the station began to use the Western Electric Company's transmitter at the West Street laboratory, which had the call letters WEAF. The switchover is recorded on the log-book page dated August 16, which has the entry "turn station over to D&R antenna."

The testing studio in the West Street building was also used as program headquarters until the installation of an emergency "equalizer" on the line from WBAY's studio. It was constructed by Mr. M. E. Strieby[1] of D&R, and consisted, according to today's recollections, of a laboratory decode resistance box, with a honeycomb radio coil and a small telephone condenser attached to its side by tire tape! With this homemade device resulting in satisfactory transmission between the two locations, the WEAF transmitter was thereafter operated by "remote" control, while D&R engineers used the WBAY apparatus for the field strength tests which have already been described.

The WEAF antenna, on the west rim of Manhattan Island, was

[1] Mr. Strieby is now Long Lines Staff Engineer of Overseas and Special Services.

more favorably located and was lower than that of WBAY; and three weeks after the station's initial evening broadcast Mr. R. G. Rich, who had been functioning at the Walker Street Station as a general "observer" for Operation B, was able to report:

> From letters received from the outside, the people seem well pleased with our programs. We get a great deal of flattery over the wire and through the mails, but very little adverse criticism. It would seem that people are not so apt to tell us what they don't like as what they do like.

In this report from Mr. Rich, which is dated August 25, is a further observation that probably pleased the telephone technicians, "The modulation from our equipment is still slightly better than at WJZ."

Thus was WEAF beginning to acquire the radio personality, based on both broadcasting technique and program quality, that was to make it an outstanding radio station. What its programs meant to radio listeners was evidenced by the letters received at the station every day, many of them from points hundreds of miles away, which the station's management acknowledged with much appreciation. One of the first of many touching letters read as follows:

> Southern Pines N. C.
> Away down in the Sticks
> September, 1922.
>
> Dear Sir:
>
> I just wish to thank you for the pleasure you gave me and our folks with your very fine music selections; tell the artists they were fine. I am a little fellow fourteen who has been operated on twice by the great New York Doctor Fred Albee at the Post Graduate New York and don't get out of bed more than a few hours a day so you can realize the pleasure radio and the good people who broadcast it give me and other shut ins. May God Bless you all.
>
> Daddy says nothing but good comes out of New York and that's why you have the best music. He was born in New York City and we are now 575 miles by Rail Road from you and the music you gave us tonight was the best that we have ever heard please tell the artist and everybody. I will close thanking you again.
>
> I remain
>
> ——— ———
>
> Southern Pines N. C.
> 75 miles South of Raleigh, N. C.
> 575 miles from New York City

The files show that Commercial Manager Drake took the time to send this boy a special letter of acknowledgment:

September 11, 1922

Dear Friend:

Of the many letters we have received since the opening of this station, I am sure that your letter is the most interesting of them all, and it gives us great pleasure to know that we have been able, by means of our broadcasting station, to reach you "way down in the sticks."

We broadcast every day except Sunday between 11 A.M. and 12 Noon; also at 4:30 P.M. to 5:30 P.M., and on Thursday nights from 7:30 P.M. to about eleven o'clock, daylight saving time. It is hardly likely that you will receive our daytime programs, as the daytime range is not as great as at night.

We are indeed glad that we can be of some service to you, and that we are able through the agency of radio to afford you some measure of entertainment and pleasure during your affliction, from which we earnestly hope you will soon entirely recover, and we shall take pleasure in conveying your thanks to the artists who entertained us on last Thursday evening.

With kindest regards, we are

Cordially yours,

———— ————

There were many letters to the station so individual and so personal as to merit a special reply, although the normal practice at the time was to mail a printed folder showing pictures of the station and including the following acknowledgment:

Thank you for your communication regarding the broadcasting which you heard from W.E.A.F. We are glad indeed to know that you received us so well, and hope that we may be able through the agency of radio to afford you much more enjoyment and pleasure.

At present we do not print programs of our concerts other than those appearing in the New York daily papers. Each selection, however, is announced by radio just before it is broadcasted.

Our 400 meter schedule is as follows: 4:30 to 5:30 P.M. on weekdays, and from 8:00 to 10:00 P.M. on Monday, Wednesday, Thursday and Saturday evenings.

Comments and suggestions regarding our programs are greatly appreciated, and we trust that we may have the pleasure of hearing from you again.

Yours very truly,
Manager of Radio Broadcasting
STATION—WEAF

It can be assumed that probably something different from this formal and impersonal acknowledgment would have been sent in reply to the following Christmas greeting, had the writer signed his name:

December 21, 1922

Dear Sirs:

It is 5:25 P.M.—you have just finished broadcasting; you have also practically finished breaking up a happy home. Our set was installed last evening. Today, my wife has not left her chair, listening in all day. Our apartment has not been cleaned—the beds not made—the baby bathed—and no dinner ready for me, her husband, and the former boss. Now, she is in love with the beautiful voice of the gentleman who announced your different soloists, etc. this afternoon, and has ordered my trunk brought up from the cellar and visaed my passport to leave tomorrow A.M. She enjoyed her day immensely and hopes it will continue forever. Hereafter, I shall sleep in the park. Merry Xmas.

Sincerely
(Signed) A Friend

P.S. Please tell Miss DeVoe that I who heard her voice, am in love with her. I am sure everyone who heard her also loves her. She must be fine to sing as she does.

The First Commercial Broadcasts

August 28, 1922, is the date of the first "commercial" broadcast; at 5:15 in the afternoon the Queensboro Corporation broadcast the first of a series of fifteen-minute announcements regarding its tenant-owned system of apartment houses at Jackson Heights, New York. Sales amounting to several thousand dollars were reported as resulting from the broadcasts, the last of which was made on September 21, which was also the date when two other business concerns, the Tidewater Oil Company and the American Express Company, made experimental announcements. The station's commercial representatives were finding that, although there had been many "prospects" at the beginning of operations, the prohibition against price references or package descriptions—the type of advertising called "direct" —made business concerns skeptical of the new medium. After two months' operation a total of only three hours of air time had been bought, and the station's revenues had amounted to only $550.

The Question of Radio Advertising

It may be useful to note, at this point in the record, the start of the discussion that was to continue for several years over the question, "Who is to pay for broadcasting?"

At first the principal debaters were the advertising journals, and the various trade publications that multiplied in number with the growth of public interest in radio matters.

There were only five radio publications listed in the long-established directory of publications issued by N. W. Ayer & Son in January, 1922, as follows:[2]

Q.S.T. (mo.) (Conn.)
Proceedings of the Institute of Radio Engineers (bi-mo.) (N. Y.)
Radio News (mo.) (N. Y.)
Wireless Age (mo.) (N. Y.)
Aviation and Wireless (mo.) (published in Ontario)

We can note the growing importance of radio broadcasting in American life from the next edition's listings of publications established to serve both the radio industry and radio listeners:

Calif.

Radio Journal (mo.)
Radio (mo.)

Conn.

Q.S.T. (mo.)

Illinois

Radio Digest Illustrated (wkly.)
Radio Topics (mo.)

Kansas

Radio Gazette (mo.)

N. J.

American Wireless Operator's Journal and Motor Inventions (mo.)

[2] *American Newspaper Annual and Directory.*

N. Y.

Radio Broadcast (mo.)
American Radio Journal (s-mo.)
Modulator (mo.)
Popular Radio (mo.)
Proceedings of the Institute of Radio Engineers (bi-mo.)
Radio Dealer (mo.)
Radio Merchandising (mo.)
Radio News (mo.)
Radio Retailer and Jobber (fortnightly)
Radio Supplies and Dealer (mo.)
Radio Trade Journal (mo.)
Radio World (wkly.)
Wireless Age (mo.)

Pa.

Radio Broadcasting News (wkly.)

Texas

Southwestern Broadcaster (wkly.)

Ontario

Radio (mo.)
Radio Broadcasting Program (wkly.)
Radio Life (mo.)

As early as the spring of 1922 the use of radio for advertising purposes was a topic for newspaper and magazine comment. The most widely circulated publication in advertising circles, *Printers' Ink,* had discussed the subject in general terms on the editorial page in its April 27th issue:[3]

It is estimated that more than 500,000 radio-receiving sets have been sold during the past six months, and already there is more or less discussion of the advertising possibilities that the new enterprise opens up. . . .

Undoubtedly the possibilities are alluring, but in our opinion, the dangers are equally so. Handled with tact and discretion, radio advertising might become effective and profitable; on the other hand, it may easily be handled in such a way as not only to defeat its own purpose, but also to react unfavor-

[3] See footnote on page 118 of this volume.

ably upon advertising in general. It will not do to forget that the public's good-will toward advertising is an asset of incalculable importance, and advertisers will do well to consider all sides of the radio proposition rather carefully.

Any attempt to make the radio an advertising medium, in the accepted sense of the term, would, we think, prove positively offensive to great numbers of people. The family circle is not a public place, and advertising has no business intruding there unless it is invited. . . .

We certainly do not wish to make advertising offensive or distasteful, for that is to defeat the very purpose for which advertising exists. And radio advertising, if it comes to anything worth while, will have to develop a technique of its own so as not to offend its auditors. The man who does not want to read a paint ad in the newspaper, can turn the page and read something else. But the man on the end of the radio must listen, or shut off entirely. That is a big distinction that ought not to be overlooked.

By the middle of the year the discussion was becoming more specific. In the third issue of *Radio Broadcast,*[4] published in July, which was before WBAY had commenced operations, there was direct reference to the American Company's experiment:

By the time this is in press a new broadcasting station will be in operation. . . .

[Several paragraphs of description of WBAY follow.]

This A. T. and T. station is being constructed, and is to be operated, purely as an experiment. It had its inception in repeated demands upon the company for supplying broadcasting transmitting sets. . . . In all there were more than sixty such requests for apparatus, to be operated in New York City.

. . . . With the idea of avoiding this situation [jamming the air] and further to get first hand information on the need and desirability of such broadcast advertising the A. T. and T. Co. decided to erect and operate themselves a first class station, renting it to those firms and institutions which think they want such service; the station is to be a regular toll station where a merchant rents the privilege of using the ether for calling his wares.

Is there a demand for such a service, and, still more important, does the radio public want the ether used for such purposes? The operation of WBAY for a few months will probably furnish an answer to these questions. Whether the answer be Yes or No the operation of this station . . . will be of benefit to the radio public because of the technical excellence of the station; the quality of transmission will probably be better than any other station now operating, so will serve as a stimulus to the others to improve the quality of their transmission to equal that of this new station.

[4] Vol. i, no. 3 (July, 1922), p. 196.

The *American Radio Journal*[5] in an editorial for June, 1922, asserted that "the broadcasting situation is in a serious muddle," and that "back of it all is the dollar problem of 'Who Pays?'" The magazine continued its discussion of broadcasting economics by concluding:

. . . . There are three solutions. One is that the municipalities should undertake to handle the programs on a civic entertainment basis.

. . . . The second method of securing adequate broadcasting, is to charge the public under some such plan as that which is now being worked out by the General Electric Company. A large corporation having the facilities to erect a national system of stations and to collect revenues from an enormous number of radio subscribers can quickly make broadcasting a matter of serious value to the public.

. . . . The third . . . method is to organize the trade and tax the members in one way or another so that a group of stations will be appointed to render programs on a basis of merit. This means taxation for the manufacturer who makes the equipment, taxation for the jobber and distributor who aid in the sales distribution, and taxation for the dealer who sells the public. All of it must eventually be paid for by the consumer.

Readers of *Radio Dealer*[6] were exhorted in July to protest against radio advertising by petitioning Congress on the subject:

. . . . The RADIO DEALER is against the broadcasting of advertising matter on the 360-meter wave length and believes that some congressional action should be taken to prohibit the use of this wave length, which has come to stand for entertainment and amusement, for advertising of any character.

Readers of the RADIO DEALER can help prevent a monopoly of the air by powerful stations broadcasting advertising by joining in this protest.

The time to speak is now, the time to act, today. Every reader of this publication is urged to write his congressmen today, demanding that stations broadcasting advertising matter be forbidden the use of the 360-wave length.

In November[7] of the same year this magazine was continuing its opposition:

"At its new station atop the Walker Street telephone building, the American Telephone and Telegraph Company has the latest apparatus, and a plan

[5] Vol. i, no. 4 (June 15, 1922), p. 4.
[6] Vol. i, no. 4 (July, 1922), p. 33.
[7] Vol. ii, no. 2 (Nov., 1922), p. 55.

Participants in the first evening program of WBAY, 1922. Miss Helen Graves, of the American Telephone and Telegraph Company Long Lines Plant Department, with Mrs. May Swayze, of the Long Lines Commercial Department, accompanist.

Experimental station 2XB at the West Street laboratory, which in 1922 became WEAF.

for broadcasting advertising to all radio fans—of selling time to soaps, home builders, razor blades, cocoa, hair tonics, and politicians, at so much an hour."

This quoted paragraph appeared in the *New York Times,* in a radio news story, which it ran in a recent Sunday issue.

It is to be hoped that the *New York Times* is in error, for the time is not quite here for conserving the air for advertising. The one million set owners haven't paid out money for radio for the purpose of listening to reasons why this or that product should be purchased.

Air advertising, meaning the *use* of the air for advertising purposes will develop, but this is not the time and New York City is not the place for any experiment, and though the *Times* carried this item it is hardly likely that the air advertising plans are really consummated. . . .

The radio industry itself, the makers of sets as well as parts, and the wholesalers as well as retailers are opposed to the use of the air for advertising purposes. . . .

Radio will suffer a severe setback if direct advertising is broadcasted. There is no need for the sale of air rights and it is a matter of regret, to most of those who realize that the radio art is in its infancy to learn that the commercial minds of the community are already prepared to take advantage of a condition developed for them—not by them. . . .

If the men who entertain the hope of broadcasting general advertising are in any manner justified in their ambition; if their desire is based upon service; if they have logical reasons to advance for desiring to monopolize the air—why don't they tell us about it?

Also in November appeared a prominent article in *Radio Broadcast*[8] entitled "Should Radio Be Used for Advertising?", referring to the noticeable effort of some radio stations to obtain some commercial benefit from their broadcasts. The writer said:

Driblets of advertising, most of it indirect so far, to be sure, but still unmistakable, are floating through the ether every day. Concerts are seasoned here and there with a dash of advertising paprika. . . . More of this sort of thing may be expected. And once the avalanche gets a good start, nothing short of an Act of Congress will suffice to stop it.

Such opinions, of course, reflected the interest of listeners in entertainment and ignored the vital question of broadcasting's support. As this record will show, it was the experiment in toll broadcasting and the resulting "sponsored" programs that provided the answer, but several years were to pass before this would be realized by radio

[8] Vol. ii, no. 1 (Nov., 1922), p. 76. Article by Joseph H. Jackson.

"fans" and station owners alike. In discussing the relation between entertainment and broadcasting economics, a later writer summed up the matter thus: "A tax upon radio sets, or radio advertising, was the only choice. Great Britain was to choose the former; the United States of America the latter alternative." If this writer had pointed out that broadcasting in Great Britain became a government activity, while in America it is a free enterprise under federal regulation, he would have epitomized the whole development that resulted from the telephone company's public-service concept.

A Separate Organization for WEAF

By the fall of 1922 it was apparent that the idea of broadcasting for hire could not be completely explored without a studio location that was more accessible to program artists, and without an expanded organization. It was also the lesson of experience that more than one broadcasting studio was essential in order to avoid confusion when one program ended and the next one began.

Accordingly, it was decided to make a fresh start with the experiment—to relieve Long Lines of the entire responsibility of promoting and developing the service, and to set about the creation of a separate broadcasting department, utilizing the existing station staff as a nucleus. To head this new operational unit Mr. W. E. Harkness was appointed Manager of Broadcasting late in October; plans were laid to build the special organization required to ensure the best possible programs while developing the station's commercial potentialities; and much study was given to questions of new studio and new transmitter locations.

It was in October, also, that the original license was superseded by a Class B license, with an assigned wave length of 400 meters, and a new schedule went into effect permitting broadcasting every weekday from 4:30 to 5:30 P.M. and evening broadcasts from 8 P.M. to 10 P.M. on Monday, Wednesday, Thursday, and Saturday. The former limit of one evening broadcast a week had indeed been a handicap.

To develop and manage the new broadcasting department, Mr. Harkness was transferred from the Long Lines organization where he was investigating the commercial development of a typewriter telegraph service—what later became the company's teletypewriter service. He had reëntered the Bell System organization in 1920 after a wide experience as a consultant in problems of organization and management, preceded by several years' service with the Western Electric Company.

The members of the station's original staff, and those selected by Mr. Harkness to join them in the responsibility of giving increased momentum to the WEAF experiment, deserve to have their names recorded at this point, since they were pioneers in what a later radio historian called "the most efficient broadcasting organization in the world." The conditions under which the "toll broadcasting" idea was brought from bud to flower can probably best be suggested by recalling the duties of those who bore the initial burdens of the undertaking.

At the beginning of the station's operation, the program unit, headed by Mr. Samuel L. Ross, included Miss Helen Hann, one of the talented Long Lines amateur entertainers, who acted both as studio hostess and as feminine announcer. Mr. V. A. Randall, another member of the Long Lines organization, who replaced Mr. G. W. Peck as announcer on August 7, 1922, was the original studio director, and had as an assistant a most versatile musician, Mr. A. V. Llufrio. Members of the original staff still speak with enthusiasm of Mr. Llufrio's emergency service in WEAF's early days, as pianist and singer, when program artists were delayed in arriving at the Walker Street studio. "It's not enough to say," reports Mr. Ross, "that he 'doubled in brass;' he tripled in it!" Well remembered, too, is Mr. Llufrio's willing and helpful coöperation with the station engineers, for he played and sang tirelessly during their innumerable tests of station equipment and wire lines.

In the fall of 1922 Miss Marion Lamphere joined Mr. Ross as program assistant; a few months later Mr. Gerard Chatfield took up similar duties, and still later Mrs. Ruth Hyde became a member of the programming group. All three rendered great assistance in connection with the program arrangements upon which the station depended for its distinction and success. Mr. Chatfield himself became program director after Mr. Ross's appointment, in 1925, as Director of the station's Artist's Bureau.

Technical Operation

Mr. J. G. Truesdell, from the Long Lines organization, was known in the broadcasting group, according to telephone terminology, as "Plant Manager," and was responsible for all technical operations.

Mr. Truesdell's technical preparation for the assignment to WBAY and WEAF had already included much experience with the Bell System's development of public-address systems. He had supervised their operation at the Republican and Democratic national conventions in 1920, and was in charge of the technical arrangements involving the use of public-address apparatus at the inauguration of President Harding in March, 1921, when the largest audience which had ever heard an inaugural address thronged the area adjacent to the Capitol. Again, on Armistice Day, 1921, when President Harding's address at the burial of the Unknown Soldier at Arlington, Va., was transmitted by wire to New York and San Francisco and heard by huge audiences in those cities as well as at Arlington, Mr. Truesdell was in charge of the operation of the circuits and the apparatus employed. To extend the record of Mr. Truesdell's technical relations with the nation's chief executive, it might be mentioned here that he was one of the telephone engineers in charge of the public-address system installed for President Harding's use on the train in which the President crossed the continent in the summer of 1923 and was invited to join the President's party on the subsequent visit to Alaska.

The Broadcasting Department was later to have two other members with experience in serving Presidents. Mr. G. W. Johnstone, who became WEAF's Press Relations Manager, had been radio operator on the U.S.S. *George Washington,* which took President Wilson on his second trip from the United States to France and return; and Mr. Herman Schoenberger, who joined the station's engineering staff, had been President Theodore Roosevelt's operator on the Presidential yacht *Mayflower.*

Serving as Assistant Plant Manager was Mr. E. R. Taylor,[9] who had been transferred from the "equipment-development" group of

[9] Mr. Taylor is now a member of the technical staff of the Bell Telephone Laboratories.

the D&R organization, headed by Mr. L. F. Morehouse, to care for studio engineering details.

Mr. Taylor's group of assistants included many engineers who later played important parts in the development and expansion of the National Broadcasting Company after its acquisition of the station in 1926. One was Mr. O. B. Hanson, who joined the department in December, 1922, after experience as Chief Operator at station WAAM. He later advanced to the position of Plant Manager, which he filled with unusual distinction because of his engineering resourcefulness and technical skill. Another was Mr. George McElrath, who was transferred from the Long Lines construction forces and became, in Mr. Taylor's words, one of WEAF's "wheelhorse" operators. Today they head NBC's engineering staff, the former as Vice-president and Chief Engineer, with Mr. McElrath as Operations Engineer.

Several other members of Mr. Taylor's pioneer group of assistants also have important responsibilities today in the NBC organization —evidence that when the station was sold there was transferred engineering talent, as well as business contracts and reputation. Mr. George Stewart, who before joining the WEAF staff had been one of the engineers engaged in the development of marine radio telephony at the Deal Beach experimental station, is now NBC's national Recording Supervisor. Mr. Albert W. Protzman is now that company's Television Technical Director. Mr. A. H. Saxton, who was Mr. Taylor's Night Chief Operator, is NBC's West Coast Division Engineer, and Mr. Howard Luttgens supervises operations centering in Chicago.

Other engineers who were identified with WEAF's early technical operations were Messrs. E. R. Cullen, J. L. Reynolds, Rufus Caldwell, Eugene Grossman, who became WEAF's Assistant Plant Manager, and Mr. E. J. Content, who is now WOR's Assistant Chief Engineer. Later the group included still others who have had prominent radio careers, including Mr. George Milne, who is now the American Broadcasting Company's Chief Engineer and Mr. R. M. Morris, who is Development and Research Engineer for NBC.

It is no wonder that WEAF, being staffed so liberally with engineering personnel, should acquire from the start an unsurpassed record for technical performance. Constantly advising the station engineers on the innumerable details connected with pickup and transmission technique was the headquarters D&R group of "transmission-development" engineers. In addition, there were the engineers of the Western Electric Company who had themselves developed and designed the transmitting equipment. The technical knowledge that was available, and that was applied, to the WEAF experiment was certainly of an impressive character.

It might be noted that Mr. R. S. Fenimore, who for many months was in direct charge of station operation and studio maintenance, still has responsibilities connected with broadcasting, for, as head of the Long Lines repeater station at Elizabethtown, N. Y., he supervises the circuits in the New York-Montreal telephone cable, which includes those serving the Canadian broadcasting stations on several networks.

Promotional Organization

One of Mr. Harkness' most important decisions in organizing his new department was to invite Mr. George F. McClelland to leave his post as Secretary of the Association of National Advertisers in order to explore, as an experienced advertising expert, the opportunities for WEAF service to the business world. The latter took up his new duties in November, Mr. H. C. Smith continuing as a commercial representative for the station.

With an immediate enthusiasm for broadcasting's power to spread the message of business, to create markets, to arouse consumer demand, and to support wholesale and retail merchandising activities, Mr. McClelland became WEAF's foremost exponent of the idea from which a national broadcasting service was developed. Gifted with imagination, with exceptional ability, and with unusual personal charm, he did more than any other one man to promote the medium of broadcasting among advertisers and their agents. From the beginning of his radio career as leader of WEAF's sales representatives, he contributed brilliantly to the station's progress. When he later became Manager of Broadcasting, he was faced with unique and difficult problems arising from the development of network broadcasting and the maintenance of WEAF's supremacy in sustaining program features. The post demanded unusual qualities, all of which Mr. McClelland possessed, and his success was notable indeed.

There are many stories still circulating about Mr. McClelland's accomplishments that testify to the affectionate remembrance in which he is held by his pioneer WEAF colleagues. It is interesting that the one most frequently repeated should not refer to any commercial activity but rather to an emergency performance as an announcer! The occasion was WEAF's first prize-fight broadcast, from Jersey City's "Boyles Thirty Acres," for announcing which the station had engaged a local celebrity. While this announcer rested between the first and second rounds, Mr. McClelland undertook to give the radio listeners some "local color." At once telephone bells at WEAF began ringing and excited voices demanded, "Switch those announcers! Let the second one describe the fight!" Manager Harkness' response to this mandate from the fight "fans," as reported to this writer, was a quick direction to Mr. Fenimore in the control-room "Get Mac on the order wire!" and WEAF's commercial manager received, to his surprise, instructions to exchange places with the regular announcer, but only at intervals, so that the latter's feelings might be spared while the fight enthusiasts were being placated.

When Mr. McClelland became Manager of Broadcasting, succeeding Mr. J. A. Holman,[10] the leadership of the station's commercial promotion fell to Mr. George Podeyn,[11] who had been invited by Mr. Harkness to join the department in 1923. He later served as the department's Sales Manager with marked success, heading a unit in the organization having responsibilities and problems that became more and more numerous and exacting as network broadcasting developed. Mr. William Ensign[12] was next to join this group in 1923, and Mr. Podeyn's staff eventually included Messrs. H. G. Foster, D. S. Tuthill, H. A. Woodman, R. L. Clark, and D. R. Buckham. All of them are well remembered in advertising circles as evangelists

[10] Mr. Holman succeeded Mr. Harkness as Station Manager in November, 1923, when the latter became an Assistant Vice-president upon the transfer of Mr. A. H. Griswold to the Pacific Telephone and Telegraph Company.

[11] Mr. Podeyn is now Manager of Station WHJB at Greensburg, Pa.

[12] Mr. Ensign is now Sales Executive of the Columbia Broadcasting System.

of the idea which generated "sponsored" programs and which therein provided the answer to the question of broadcasting's economic support.

THE OFFICE FORCE

To supervise the establishment of a system of accounts for the new Broadcasting Department, Mr. Frank S. Spring was transferred from the Comptroller's organization of the American Company. He joined the department in November, 1922, bringing with him Mr. H. F. McKeon as assistant, and selecting soon afterwards another able assistant, Mr. Mark J. Woods, from the New York Telephone Company's accounting staff.

With the department's expansion it was inevitable that the scope of Mr. Spring's activities should broaden in order to utilize his executive talents, and for some time before the sale of the station in 1926, he was Assistant Manager of Broadcasting, supervising all the department's functions except that headed by Plant Manager O. B. Hanson. He contributed enormously to the station's success in meeting the changing and difficult problems arising from broadcasting's growth and network development.[13]

Mr. Spring's early assistants, Mr. McKeon and Mr. Woods, also made important contributions to this success as their responsibilities increased with the department's steady growth. By 1926 Mr. McKeon, as Chief Clerk, headed a departmental division of 30,[14] with Mr. Woods functioning as supervisor of accounts and office routines. When the station passed into the hands of the National Broadcasting Company in the fall of the year, Mr. McKeon was auditor, and his NBC office today is that of Comptroller. Mr. Woods, too, has had an unbroken career in radio, being today the President of the American Broadcasting Company.

WEAF's fundamental problem as an experimental "toll" station was to attract, hold, and increase its audience through the character

[13] Mr. Spring today is President of the Associated Telephone and Telegraph Company.

[14] One member was among the best known and most popular of WEAF's personalities, Miss Betty Lutz, who as general "hostess" greeted artists and studio visitors from her desk in WEAF's reception room with well-remembered tact and charm. She is well known today to radio listeners in the Midwest through her broadcasts as "Betty Crocker."

and quality of its programs. To this end the station made an unusual and continuing effort to explore the tastes, desires, and program reactions of radio listeners. The study of the station's audience mail was therefore, from the start, one of the staff's most important concerns.

Under Miss Alice Hunt, now Mrs. E. R. Taylor, the mail-analysis function quickly expanded to become a "key" activity, with many assistants required for the tabulation, acknowledgment, and circulation of the correspondence that reached the station in ever increasing amounts. One of Mrs. Taylor's interesting recollections today is the significant increase in the station's mail when, following a talk by Miss Marion Davies on January 27, 1923, on "How I make up for the movies,"[15] an autographed photograph of the actress was offered to all requesting one. It was the first free offer in WEAF's history. "Before that broadcast," Mrs. Taylor recalls, "the station was receiving a few dozen letters a day; immediately after it there were hundreds. It was tangible proof that people were listening to WEAF programs and Commercial Manager McClelland simply bubbled with enthusiasm and rushed out to tell prospective advertisers about it."

Miss Hunt's successor, late in 1923, as supervisor of files and correspondence, was Miss Adelaide Piana, who is today in charge of Blue Network files. Many reports by Miss Hunt and Miss Piana are in the station's old files and show with what ability and care they analyzed and interpreted, for the station's management, the public's written response to WEAF's program offerings.

This public response, from the beginning of the broadcasting experiment, gave valuable clues as to program preferences, and every program experiment brought a new burst of comment that revealed something about WEAF's growing audience through such details as age, sex, handwriting, stationery, and location. The first broadcasting of symphony music, for example, at once changed the character of the audience mail, as did the venturesome addition to the programs of informative talks on personal, household, and business matters. Even when the broadcasting schedule was so limited, the

[15] This talk was sponsored by a manufacturer of cosmetics.

letters and postal cards were numerous. Before the end of 1923 they were reaching the station at the rate of 800 a day and some 25,000 were received, according to the records, during the first two weeks of 1924. They were all studied with minute care so that the station and its advertisers might have the clearest possible conception of the public that WEAF's experimental policies were attracting.

A retrospective remark by Miss Piana in the summer of 1944, during her splendid coöperation with the present writer in locating documents pertaining to the station's history, suggests the importance and usefulness of WEAF's mail-handling methods. "When I first went to NBC," she said, "after WEAF became its key station, I expected to be told to use the WJZ system of analysis and filing. But WJZ didn't have a really good system then, and I remember how complimented I felt that WEAF mail was not turned over to WJZ people for handling but, on the contrary, all fan mail was turned over to the WEAF staff!"

Another of WEAF's "key" activities was that carried on by Mr. R. G. Rich, who had the all-important task of obtaining the data from which the "radio market" could be quantitatively and qualitatively analyzed. Prior to his service during World War I, Mr. Rich had been one of Western Electric's engineers and returned to the Bell System in 1922 as a member of the Operation B group headed by Mr. Elam Miller and later transferred to the Broadcasting Department.

Information about the character of WEAF's radio audience that would enable advertisers to judge the value of the radio medium was non-existent, as WEAF's programs were winning an ever growing popularity. Mr. Rich's investigations were of a pioneering character and resulted in valuable statistical information regarding the types of receivers and loud-speakers in use, the number of listeners per set, and the economic status of the listeners. Such economic research was, of course, fundamental to the success of the WEAF experiment and was carried on continuously. Through it, when there was a network available for broadcasters, the department's commercial representatives were enabled to provide advertisers and their agents with accurate market and economic data for all territories covered. It was thus an important factor in the promotion of the network idea that proved how broadcasting could be financially supported.[16]

The First Station Accompanist

A glimpse of WEAF's early environment is given by Mrs. Howard Hunter, formerly Miss Barr, who thus described for the writer the circumstances of her first broadcast:

> I was a regular WEAF listener, and having a holiday from my bank job on Washington's Birthday, 1923, I visited the studio out of curiosity where a hostess received me most cordially, and an engineer explained the equipment. While I was being conducted through the premises a singer arrived to begin a scheduled broadcast. The studio was in consternation because he had failed to bring his own accompanist and there was nobody in the studio who could play. Mr. Llufrio, who was on the staff as announcer, also acted as accompanist when needed, but he wasn't on hand. It was just one of those early studio emergencies; we had lots of them later. So I volunteered to play the accompaniments. While the singer rested, I played piano solos, and we alternated that way for two hours, with Mr. Randall announcing the numbers.

That was how WEAF's listeners first heard the name, and the music, of Winifred T. Barr, who was asked by Program Director Ross, several weeks later, to become the station's first staff accompanist. Her service at WEAF embraced many duties, for she acted as studio hostess, announcer, and soloist, besides giving auditions to prospective studio entertainers. Of all the names identified with the station, hers and Graham McNamee's were undoubtedly the most familiar to the station's listeners. It was Miss Barr's distinction to be the first broadcasting artist to dedicate a new radio broadcasting station from a studio many miles distant from it. On July 4, 1923, her 15-minute program, played at WEAF, constituted the formal opening of the Bell System's second station, WCAP, at Washington, D. C.

[16] Following the sale of WEAF in 1926 Mr. Rich transferred to the Long Lines Department to study commercial problems relating to the wire transmission of pictures. From December, 1928, until his retirement in 1945 he was engaged in commercial research and statistical activity on the staff of the Commercial Department of the New York Telephone Company in Albany, N. Y., the headquarters for the company's "Upstate Area."

DEPARTMENT SPIRIT

As Mrs. Hunter now recalls this four-year radio experience:

> It was a strenuous time, but the returns in personal satisfaction and fun were tremendous. It was the exceptionally cooperative spirit of the station personnel that made the work so rewarding. We had all caught the infection of being good telephone people, of doing the very best possible job that could be done. Long hours meant nothing to us in comparison with getting good results. Even when we could have had time off on a holiday, many of our staff would show up to be there just in case they were needed. We all wanted to make the experiment a success. If the Bell System would only start a station again, I'm sure the original staff would like to be taken back.

One of the pleasures of the present chronicler in collecting and collating the memories of pioneer members of the Broadcasting Department has been to note the affectionate references to the station and to Manager Harkness personally and to note, too, how many of these members expressed the thought of the one who wrote, after checking this record, "I am sure that I would be as enthusiastic as the other old timers to do it all over again under the guidance of A. T. & T." All the recollections which have been drawn upon in compiling this account reveal that it was truly an enthusiastic and coöperative band that made WEAF an institution in itself and that built the station's reputation for program personality and studio courtesy, as well as for broadcasting technique.

It was a group that expanded rapidly to include staff writers and musicians, engineers, commercial representatives, statisticians, receptionists, clerks, and famous announcers, as the scope of the broadcasting experiment constantly broadened. When the company relinquished operation of the station, the department's personnel numbered more than a hundred. Although functioning outside the orbit of normal telephone activity, it nevertheless felt itself to be part of the Bell System recognized as giving the best telephone service in the world, and it worked devotedly to win the same distinction for its broadcasting service. In the entire telephone organization, so noted for its teamwork, there was no group more efficient or more loyal, and all who were interviewed during the preparation of these pages shared the nostalgic feeling that "Those were the days!"

Selection of a Downtown Studio Location

At first it was believed that the new studio should be established in the theatrical district of New York's Times Square. Such a location would have met the convenience of entertainers but would have placed the new department several miles away from headquarters supervision. It was because the headquarters building was well situated from the standpoint of transportation facilities that the decision was reached to centralize both operation and supervision at 195 Broadway. By the end of November plans[17] were ready for two fourth-floor studios—which, however, were not opened for use until April of the next year—a large one for choral groups and orchestras, and a smaller one for speakers and soloists, with a control-room between them, for the operation of which Engineers Taylor and Hanson designed a unique and most effective system of switches and signal lights.[18]

[17] Drawings and other technical data pertaining to this fourth-floor layout are in the Bell Telephone Laboratories Central Office files.

[18] Engineer B. S. McCutcheon should be recorded as having had important responsibilities in connection with the acoustic treatment of both the WBAY and WEAF studios. At the latter the acoustic problems were specially challenging since the ceilings were low and there were the street noises of a busy business district.

CHAPTER VII

PROGRAM EXPERIMENTS AT WALKER STREET

Commercial Broadcasts

WHILE the new studio quarters were being prepared, the Broadcasting Department began to meet with some success in stimulating the commercial use of the station's facilities. During November, 1922, the first month of the new department's activity, there were seven broadcasters, all of whom used evening hours for their presentations. Among them was the first department store to engage the service, R. H. Macy and Company. The number also included a dentifrice manufacturer, with a discreet talk on the care of the teeth; a political organization, with November talks to the voters; and a motion-picture producer, who broadcast details about a film story, bringing members of his cast to the microphone.

The Broadcasting Department's accounting records show that in the following month, December, there were 13 broadcasters, three of them representing New York department stores, one of which was Gimbel Brothers. The extensive series of broadcasts which this well-known retail concern inaugurated through WEAF in March emphasizes in an interesting way the motive behind the American Company's broadcasting venture.

This store was one of the many business organizations that had been considering the erection of a private broadcasting station and had inquired, in October, 1922, as to the availability of Western Electric equipment. The American Company's station had been established in order to provide facilities for the use of such concerns and thus save them the investment and expense of operating private stations in an area where the air was already congested.

Through the arrangement[1] worked out with Gimbel Brothers, the store built a studio on an upper floor in which speech-input equipment was installed by the American Company and a wire connection provided to the WEAF control-room. With WEAF personnel in charge of operation and maintenance, the store became, in March, 1923, the first "sponsor" of entertainment programs, and its studio was the first broadcasting location where the general public could observe broadcasting in progress.

The programs of Browning King, Inc.,[2] that began in April have also been called the first that were "commercially sponsored." They differed from those sponsored by Gimbel Brothers in that the orchestra which provided the entertainment was obligated to give no other radio performances. The historical distinction is that while the department store was the first WEAF client to provide radio entertainment, Browning King, Inc., was the first commercial sponsor of an entertainment program designed for its own exclusive presentation. The latter company also had been considering the establishment of a broadcasting station of its own for which the WEAF toll facilities afforded a practical and far less costly substitute.

Of the 13 broadcasters in December, 1922, one was the William H. Rankin Company, a New York advertising agency which was the first concern in its field to use radio. Later, in the September, 1929, issue of *Broadcast Advertising,*[3] the manager of the Rankin Company's radio department recalled the experience:

. . . Mr. G. F. McClelland, called on the head of our company for the purpose of enlisting his aid in selling some of our customers a ten-minute talk on station WEAF for $100. That was the conception of the value of the Commercial Radio Broadcasting the latter part of 1922. . . . Our president told

[1] Broadcasting Department Contract #38. Later, Gimbel Brothers had their own broadcasting station at the New York store and also in Philadelphia.

[2] Broadcasting Department Contract #47. The first program was on April 25. The music was "Anna C. Byrnes and her orchestra." The station's strict attitude at the time toward advertising announcements is shown by the record that no reference to the sponsor as a clothing manufacturer was permitted.

[3] Vol. i, no. 6, p. 10, "Broadcasting in America," by Robert H. Rankin.

Mr. McClelland he would be his first customer and pay $100 to talk ten minutes on station WEAF—and he took as his subject "Advertising and Its Relation to the Public," broadcasting on December 30, 1922. At the end of his talk he offered to send a copy of it to any interested advertiser. We received about ten telephone calls and 15 letters and postcards, among them a prospective client who telephoned saying that he was very favorably impressed with the talk and the enterprise behind it.

Thus was born in our organization the belief that Radio Broadcasting could be made to increase the value of the advertising dollar of our customers in other media. Later, we learned by experience that Radio Broadcasting would create consumer demand in territories where the product never before had been sold or asked for. It would increase sales, stimulate intense dealer interest, build good-will not only among consumers, but the sales, the manufacturing departments and entire force of the manufacturer as well.

A memorandum in the files discussing some of these commercial presentations also has this to say about the station's experimental policies:

We have put on certain educational and benevolent subjects without pay for two reasons: first, to assist the various causes presented, and second, to determine the reaction of the public. Among these have been the following: The American Red Cross, the Federation of Jewish Charities, Anti-tuberculosis Association, American Society for the Control of Cancer, Mosquito Exterminating Commission. A further type of work we have done is the broadcasting of public notices for departments of the government and state, such as a message from the Postmaster to mail Christmas packages early, and one from the Department of Vehicles to remind automobile owners to secure their 1923 licenses promptly. We have also put on a number of sports events such as the principal football games of the leading colleges, and also important musical events like the broadcasting of an opera or symphony orchestra.

A Football Game Makes Radio History

One of the football broadcasts referred to in the memorandum just quoted made radio history, for it involved the first combination of long-distance telephone lines, radio broadcasting, and a public-address system.

The game was one between teams of Princeton and the University of Chicago and was played at the latter's Stagg Field on October 28, 1922. By means of high-quality transmitters and amplifiers located at the football field, announcements of the plays and the ap-

Miss Helen Hann, of the American Telephone and Telegraph Company Long Lines Department, was WEAF's first studio hostess and an announcer.

The Broadcasting Department of the American Telephone and Telegraph Company, August 1, 1923. Left to right, front row: B. J. Donnelly, E. R. Raguse, E. F. Grossman, E. J. Content, W. A. Irvin, G. E. Stewart, D. B. McKey, M. J. Woods, E. H. Felix, G. W. Johnstone, H. F. McKeon; second row: R. H. Caldwell, H. Schoenenberger, O. B. Hanson, E. R. Taylor, F. S. Spring, W. E. Harkness, G. F. McClelland, S. L. Ross, V. A. Randall, H. C. Smith, G. Chatfield, G. J. Podeyn; third row: A. V. Llufrio, M. L. Rackle, N. A. Conner, A. Hunt, A. Cheuvreux, E. E. Sniffin, G. Weightman, A. Piana, H. F. Starrett, E. L. Schneeweiss, J. Land, H. M. Hann, W. T. Barr, G. Turner, E. E. Howland, A. F. Castleman, M. Jackson, E. M. Charles, W. Rickert, M. Adler; fourth row: (left) A. Ropps, G. McElrath, A. H. Saxton, (right) J. J. Beloungy. Away on duty: J. G. Truesdell, J. L. Reynolds, R. S. Fenimore, A. W. Protzman, M. B. Lorenzen, G. McNamee, A. I. Healy, W. P. Sweeny, E. R. Cullen.

plause of the spectators were delivered to a cable circuit extending to the toll office of the Telephone Company in Chicago. This circuit was connected there to a long-distance line to New York. Not only did WEAF broadcast what the Stagg Field microphones picked up, but in Park Row, New York, a truck was provided with a radio receiving set which was arranged to operate a public-address system from which street crowds could also hear the program transmitted from Chicago.

It was possible to undertake this historic long-distance transmission experiment because Long Lines men along the route were already skilled in the technique of preparing the circuits through their experience during many demonstrations of the first transcontinental telephone line which had been opened for service in 1915.

Such demonstrations were favorite performances for Mr. John J. Carty, when Chief Engineer and later when Vice-president of the A. T. & T. Co.; he would call the roll of repeater stations between New York and San Francisco, and the answering voices along the line would give dramatic emphasis to the telephone's conquest of time and space. One of these roll calls was later broadcast, thrilling public and telephone employees alike with the revelation of communications progress.[4]

Other Sports Broadcasts

In the light of present-day popularity of football broadcasts, it is interesting to read in WEAF's files of the interest created by the broadcast of the Chicago-Princeton game of 1922. The report in question came from Princeton University and stated that following the broadcast a radio receiving set was installed in one of the lecture halls so that students could hear the play-by-play accounts of other Princeton games. When WEAF announced a broadcast of the Yale-Harvard game for November 25, this receiving set was installed in a small room for the benefit of a few university executives, since it was thought that Princetonians would not be concerned with the game, their team not being a participant.

As game time approached, however, the students began to pour into the lecture hall and vigorously demanded "service" on the Yale-

[4] See below, page 199.

Harvard game. The clamor grew to such proportions that the set was quickly reinstalled in the hall and more than 500 students stayed to listen. The file report reads: "The reception from WEAF was especially good, no wire line or transmitter distortion being apparent. Radio reports of football games will hereafter be a regular fixture at Princeton for the benefit of those who cannot attend."[5] The growth of radio's service to the nation, through network broadcasting, is well shown by the contrast between a Princeton audience of 500 and today's audience of many millions for sports broadcasts.

Program Distinction

From the beginning of the broadcasting experiment it was recognized that the company's station could occupy no other place in broadcasting than the lead, if it was to test thoroughly the desires and tastes of radio listeners. The Broadcasting Department was tireless in its effort to maintain this position of leadership and in its analysis of public comment on its programs. Technical excellence in broadcasting was of course assured by the knowledge and experience of telephone scientists and engineers, and the station's growing reputation for entertainment of unusual interest and variety made it possible to obtain program events that blazed new broadcasting trails.

One of these events was the broadcasting on November 11, 1922, of a performance of Verdi's opera "Aïda" by the Metropolitan Opera Company. The performance was given in the Kingsbridge Armory, several miles distant from WEAF's transmitter and was the first "remote control" experiment. The electrical installation required to control the broadcasting apparatus in the laboratories building was perhaps the most difficult of its kind that had yet been attempted anywhere, telephone engineers working for several days in prepar-

[5] "These Long Lines circuits, normally passing from 250 to 2500 cycles, were especially engineered to improve their quality for broadcasting purposes, and an attempt was made to equalize these circuits from 100 to 5000 cycles. . . . It must be borne in mind that in those days it took a week or so of preparation to arrange facilities and equipment for broadcasts of this nature, and only the A. T. & T. Co., with its vast telephone facilities and coordinated equipment could have made these events possible in the early days when revenue from broadcasting was unheard of." From report of Mr. O. B. Hanson to the Federal Communications Commission, referred to on page 33.

ing the telephone circuits for the transmission of music. It was a piece of engineering that soon became commonplace and routine, but at the time it was a pioneering accomplishment. Some of the engineers whom the writer has consulted still remember the technical preparation involved, chiefly because, as one of them asserted, it was "the first time on Manhattan Island that we used an intermediate amplifier."

Another "first" can be credited to WEAF in the same month. Satisfactory telephone circuits had been arranged to connect the Great Hall of the College of the City of New York with WEAF's transmitter so that the popular Sunday afternoon recitals of the college organist, Dr. Samuel Baldwin, could be broadcast; and a Philharmonic concert on November 22 in the same hall, four days before the series of organ recitals began, marked the first time that a public recital of a symphony orchestra had ever been broadcast direct from an auditorium. From five of these Philharmonic concerts the music of the masters went out on the radio waves, to aid greatly in WEAF's careful study of the desires of the radio audience.

The Capitol Theatre Broadcasts

Of the many entertainment features that distinguished WEAF programs while its new studio was being put in readiness, none proved more popular than the Sunday night broadcasts from the Capitol Theatre, the first of which occurred on November 19, 1922. There is a story to tell in connection with them because it accents the technical resources behind the American Company's broadcasting experiment.

The Capitol Theatre in New York was, at the time, the world's largest motion-picture theatre and was under the direction of Mr. S. L. Rothafel, who was later to be known to millions of radio listeners as "Roxy." It was famous for its elaborate stage shows which called for long and tiring rehearsals, with Mr. Rothafel using a megaphone to direct them from the auditorium. It was famous also for its acoustics, and telephone engineers engaged in the development of public-address systems were exceedingly anxious to use the auditorium for more extensive tests than were possible in the Western Electric laboratory.

When it was suggested to Mr. Rothafel that he discard his megaphone at rehearsals and conserve his energy by using instead a microphone, an amplifier, and a loud-speaker he was frankly skeptical but consented to try the apparatus. Its usefulness was, of course, apparent at the first demonstration, and the delighted director gave the engineers permission to utilize an off-stage dressing-room for their testing equipment, and to install microphones at various places on the theatre's great proscenium arch to pick up the music of the Capitol's large and distinguished orchestra.

The dressing-room in question can truly be given a noteworthy place in communications history. Not only did it become the control-room for the WEAF broadcasts of the Capitol's orchestra, and of the subsequent broadcasts of the artists known as "Roxy's Gang," but it played a part in experiments that led to the development of talking motion pictures and other products of electrical recording. The public-address development itself was an important influence in the architectural design of future auditoriums.

The Capitol Theatre broadcasts were notable as program features, but they were also important in broadcasting history because they began when theatre managers considered broadcast entertainment a dangerous competition. The attitude of the Metropolitan Opera management, with regard to broadcasts from the Opera House was even more antagonistic to radio, the opinion being that such broadcasting would "cheapen" opera. One of the definite results of WEAF's program policies was the proof, so important both to entertainment enterprises and to radio listeners, that broadcasting increased rather than diminished the demand for entertainment.

The answer to those who contended that the broadcast of a theatrical performance might decrease the attendance was in the public reaction to WEAF's broadcast, on April 11, 1923, of the first act of the musical comedy "Wildflower," direct from New York's Casino Theatre. For weeks afterward the house was sold out, and the sale of phonograph records and sheet music of popular numbers increased markedly. As for the broadcasts of the Capitol's splendid orchestra, Mr. Rothafel had only one thing to say when asked about their effect: "I nationalized the Capitol Theatre in one day!"

Sunday at WEAF

Sunday became an eventful day for WEAF listeners because of "remote-control jobs," as the telephone men classified them—undertaken only when a high standard of transmission could be maintained. One was an afternoon broadcast of the Men's Conference of the Bedford Branch of the Brooklyn Y.M.C.A., an exceptionally interesting broadcast because of the regular address by Dr. S. Parkes Cadman, one of the day's most forceful speakers, who extemporaneously answered questions asked by conference members after each talk.

The first of these broadcasts occurred on January 7, 1923. The first of the Capitol Theatre broadcasts from a specially constructed studio, with "Roxy" acting as master of ceremonies, was made on February 4, and on the following Sunday, February 11, these two outstanding features were combined with another to form a regular Sunday program. The third feature was an early afternoon talk given in the WEAF studio by another gifted speaker, Dr. Newell Dwight Hillis. Two weeks later the Sunday schedule was augmented by regular recitals from the Skinner Organ studios on Fifth Avenue, New York. Thousands of letters received at WEAF evidenced the widespread appeal of these distinctive broadcasts. A sample Sunday program for a slightly later date is given on page 117.

Let there be one more event recorded in this sketch of WEAF's early program undertakings. On December 23, 1922, more than 2,000 Bell System telephone workers assembled in the lobby of the headquarters building of the American Telephone and Telegraph Company to sing Christmas carols in accordance with their annual custom. It was the largest chorus to broadcast from a radio station up to that time.

The Growing WEAF Audience

As the time approached for transferring operations to the Broadway location, an ever growing audience regularly awaited WEAF broadcasts. Letters like the following, in the station mail of the period, were evidence of eager listeners hundreds of miles away when transmission was good on cold winter nights:

I am located in the Temagami Forest Reserve, seven miles from the end of steel in northern Ontario. I have no idea how far I am from New York, N. Y., but the range as shown in the various radio journals of your station is given at 900 miles. Anyway, you come in here swell, just like right in the room with you folks over there, and your operator is an old friend of ours—we know his voice so well.

Last week I took the set back into the bush about twenty miles to a new camp—and mineralized rock for miles—gold and silver mines all through this country—and after scratching around for some soft places for a ground wire, I discovered a place where I could drive an iron pipe in between two huge boulders. Got in down about three feet and then threw a wire over a tree.

Just as I thought—in comes old WEAF and the miners' wives tore the headphones apart trying to all listen in at once.

I stepped outside the shack for a while, while they were listening to you inside. It was a cold, clear, bright night, stars and moon hanging like jewels from the sky; five feet of snow; 42 below zero; not a sound but the trees snapping in the frost; and yet, if everybody only knew it, the air was full of sweet music.

I remember the time when to be out here was to be out of the world—isolation complete; not a soul to hear or see for months on end; six months of snow and ice, fighting back a frozen death with an axe and stove wood in a seemingly never ending battle.

But the long nights are long no longer—WEAF is right here in the shack shortly after sundown, and you come in so plain that the dog used to bark at you even though I had the headphones clamped tight on my head. He does not bark any more—he knows you the same as I do—just pricks up his ears at first, then sits blinking at the bulbs, and listens.

Long life and prosperity, WEAF.

WEAF's audience heard arresting words on February 14, 1923, during a broadcast of the proceedings of a joint meeting of the American Institute of Electrical Engineers, held simultaneously in New York and Chicago. Dr. Frank B. Jewett, then Vice-president of the Western Electric Company, who opened the meeting, said:

For the first time groups of men and women, separated by hundreds of miles, are gathered together in a common meeting under a single presiding officer to listen to papers presented in cities separated by half the span of a continent and to take part in the discussion of these papers with an ease characteristic of discussions in small and intimate gatherings. At the same time unnumbered thousands in their homes are auditors of our deliberation through radio broadcasting.

PROGRAM—SUNDAY, AUGUST 10, 1924
STATION WEAF—AMERICAN TELEPHONE & TELEGRAPH COMPANY
(492 Meters 610 Kilocycles) (Daylight Saving Time)
195 Broadway, New York City

3:00 to 4:00 P.M.	"Sunday Hymn Sing" under the auspices of the Greater New York Federation of Churches, Mr. Frank Goodman, Secretary of Religious Work Department, presiding.
4:00 to 5:00 P.M.	Interdenominational services under the auspices of the Greater New York Federation of Churches. Mr. Herbert F. Laflamme, Field Secretary, presiding. Music by the Federation Radio Choir; Carlos Abba, Harpist; George Vause, Pianist, and Arthur Billings Hunt, Baritone and Musical Director. Address by Rev. Henry T. Sell, D.D., Author-Lecturer.
(a)	Harp Prelude by Carlos Abba.
(b)	"Hold the Fort" (Bliss) and "Saved by the Blood" (Towner) by the Federation Radio Choir.
(c)	Scripture.
(d)	Harp Revery by Carlos Abba.
(e)	Prayer.
(f)	"Crossing the Bar" (Willeby) by Arthur Billings Hunt, Baritone.
(g)	Address by Rev. Henry T. Sell, D.D.
(h)	"No Other One But Jesus" (Morton) by the Federation Radio Choir.
(i)	Benediction.
(j)	"While Jesus Whispers" (Palmer) by the Federation Radio Choir.
5:00 to 5:20 P.M.	"Songs of Faith" the ninth of a series of Lectures on "The Literature of the Old Testament" by Professor Herbert B. Howe of Columbia University.

....

7:20 to 9:15 P.M.	Musical program from the Capitol Theatre, New York City, by courtesy of the Capitol Theatre management, and Mr. S. L. Rothafel (Roxy). The first part of the program will be taken direct from the stage of the theatre and will consist of music by featured artists and selections by the Capitol Grand Orchestra. The second part of the program will consist of a special presentation by Mr. Rothafel of vocal and instrumental artists direct from the broadcasting studio in the theatre.
9:15 to 10:15 P.M.	Organ recital direct from the studio of the Skinner Organ Company, New York City.

The remarks of Mr. Edward B. Craft, Chief Engineer of the Western Electric Company, who spoke at the New York meeting, foreshadowed the enormous benefits which the development of network broadcasting was destined to bring about. Mr. Craft said:

When Thomas Willett was appointed the first Mayor of New York by Governor Richard Nicolls in 1685, he could easily have addressed his entire constituency of 1,100 people without raising his voice. The ideas on which this nation was founded were spread abroad largely by word-of-mouth. With the growth of population, of the newspaper and of the mail service, the printed word gradually displaced the spoken word. The loud speaking telephone system will tend to re-establish oratory by making it worth while for the nation's leaders to sway the emotions of tremendous audiences. The telephone system now carries more messages daily than all other forms of communication combined. We may expect that the combination of loud speakers, radio and wire lines will give an equally good account of itself.

Radio's Commercial Usefulness Still Doubted

There were 14 commercial broadcasters during February, 1923, to indicate that, because of WEAF's growing reputation for programs of musical interest, novelty, and quality, the usefulness of the station's facilities was being increasingly considered by business concerns to promote public good will. On the last day of the month a revision of the broadcasting schedule was authorized by the Department of Commerce, thus giving Messrs. McClelland and Smith, the station's active business representatives, more "radio time" to offer. The new schedule was as follows:

10:00 A.M. to 2:00 P.M.—As needed
4:30 P.M. to 5:30 P.M.—Daily
7:30 P.M. to 10:30 P.M.—Monday, Wednesday, Thursday, Saturday
7:30 P.M. to 8:00 P.M.—Tuesday and Friday
Sundays, as desired

Printers' Ink, however, the leading publication in the advertising field, was dubious as to the usefulness of radio for commercial presentations. Its February 8, 1923, editorial,[6] headed "Radio an Ob-

[6] The editor of *Printers' Ink*, in graciously extending permission to the author to quote this and other statements appearing on pages 92 and 260, has pointed out that the views expressed were not, at the time, concurred in by any members of the editorial staff who are

jectionable Advertising Medium," was not encouraging to the men endeavoring to persuade advertisers and their agents to adopt the new medium:

It is a matter of general advertising interest to record that the American Telephone and Telegraph Company is trying to establish a new advertising medium. Through its station, WEAF, New York, it is permitting advertisers to broadcast messages. So far the company's venture is only in the experimental stage. As a tryout, it has placed a nominal charge of $100 on a ten-minute talk. During this time about 750 words can be delivered.

The fact that several advertisers have already availed themselves of this service would seem to indicate that there is a demand for it. Just the same, it is our advice to the American Telephone and Telegraph Company to "stop, look and listen" before extending this new branch of its business. The plan is loaded with insidious dangers. The company, itself, evidently recognizes this, as it is proceeding cautiously in this advertising broadcasting experiment. For one thing, it is restricting the number of times a product may be mentioned during the course of a talk. It feels that the radio audience may regard the advertising message as an unwarranted imposition on its time. For this reason, it is insisted that the advertiser make his announcement subtle. No bald statements are permitted.

But regardless of how carefully censored the messages may be, the objection to this form of advertising still stands. Station WEAF has built up its reputation on the fine quality of its programmes. Radio fans who tune in on this station are accustomed to get high-class entertainment. If they are obliged to listen to some advertiser exploit his wares, they will very properly resent it, even though the talk may be delivered under the guise of a matter of public interest or even of public welfare. An audience that has been wheedled into listening to a selfish message will naturally be offended. Its ill-will would be directed not only against the company that delivered the story, but also against the advertiser who chooses to talk shop at such an inopportune time.

There are several objections to the sending out of advertising through radio broadcasting stations, but we are opposed to the scheme principally because it is against good public policy. We are opposed to it for the same reason that we object to sky writing. People should not be forced to read advertising unless they are so inclined. We are opposed to it on much the same grounds that we object to "readers" or press agent dope or any other kind of disguised publicity that inveigles persons to read it on the promise that it is news. Forcing a business proposition under people's noses or into their ears when they are trying to do something else is not the way to win the good-will of these people.

Another point that the American Telephone and Telegraph Company should

now associated with the publication; and they did not, and do not, represent the belief of the present owners of *Printers' Ink*.

consider: Much of the radio's popularity is due to the way the newspapers have been playing it up. In many cases they are devoting whole pages and in some cases entire sections to radio developments. The programmes of the various broadcasting stations, which the newspapers publish, is of inestimable value to radio users, and in fact without these published programmes the broadcasting stations would be seriously handicapped. It is certain that the newspapers will not continue to give the radio interests all of this generous co-operation if the broadcasters are themselves going to enter into advertising competition with the newspapers.

Revenues, at the time, covered only a fraction of the station's expenses. They would not materially increase until the advent of programs of entertainment "sponsored" by business concerns that were willing to experiment with that form of indirect advertising. "Direct" advertising was not allowed and the prohibition not only affected station income but also had other results, as in the case of a suit for $100,000 filed against the station, alleging "discrimination," when the facilities were refused to a business man wishing so to use them.

WEAF's New Studios Dedicated

But revenues from broadcasting were not so important at this stage of the experiment as the foundation for broadcasting's practical development. This foundation had been laid by establishing the station's reputation for distinctive programs, distinctively presented from both technical and artistic standpoints. When the new studios were formally opened on April 30, 1923,[7] in the presence of a distinguished gathering of music critics, radio editors, and newspaper men, Vice-president Bloom, as master of ceremonies, was able to tell his guests that during nine months of broadcasting experience some 200 of America's leading statesmen and citizens, as well as stars of the first magnitude in the theatrical and educational world, had faced WEAF's microphones and that the station had presented over 200 separate programs involving a total of 3,000 people.

To include in this record a typical report of the studio's opening, here is the account that appeared in the New York *World:*[8]

[7] Actual broadcasting from the new studios began on April 10.

[8] Sunday, May 6, 1923, p. 10m.

NEW WEAF STUDIOS OPENED WITH INTERESTING CEREMONY

Latest Apparatus Installed to Give Radio Fans Splendid Concerts

The formal opening of WEAF's new broadcasting studios at No. 195 Broadway, on the evening of April 30, was attended by many of America's foremost musical and dramatic critics and newspaper editors who listened to a varied program which demonstrated the perfection of technique attainable with the new facilities. A loud speaking equipment in the reception room reproduced the concert rendered by the artists in the studios with a fidelity which proved a revelation to many present.

Special features of the program were John Charles Thomas, concert baritone; Walter Charmbury, pianist and composer, and Nadia Riesenberg, pianist. Among the singers were Evelyn Herbert, Helen L. Rush, lyric soprano; Jascha Bunshuk, first cellist of the Capitol Symphony Orchestra, gave a cello recital. Entertainment of a lighter character was furnished by Phil Ohman's Famous Trio, Billy Jones, Ernest Hare and Elsie Mae Gordon.

The Studio Layout

The announcer's microphone is located in a sound-proof booth having double plate glass windows and giving clear vision to both studios. Special walls render the booth practically impervious to sounds from the studios. The loud speakers in the studios repeat the announcer's introduction of artists and also enable him to give directions regarding placement of instruments and singers while the studio is idle. Switches on the announcer's control panel enable him to switch in his own announcing microphone or those in large and small studios. The announcer's loud speaker enables him to hear the performance as heard by the radio audience so that his directions are given from the audience's point of view. The signal lights indicate by colored lights, whether or not the studio is on the air, the carrier wave is being sent out, the microphones are switched in or studio director or announcer are wanted on the telephone. Each door to the station has a red signal light which indicates that the studio is on the air.

Doors Have Safety Knobs

As a further precaution the doors are equipped with special knobs which can be opened only by some one familiar with them. A loud speaker concealed in a horn closet, reproduces the broadcast entertainment for the reception room. A ventilation system through ducts keeps the studios and reception room cool and comfortable under all conditions even though all windows are closed. Adjustable deadening curtains are readily adapted to suit the music being transmitted. A double wall with dead air space prevents radiation of hall and elevator noises from the main corridor to the studio. The announcer, who is the key to the whole situation, is in direct communication with the engineers through desk telephone. The equipment panels are mounted with all the necessary apparatus for controlling the microphone amplifiers and input currents to the special cables connecting the studio with the broadcasting station as well as controlling and adjusting remote control telephone lines which operate the station from outside points. Behind the panels is a large loud speaker which provides the monitoring engineers with either the studio output or with the output of a loop radio receiver.

Thus, the Broadway-Fulton Street neighborhood once more became New York's chief entertainment center, for WEAF's new home was only a few hundred feet from the spot where had stood a half-century earlier the headquarters of the famous enterprise of Barnum and Bailey—its posters and handbills proclaiming "the greatest show on earth."

WEAF was already more than a local institution. Its heavy mail revealed that its programs had been heard in every State in the Union, as well as in Canada, Mexico, and England; and the coming months were to make its call letters symbolize outstanding programs wherever there were radio receivers in its kilocycle path.

W——E——A——F

Over the two Broadway entrances of the American Company's headquarters building, entrances through which passed thousands on the way to WEAF's fourth-floor studios, are grilles of which the distinguished architectural critic, Mr. Kenneth Clark, wrote in the *Architectural Record:* [9]

. . . . The treatment of the bronze grille work between the columns on the Broadway front, is notable in that each bay, over the doorways, has for a central motive, a panel modelled by Mr. Paul Manship. The subjects are: Earth, Air, Fire, and Water. The inspiration for these panels was derived from the famous figures on the Tower of the Winds at Athens, and these modern derivations stamp the artist as one of the greatest of decorative sculptors. Almost Oriental in their richness and fullness of effect, and superb in execution, these panels will live as a joy forever and had they emerged from the largess of the Renaissance Period, the columns framing them would have been decorated with the sonnets of their admirers. As it is in blasé modern New York that

[9] Jan. 24, 1924, no. 304, p. 81.

they have appeared, the passerby barely glances at them. It remains for a future age to place them where they belong, in some museum, to be studied and admired as they deserve.

It was an observant telephone employee who noted the coincidence that the initial letters of the four subjects represented in these panels—Water, Earth, Air, and Fire—were the identification of the broadcasting station harbored within.

CHAPTER VIII

"HELLO, ENGLAND"

A One-Way Transatlantic Talk

SINCE Bell System chronology records another "radio debut" in the headquarters building a few weeks before the dedication of the new WEAF studios, this résumé of broadcasting activities will be interrupted in order to include a brief and personal reference to it. The event was historic because it demonstrated the success of telephone engineers in developing a radio technique for extending telephone service overseas.

When these engineers first transmitted speech across the Atlantic in 1915, several hundred 15-watt tubes were necessary in the experiment in order to obtain sufficient power for transmission. Important research was begun after the war to develop tubes of substantial transmitting power, and a copper-anode water-cooled tube evolved which pointed the way to a solution of the problem of overseas telephony. This development work continued, and in 1922 a powerful water-cooled amplifier was installed in space leased at the R.C.A. transatlantic radio telegraph transmitting station at Rocky Point, Long Island, where an antenna was available. Telephone engineers went to England where, through the coöperation of British Post Office engineers, they were able to study and measure every variation in the transmission tests originating on Long Island. Since there was no suitable transmitting equipment on the other side of the Atlantic, these tests could be of only west-to-east transmission.[1]

[1] The group of engineers in charge of the Rocky Point installation was headed by Mr. A. A. Oswald. Those who carried on the transmission tests in England were Dr. H. W. Nichols and Mr. H. T. Friis. Later in the year Dr. Nichols was awarded the Fahie Premium

January 14, 1923, was the day selected for a demonstration of the technique which had resulted from the long and detailed experimentation, and nine o'clock in the evening was the time set, since transmission was best in the hours of darkness. The only arrangements were that President Thayer and Vice-president Gifford, and Vice-president Carty, who had technical supervision of the demonstration, would speak, and that a distinguished gathering of scientists and others would be waiting, at two o'clock in the morning, at New Southgate, near London, to hear the voices from America.

The technical importance of the demonstration has, of course, been reported in many places. Other details, of the human-interest variety, are set down in the personal notes of the present writer, who was delegated to inform the press of the event and who was on hand during the day to observe the preparation. These notes refer, for example, to the D&R engineers who equalized and provided amplifiers for the wire lines connecting the headquarters building with the Rocky Point apparatus. They picture the afternoon scene in President Thayer's office where engineers sat before a special transmitter, reading aloud newspaper items or long lists of words, while cablegrams arrived at intervals from London reporting "60% intelligible," then "70% intelligible"—then "80% intelligible"—the percentage climbing higher as daylight faded.

In the notebook also is the record of a conversation in the office of Vice-president Carty, who had remarked about six o'clock, after giving some final instructions, "Now I'll get a little nap." "What!" said this astonished publicity manager, "Aren't you nervous? Can you really sleep?" "There's nothing to worry about," was the answer. "The tests are what I expected. There was sleet on the wires just before we opened the first transcontinental line, but I slept, on that very sofa, for 30 minutes. You see, I knew that line was being watched—by telephone men."

And besides such random jottings, the notebook also records historic messages, together with an incident which, though inconsequential, still stands out in the writer's memory. Before nine o'clock arrived there were many reassuring messages "100% intel-

by the Institution of Electrical Engineers in London for a lecture before the Institution on Transatlantic Wireless Telephony.

ligible," and promptly on the hour Mr. Thayer laid aside his cigar and began to read the words addressed to an audience 3,000 miles away on another continent.

Eleven minutes later came the cabled message:

"THAYER GOT THROUGH TO ALL"
Signed, Gill [2]

As the tests proceeded other cablegrams arrived in thrilling sequence:

TO	*TIME*	
General Carty	9:14 P.M.	Purves[3] recognized Carty. Signed, Gill
General Carty	9:21 P.M.	Audience wants some local color. Going fine. Press wants pause between speakers and clear announcements of names. Signed, Gill
General Carty	9:26 P.M.	A few listeners have trouble with the American language. General impression fine as far as we can judge during intermission. Signed, Gill
General Carty	9:35 P.M.	I have listened with great interest and pleasure to the far-flung voices of Mr. Thayer and Mr. Carty. Of Mr. Thayer's message, I recognized every word. I missed a little of Mr. Carty's but recognized absolutely his well-known intonations. Send best respects and warmest good wishes to our friends in the A. T. & T. and W. E. Cos. Signed, Purves
General Carty	9:36 P.M.	For Mr. Thayer. I heard every word you said and recognized your voice perfectly. Signed, Wilkins[4]

[2] Mr. Frank Gill, Chief European Engineer of the International Western Electric Company and also President of the British Institution of Electrical Engineers, who was in charge of technical arrangements in England.

[3] Engineer-in-Chief of the General Post Office of Great Britain.

[4] Mr. F. H. Wilkins, Vice-president and European General Manager, International Western Electric Company.

President Harry B. Thayer, of the American Telephone and Telegraph Company, speaking in a one-way radio telephone test to England, January 14, 1923. Photo by Rosenfeld.

Transmitting equipment for transatlantic radio telephony, installed at Rocky Point, in 1923 by telephone engineers. The picture shows the water-cooled tubes referred to on page 124.

General Carty	10:01 P.M.	Representatives of British press congratulate A. T. & T. Co. and Radio Corp.[5] on their epoch-making experiment, the success of which has exceeded their expectations, and in which they see the dawning of a new era in long distance speaking which will be of the greatest value to the press of the world. Press Representatives
President Thayer	10:10 P.M.	I have just listened to your radio telephonic message which I have heard very distinctly. I congratulate you and all those connected with the research which has led to this achievement. G. Marconi
General Carty	10:45 P.M.	To your engineers the most sincere fraternal greetings from their British confreres. Signed, Gill
General Carty	10:58 P.M.	On conclusion of these most successful and historic tests which have made a profound impression, all those assembled at the London end wish to congratulate most heartily the A. T. and T. Co. Signed, Gill
President Thayer	10:58 P.M.	Heartiest congratulations on what has been achieved and on the complete success of its demonstration. Your voice was just like a personal talk. Would not have missed it for world. Signed, Kingsbury[6]
General Carty	10:58 P.M.	Loud speaker now being used. Good results. Great enthusiasm. Signed, Gill
General Carty	11:00 P.M.	Your interview on loud speaker came through fine. Signed, Gill

[5] The American Company had announced the experiment as "coöperative" because of contractual relations with RCA and because of the use of certain large RCA antennas on Long Island in connection with the radio telephone apparatus installed there.

[6] J. E. Kingsbury, author of *The Telephone and Telephone Exchanges* (London, 1915) and a director of Western Electric, Ltd. of London. This well-known telephone authority was one of the speakers at the unveiling on November 24, 1937, in Edinburgh, Scotland, of a tablet marking the birthplace of the telephone's inventor.

General Carty 11:01 P.M. There is only one word—magnificent.
Signed, Gill

With communications history thus being made every moment, the press representatives were invited to come downtown for the news. Yet when they arrived, there was little to give them but a technical explanation of the test and copies of the congratulatory messages as they arrived.

This chronicler sensed that the newspaper men did not fully realize the import of the occasion and reported with disappointment to Vice-president Gifford that they seemed unimpressed. "I know what's the matter," said Mr. Gifford, "they want evidence! General Carty has that door closed to keep out noise, but I'm going to open it so these men can see what's going on!" And, beckoning to the skeptical reporters, he opened the door to the President's office, disclosing a smiling man with a sheaf of telegrams in his hand, speaking into a strange-looking transmitter.[7] "That's Mr. Thayer, gentlemen," said Mr. Gifford, quietly, "and he's talking to England!"

And so, among the memories of an eventful evening, is that unplanned, informal scene—a prideful president saying for his colleagues, "Thanks for your message," and a group of newspaper men clustered at his door, listening intently, and almost unbelievingly, to words that were flashing across the sea, heralds of a service to reach all parts of the globe.[8]

[7] This instrument is one of the exhibits in the collection of transmitters used on historic occasions in communications history in the Bell System Historical Museum at Bell Telephone Laboratories.

[8] One who wishes to trace the technical development and the practical extension of the Bell System's overseas service, which was inaugurated four years later, after facilities were available in England for east-to-west transmission, will find a great number of pertinent articles listed in the *Bell System Technical Journal* and the *Bell Telephone Quarterly.*

PART III

POLICIES AND PROGRESS, 1923

CHAPTER IX

PATENT INFRINGEMENT PROBLEMS

Problem of Institutional Behavior

THE organization within the Bell System for the study of problems arising from broadcasting's wildfire growth consisted, as was explained on a previous page, of the headquarters unit known as Department of Operation B and the specially appointed radio representatives of the System's operating units. In February, 1923, a few weeks before the opening of WEAF's new studios, all who were thus dealing with radio matters met in New York—it was the second such conference—to compare experiences and to shape policies consistent with the public's growing interest in broadcasting and with the Bell System's service obligations.

The spread of broadcasting enthusiasm had been astonishing since telephone engineers in December, 1921, began to explore the practical problems suggested by the original concept of toll broadcasting. There were then but 8 stations with commercial licenses to broadcast news and entertainment, but the number exceeded 200 even before the American Company's experimental station sent out its first program in the summer of 1922. By the spring of 1923 the Department of Commerce had issued nearly 600 commercial licenses. Its official bulletin of February 1, 1923, listing 576 stations,[1] showed how varied in character were the enterprises that had sought

[1] Not all of these were in active operation. Accurate statistics were not available from government records, since several weeks might elapse between the abandonment of broadcasting activities and the deletion of stations from those listed in the government's radio bulletins.

TABLE 1. BUSINESS ENGAGED IN BY OWNERS OF BROADCASTING STATIONS, FEBRUARY 1, 1923

	Radio & Electric Mfr's. & Dealers	Educational Institutions	Newspapers & Publications	Department Stores	Auto & Batt. Cos. & Cycle Dealers	Music & Musical Inst. & Jewelry	Churches & Y.M.C.A's	Police-Fire & City	Hardware Stores	Banks & Brokers	Mine Supplies, Marble Oil Cos.	Tel. & Tel. Cos.	Stock Yards, Poultry Farms, & Grain Dealers	Railroads & Power Companies	State Bureaus	Clubs & Societies	Parks & Amusements	Theatres	Laundries	Unknown	TOTAL
Ala.	2	1	..	..	..	..	..	..	..	..	..	..	..	1	..	..	..	..	..	1	5
Ariz.	1	1	1	1	..	..	..	..	..	..	..	..	..	..	..	..	..	..	..	1	5
Ark.	1	..	1	..	..	1	..	..	..	..	..	..	..	..	..	..	..	..	..	2	5
Calif.	23	2	6	4	1	..	2	2	..	2	..	..	1	1	..	..	1	1	1	12	59
Colo.	8	1	1	..	1	1	1	..	..	..	1	..	..	..	..	..	..	..	..	2	16
Conn.	4	..	1	..	1	..	..	..	..	..	..	..	..	..	..	..	..	..	..	1	7
Del.	2	..	..	..	..	..	..	..	..	..	..	..	..	..	..	..	..	..	..	1	3
D.C.	4	..	..	2	1	..	1	..	..	..	..	..	..	..	..	..	..	..	..	..	8
Fla.	5	..	3	..	..	..	..	..	..	..	..	..	..	..	..	..	..	..	..	2	10
Ga.	4	2	2	..	..	..	..	..	..	..	..	..	..	1	..	..	..	..	..	..	9
Id.	1	1	..	1	1	..	1	..	..	..	..	..	..	..	..	..	..	..	..	..	5
Ill.	4	3	5	1	1	1	..	1	..	..	..	1	..	..	..	..	..	1	..	2	20
Ind.	7	1	6	..	..	1	..	..	..	..	..	..	..	..	..	..	..	..	..	..	15
Ia.	11	3	2	..	1	1	..	..	..	2	..	..	..	..	..	..	..	..	..	4	24
Kans.	11	1	1	..	2	..	..	..	..	..	1	..	..	..	..	..	..	..	..	2	18
Ky.	1	..	2	..	..	..	..	..	1	..	..	..	..	..	..	..	..	..	..	4	8
La.	2	2	2	..	..	..	..	..	..	..	..	..	..	..	..	..	..	..	..	1	7
Me.	2	..	..	..	..	..	..	..	1	..	..	..	..	..	..	..	..	..	..	..	3
Md.	3	..	1	..	..	1	..	..	..	..	..	..	..	..	..	..	..	..	..	..	5
Mass.	4	2	..	1	..	..	..	..	2	..	..	..	..	..	..	..	..	..	..	..	9
Mich.	3	2	4	..	1	..	..	1	..	..	..	..	..	..	..	..	..	..	..	3	14
Minn.	7	4	1	..	..	..	..	..	..	..	..	..	..	..	..	..	..	..	..	2	14
Miss.	..	..	..	..	..	..	..	..	..	..	..	..	..	..	..	..	..	..	..	..	0
Mo.	3	5	4	2	1	2	1	..	..	..	..	..	..	..	1	..	..	..	..	6	25
Mont.	1	1	2	..	..	..	..	..	..	..	..	..	..	..	..	..	..	..	..	1	5
Nebr.	7	3	3	..	..	1	..	..	..	..	..	..	1	..	1	2	..	..	..	4	22
Nev.	1	..	..	..	1	..	..	..	..	..	..	..	..	..	..	..	..	..	..	..	2

TABLE 1 (*continued*). BUSINESS ENGAGED IN BY OWNERS OF BROADCASTING STATIONS, FEBRUARY 1, 1923

	Radio & Electric Mfr's. & Dealers	Educational Institutions	Newspapers & Publications	Department Stores	Auto & Batt. Cos. & Cycle Dealers	Music & Musical Inst. & Jewelry	Churches & Y.M.C.A.'s	Police-Fire & City	Hardware Stores	Banks & Brokers	Mine Supplies, Marble Oil Cos.	Tel. & Tel. Cos.	Stock Yards, Poultry Farms, & Grain Dealers	Railroads & Power Companies	State Bureaus	Clubs & Societies	Parks & Amusements	Theatres	Laundries	Unknown	TOTAL
N.H.	1	..	..	..	..	..	..	..	..	..	..	..	..	..	..	..	..	..	..	..	1
N.J.	6	1	..	1	1	..	..	1	1	..	1	..	..	..	..	1	..	..	..	1	14
N.M.	..	1	..	..	..	..	..	..	..	..	..	..	..	1	..	..	..	..	..	..	2
N.Y.	13	5	2	1	..	..	1	1	..	..	..	3	..	..	..	..	..	..	..	3	29
N.C.	2	1	..	..	..	..	..	..	..	..	..	..	..	..	..	..	..	..	..	..	3
N.D.	3	2	..	..	..	..	..	..	..	..	..	..	..	..	..	..	..	..	..	..	5
O.	18	8	3	..	..	1	1	..	..	1	..	..	1	..	..	..	..	..	..	1	34
Okla.	6	..	1	..	..	..	..	..	..	..	1	..	..	..	..	..	..	..	..	1	9
Ore.	6	2	2	..	..	2	..	..	..	..	..	..	1	..	..	..	..	..	..	2	15
Pa.	8	3	..	10	1	..	..	..	..	..	..	..	..	..	1	..	..	..	..	6	29
R.I.	1	..	..	2	1	..	..	..	..	..	..	..	..	..	..	..	1	..	..	..	5
S.C.	4	..	..	..	..	..	..	..	..	..	..	..	..	..	..	..	..	..	..	..	4
S.D.	1	2	1	..	..	..	..	..	..	..	..	..	..	..	..	..	..	..	..	..	4
Tenn.	..	..	1	..	..	1	..	..	..	..	..	1	..	..	..	..	..	..	..	2	5
Tex.	14	4	5	1	..	..	1	1	..	..	1	..	..	..	..	..	..	..	..	10	37
U.	1	..	2	..	..	..	..	..	..	..	..	..	..	..	..	..	..	..	..	2	5
Vt.	1	1	..	..	..	..	..	..	..	..	..	..	..	..	..	..	..	..	..	1	3
Va.	1	1	..	..	..	..	..	..	..	..	..	..	..	..	..	..	..	..	..	1	3
Wash.	8	2	2	1	1	..	2	..	..	..	..	..	..	..	..	..	..	..	..	7	23
W.Va.	..	1	..	..	..	..	..	..	1	..	..	..	..	..	..	..	..	..	..	1	3
Wis.	3	2	1	1	1	..	..	..	..	..	..	..	..	..	1	..	..	..	..	2	11
Wyo.	1	..	..	..	1	..	1	..	..	..	..	..	..	..	..	..	..	..	..	..	3
Alaska	..	..	..	..	..	..	..	..	..	..	..	..	..	..	..	..	..	..	..	1	1
Hawaii	1	..	1	..	..	..	..	..	..	..	..	..	..	..	..	..	..	..	..	1	3
Puerto Rico	1	1	..	..	..	..	..	..	..	..	..	..	..	..	..	..	..	..	..	..	2
TOTAL	222	72	69	29	18	13	12	7	6	5	5	5	4	4	4	3	2	2	1	93	576

licenses permitting them to test the usefulness of the new medium. These included 72 educational institutions, 69 publishers, 29 department stores, and 12 churches and Y.M.C.A.'s, besides the business concerns of which radio and electric manufacturers and dealers composed the largest category.

Because of the number and location of these broadcasting ventures, both the American Company and the local Bell companies were confronted with a perplexing problem in what might be called institutional behavior. It was a problem compounded of many elements and was "not the kind," as Vice-president Gifford observed during the 1923 meeting of radio representatives:

> which we in the telephone company have been accustomed to deal with. . . . It is a new problem, one which is very much involved with public relations. The public is interested in it. Perhaps the public is more sensitive to the radio end of the business now than to the telephone end. It is a problem that not only involves us but also involves other companies with which we have made cross-licensing arrangements; and it is a problem which the governmental authorities at Washington are attacking from various angles. So we have something to solve which is not simple. . . . Really, we are blazing the trail, and we must blaze that trail without offending the sensibilities of the public, without giving legislators any just cause for complaint against us and without offending our associates in contractual relationships that we have; and it needs patience, it needs tact, and it needs consideration each for the other in working it out.

General Nature of Infringement Problems

The characteristic institutional regard for the "sensibilities of the public" was being tested, at the time of the 1923 meeting of the Bell System radio representatives, by a serious and challenging situation. This was the extent to which nearly all active broadcasting stations, aside from the 35 which were using Western Electric equipment and 6 which were operated by the other companies licensed by the cross-licensing agreement of 1920, were infringing on the American Company's patent rights. These rights covered broadly, and in specific details, the fundamental features of broadcasting systems, such as the arrangements for producing oscillations and for modulating currents, negative grids, and so forth, as well as the vacuum tubes themselves. As one radio historian later referred to the in-

Table 2. Distribution of Radio Broadcasting Stations by States
January 1, 1922, to February 1, 1923

Number of Stations at the First of Each Month

	Jan.	Feb.	Mar.	Apr.	May	Jun.	Jul.	Aug.	Sept.	Oct.	Nov.	Dec.	Jan.	Feb.
Ala.	..	..	1	2	2	3	2	3	4	4	5	4	5	5
Ariz.	..	..	..	..	..	2	3	3	3	5	5	5	6	5
Ark.	..	..	1	2	3	5	6	6	6	6	6	5	5	5
Calif.	14	16	21	27	45	59	61	66	67	66	67	68	68	59
Colo.	..	..	1	2	3	5	8	8	8	9	10	11	13	16
Conn.	..	..	..	..	1	2	3	3	4	5	5	5	6	7
Del.	..	..	..	..	..	..	..	1	1	1	1	1	3	3
D.C.	3	3	3	6	6	5	6	8	8	8	8	8	8	8
Fla.	..	..	..	..	..	3	6	7	9	10	9	9	9	10
Ga.	..	..	..	2	3	5	7	8	9	9	9	8	9	9
Id.	..	..	..	..	..	..	..	3	4	5	6	6	4	5
Ill.	..	..	2	4	8	12	14	17	19	19	21	21	21	20
Ind.	..	1	3	3	6	7	10	13	14	14	15	14	15	15
Ia.	..	..	..	2	3	5	11	18	18	22	24	23	25	24
Kans.	..	..	..	2	6	9	11	12	13	15	15	16	17	18
Ky.	..	..	..	..	..	..	..	2	3	5	5	6	7	8
La.	..	..	..	2	6	8	9	10	10	10	10	9	7	7
Me.	..	..	..	..	1	1	2	3	3	4	4	4	3	3
Md.	..	..	..	1	1	2	3	3	3	3	3	4	5	5
Mass.	..	..	1	2	3	6	7	9	9	12	9	9	9	9
Mich.	1	1	2	5	5	7	7	9	10	11	12	13	14	14
Minn.	..	1	1	1	6	8	10	10	11	13	13	13	14	14
Miss.	..	..	..	..	..	..	..	1	1	1	0	0	0	0
Mo.	..	..	2	4	9	12	14	18	22	21	22	24	25	25
Mont.	..	..	..	..	..	1	1	4	4	4	4	5	5	5
Nebr.	1	1	1	2	3	4	7	12	17	18	21	23	22	22
Nev.	..	..	..	..	1	2	1	2	2	2	2	2	2	2
N.H.	..	..	..	..	..	1	1	1	2	1	1	1	1	1
N.J.	2	3	4	6	9	10	10	12	12	13	13	13	14	14
N.M.	..	..	..	..	2	2	2	2	2	2	2	2	2	2
N.Y.	2	2	5	12	14	19	24	27	28	30	29	28	29	29
N.C.	..	..	..	1	1	2	2	2	3	3	3	3	3	3
N.D.	..	..	..	..	..	1	1	1	2	2	4	3	4	5
O.	2	3	9	11	21	25	27	31	32	36	34	35	32	34
Okla.	..	..	..	2	2	3	4	5	6	11	11	10	10	9
Ore.	..	..	..	5	6	9	10	11	14	15	17	15	16	15
Pa.	2	3	4	10	15	19	22	23	25	28	31	33	34	29
R.I.	..	..	..	..	..	1	2	2	5	5	5	5	5	5
S.C.	..	..	..	..	..	..	2	2	2	2	2	4	4	4
S.D.	..	..	..	..	..	2	3	3	4	4	4	5	5	4
Tenn.	..	..	..	2	2	3	3	3	3	3	3	4	4	5
Tex.	..	..	..	4	5	10	16	20	24	28	33	34	36	37
U.	..	..	..	..	1	4	4	4	4	4	4	4	4	5
Vt.	..	..	..	..	..	1	1	1	1	2	2	2	3	3
Va.	..	..	..	..	2	3	3	3	3	4	3	5	4	3
Wash.	1	1	3	8	13	18	20	22	23	23	22	24	24	23
W.Va.	..	..	..	1	3	3	3	5	5	5	4	4	2	3
Wis.	..	1	1	1	2	3	6	9	10	10	10	11	11	11
Wyo.	..	..	..	..	..	..	..	..	..	1	1	3	3	3
Alaska	..	..	..	..	..	..	..	..	..	1	1	1	1	1
Hawaii	..	..	..	1	1	2	2	2	2	2	2	3	3	3
Puerto Rico	..	..	..	..	..	..	1	1	2	2	2	2	2	2
	28	36	65	133	220	314	378	451	496	539	554	570	583	576

fringement conditions, "squatters had taken possession" of these rights.

Positive action to prevent broadcasting operations by these "squatters," of course, "very much involved public relations." For one thing, such a step could easily be construed as an arbitrary and selfish effort to deprive the public of entertainment on which it was relying. And any such local feeling would necessarily react on telephone service itself which depends, for general usefulness and for growth, upon coöperative and understanding relations between company and customer. Furthermore, many of the infringing broadcasters had undoubtedly begun operations without realizing that these operations involved an unlicensed use of patented inventions. For example, an assembly of transmitting apparatus by local radio enthusiasts could easily be made because of the availability of vacuum tubes that were manufactured and sold for amateur experimentation. If, however, such assembled transmitters were then used for broadcasts of entertainment and news, there was an infringement of the American Company's patent rights.

These were among the reasons why the company's policy toward infringers was one of tolerance. Another was the belief that sooner or later the expense of broadcasting would eliminate considerable infringement by causing stations to discontinue operations. This belief must have been founded on accurate knowledge of local conditions, since the record shows some 150 broadcasters vanishing from the official station roster between the beginning of March and the end of July, 1923.

But when, besides infringing the patents, the stations in question also sought speech-input equipment and wire connections in order to pick up programs, a dilemma was created for the telephone organization which, having the habit of considering communications objectively as services, hoped for a national and publicly useful broadcasting development, for which the use of wires was essential. This dilemma arose because the Bell System was in possession of the general type of circuits best suited for such use; it was recognized as the agency best fitted to provide them; its patents controlled much of the necessary equipment; and it had the trained personnel necessary to ensure successful operation. A growing demand for wire facilities was clearly inevitable; and, since the desire of the Bell System was that the public be served, it had no reason to withhold wire facilities as an adjunct to broadcasting if they could be provided without interfering with or imperiling the nation's telephone service.

On the other hand, there were important legal considerations involved. The one particularly impressing the company's attorneys, as they weighed developments in the broadcasting field, was that the patents being infringed were not only valuable in connection with the radio art but covered inventions which were indispensable in connection with the regular telephone service being rendered by the Bell companies. There was strong legal opinion that the routine provision of circuits to infringing stations, together with the requisite speech-input equipment, might imply a tacit approval of infringing broadcasting activities.

On this account the conclusion reached at the February meeting of Bell System radio representatives was that wires and equipment for picking up programs ought not to be furnished to any infringing broadcaster. It was decided at the same time that the public interest necessitated the establishment of a procedure for the licensing of infringing stations by the American Company so that, pending further study of the System's relationship to broadcasting's development, wire telephony as an adjunct to broadcasting might be provided in specific cases where facilities could be made available.

As Operation B wrote to Bell System operating units, when reporting the tentative licensing procedure that was adopted:

> The public is demanding these facilities and it is the desire of the Bell System to meet this demand in so far as it reasonably can do so. This bulletin establishes a procedure for doing this and has as its intent the desire to be helpful to those interested in radio broadcasting. The procedure for the licensing of unlicensed broadcasting stations is established not as a basis of revenue to the Bell System but in order that the broadcaster may be in a position to obtain advantages which he could not otherwise secure. Therefore, whenever we can provide wire telephony as an adjunct to radio broadcasting subject to the conditions outlined in this bulletin it is our feeling that it should be provided in a wholehearted and enthusiastic manner.

"The Broadcasting Station of the Future"

Since the purpose of this commentary is to record as well as to describe, a few paragraphs from the bulletin itself belong here as further evidence of the company's recognition of the function of wires in extending and increasing broadcasting's value to the public:

Wire telephony as an adjunct to radio broadcasting is being widely sought and it is now desirable that the position of the Bell System with reference to it be definitely outlined.

Without the use of wire telephony as an adjunct to radio broadcasting it was necessary that the musicians, singers, or speakers be present at the studio closely associated with the transmitting apparatus at the broadcasting station. With the increase in popularity of radio broadcasting, owners of broadcasting stations in an effort to improve the quality of their programs began to cast about for material which would be available to them without the necessity of having the performers appear at the studio.

Speakers of prominence, having messages of real moment, usually speak in halls, auditoriums or at banquets to relatively limited audiences. They would often welcome the opportunity of having their speeches broadcasted and the radio audience would generally be eager to hear them. Obviously this can be done only by wire telephony as an adjunct to radio broadcasting.

In larger centers excellent musical programs are in progress in theatres, halls and auditoriums throughout a considerable part of the year. Such material provides excellent subject matter for broadcasting and frequently can be broadcast satisfactorily only if wire telephone communication is afforded from the places where rendered, as the studios usually associated with broadcasting stations are unsuitable for such performances and also the cost of bringing the artists to the studio would often be prohibitive.

In the Autumn of 1922 all of the more important college football games held in the East were broadcast play-by-play directly from the field by wire telephony as an adjunct to radio broadcasting. This was decidedly popular with the radio audience and there is reason to believe that there will be a large demand for it in the future.

The broadcasting of sermons and church services also has been a prominent feature throughout the country and the demand for these services is increasing steadily. It seems probable that the more prominent churches will seek the permanent installation of speech input equipment and that broadcasting soon will become one of their established activities.

One broadcasting station in the East has recently arranged for the permanent installation of speech input equipment in a prominent cafe which has an exceptionally high-grade orchestra. This enables the broadcasting station to fill in its program at will with material highly acceptable to the radio audience. It is expected that a considerable number of broadcasting stations throughout the country will attempt soon to follow this practice.

Our observations lead us to predict the rapid increase in importance of wire telephony as an adjunct to radio broadcasting and something of a decrease in importance of the studio associated with the broadcasting station. If wire telephony as an adjunct to radio broadcasting can be provided the broadcasting station of the future bids fair to be the means by which a great number will be given the benefit of hearing many entertainment features of a high type which are available now only to the restricted audiences in the particular halls, theatres or auditoriums in which the performances are being given.

Steps to License Infringing Stations

The license agreement that was prepared for local Bell companies to submit to infringing stations in their territories was a license to continue to operate under patents which the American Company owned or controlled.

The scale of fees finally arrived at, after long consideration of many factors in the situation, was as follows:

$500 for stations of from 5 to 100 watts antenna input
$1,000 for stations of from 150 to 250 watts antenna input
$1,500 for stations of 300 watts antenna input
$2,000 for stations of 500 watts antenna input

These fees were not required, however, from broadcasting stations operated by colleges and universities. The headquarters' announcement to the Bell companies of the proposed fees read:

We are reserving decision on the license treatment of university cases, and to assist us in formulating a uniform policy throughout the Bell System, we will appreciate a statement listing the university stations in your territory under the classifications (1) experimental or educational work only, (2) experimental or educational work mainly, supplemented by broadcasting, (3) broadcasting as usually understood.

Within a few months the scale of license fees was changed to $4.00 per watt of antenna input, with a minimum fee of $500 and a maximum fee of $3,000.[2] This meant that for the fee of $3,000 the li-

[2] "The license forms seem reasonable enough and . . . the fee is certainly no more than adequate to cover the various costly developments which the Telephone Company puts at the disposal of the licensee when he is operating one of their equipments." *Radio Broadcast,* vol. v, no. 4 (Aug., 1924), p. 300.

censed station could operate with any power it might wish so far as Bell System patents were concerned. These license fees were single and not recurring payments, and the licensee could pay them in monthly installments if he so desired. When the scale was thus revised, licenses for the nominal fee of $1.00 were offered to stations operated by (1) colleges, universities, and other educational institutions, (2) churches and other religious institutions, and (3) State and municipal governments; these licenses did not include the right to operate for toll or hire.

The prevalence of infringement was, of course, one of the reasons for Mr. Gifford's remark at the 1923 conference, "It needs patience, it needs tact." In the following year, as will be seen, the company's policy of patience had to be changed, under legal advice, to positive action, in order to protect the company's patents.

CHAPTER X

WEAF AT 195 BROADWAY

An Able Program Director

THAT WEAF's popularity with listeners and entertainers was so firmly established when the studios were moved to "195" was the result in great measure of the ability and judgment of the station's program director. Mr. Ross brought to this position a valuable sense of musical and entertainment values and of program balance, which he employed most effectively to further the Broadcasting Department's investigation of public tastes and desires, an exploration that definitely began in November, 1922, when the station's first elaborate questionnaire was distributed to listeners, and which involved a continuous analysis of the station's mounting correspondence. Guided by the public preferences that were being constantly expressed, Mr. Ross was notably successful in arranging station programs of engaging variety, and besides his talent in this respect, he also had a gift for maintaining happy relationships with artists and entertainers.

Perhaps one of Mr. Ross's most important services in establishing and maintaining WEAF's broadcasting standards was his choice of men who, as station announcers, had the responsibility of representing WEAF while presenting programs to the public. All those who thus helped to make WEAF's microphone so famous were of his personal selection. And no individual choice contributed more greatly to the enjoyment of WEAF's listeners than one that he made on a day in May, 1923, when a visitor appeared at the studio bearing an introduction from a mutual friend who was a music supervisor of the New York City Board of Education.

Graham McNamee: "The World's Most Popular Announcer"

The visitor was Mr. Graham McNamee who was destined, as a member of WEAF's staff, to have the most spectacular career of any radio announcer in the history of broadcasting. Presenting his introduction to Mr. Ross during a respite from jury duty in the neighborhood, Mr. McNamee in a few moments found himself considering an unexpected and a momentous offer to become a member of the WEAF family.

The visit was to Mr. Ross a most opportune and even a providential one, for another announcing job was developing. Colonel Edward H. R. Green, who was operating Station WMAF as a hobby at Round Hills, Massachusetts, had installed a Western Electric transmitter there and had arranged to receive the "sustaining" features of WEAF programs by telephone wire as special entertainment for his listeners. The union of the two stations during the summer of 1923, through circuits temporarily arranged to transmit the requisite band of frequencies, constituted what was actually the first broadcasting "chain" in history. This arrangement brought an announcing problem to WEAF since, when its programs were switched to the wires reaching WMAF, an announcer would be needed to speak for that station, while another was simultaneously addressing the audience of the New York station.

This matter was under consideration when Graham McNamee appeared. Mr. Ross's recollection of the situation is as follows:

> I offered him a temporary job because I was immediately attracted by the quality of his voice and also discovered that he had a good musical background, for he was a trained singer, was experienced in church work, and had appeared in many concerts. Furthermore, I discovered that he had played semi-professional baseball and hockey, and so had an interest in sports to match his interest in music. But it was his voice, after I had given him an audition, that impressed me most.

And so a new face appeared in the WEAF studios, and a new voice began to identify the station—a voice which, when transmitted through the ether, challenged attention through an arresting and appealing quality all its own. When radio listeners heard it between

Graham McNamee in an early WEAF sports broadcast. Photo by International Newsreel.

The Happiness Boys of 1923, Ernest Hare and Billy Jones, probably radio's first comedy team. Photo by Foto Topics, Inc.

rounds of the Greb-Wilson prize fight in August, 1923, and between innings of the World Series baseball broadcasts from New York's Polo Grounds in the autumn, they were quick to manifest their approval of the new radio personality that it revealed. Mr. McNamee's assignment for each of these sports events was to talk while another announcer, responsible for presenting "play-by-play" details, was resting. But his "fill-in" reporting of the general scene, and of notables within the range of his vision, was so graphic and alert that listeners immediately called for more. After the first three World Series broadcasts it was Mr. McNamee who took over the full announcing responsibility, his vivid and thrilling descriptions setting a new standard in sports announcing.

When the development of network broadcasting made it possible to broadcast accounts of political conventions or inter-sectional football games to millions, Mr. McNamee's colorful reporting and the infectious excitement conveyed by his manner made him the "world's most popular announcer," as was inscribed on the cup presented to him by *Radio Digest* in 1925, after a nationwide competition in which the names of 133 announcers were entered.

Significant of Mr. Graham McNamee's radio personality, as well as the pleasure given by WEAF broadcasts to inmates of hospitals and other institutions—the people once referred to on a broadcast by "Roxy" as "those real indoor sports"—is the following letter:[1]

> Please accept our sincere thanks for your wonderful broadcasting of the first game of the 1924 season between the Giants and the Brooklyn Dodgers. Your knowledge of the game and your colorful description made a hit here; and it was no ordinary "bunt" but a powerful "wallop" that has had us talking ever since.
>
> The Hospital is really a home for some eight hundred patients, a majority of whom are playing their last game and waiting for the exit gates to open. Their little Main Street is quite narrow, and the radio is bringing the world to their feet, as it were.
>
> I wish you could see these helpless men listening to your voice; some are blind and many bedridden, but the smile on their faces as the game progressed certainly would repay you, had you any doubts as to the success of your reception.

[1] Reprinted from *You're on the Air* by Graham McNamee, published by Harper and Brothers in 1926.

Mr. McNamee received mail in enormous amounts, some 1,700 pieces arriving at the WEAF studio after his first broadcast of a World Series baseball game in October, 1923, and 50,000 pieces following the series of 1925. Naturally much of it was critical, ranging from good-natured correction of mistakes in pronunciation to definite accusations of favoritism and bias. Eager partisans of one contestant would angrily accuse him of favoring the other in a football or baseball game, but there was always an equal division of the partisanship thus expressed, to prove his remarkable ability to handle broadcasts requiring extemporaneous but exacting reporting.

There were, of course, other announcers, selected by Mr. Ross with the greatest care for their musical background, voice characteristics, entertainment versatility, and ability to meet studio emergencies, who joined the staff as the broadcasting schedule was extended and more and more sponsored programs were initiated.

All of them contributed enormously to the establishment of WEAF's personality. Besides Mr. V. A. Randall and Miss Helen Hann from the original WBAY organization, there was Mr. Phillips Carlin,[2] who came to WEAF in November, 1923, to team up with Mr. McNamee in many a thrilling broadcast, the two often being referred to as "the twin announcers" because of similarities in voice and style. Others who helped to give the station's announcing staff its distinction were Mr. R. C. Wentworth, Mr. Leslie Joy, Mr. A. Morgan, and Mr. James Haupt, who frequently appeared on WEAF programs as a tenor soloist and who later acted as WEAF's Assistant Musical Director.

Yet, although every member of this group deserved and enjoyed great personal popularity among radio listeners, it was Mr. Graham McNamee whose flair for radio and breeziness of manner gave a special character to what a radio historian has termed the "WEAF school of announcing."[3] The zest of his well-remembered personal

[2] Mr. Carlin later became WEAF's studio director. He is now Vice-president of the Mutual Broadcasting System in charge of programs.

[3] After a series of meetings of the Radio Voice Technique Committee of New York University, held to select the best local radio announcers, Mr. McNamee received the highest score of the ten men chosen. The other nine were Messrs. Brockenshire of WJZ, Barnett of WOR, Reed of WJZ, Carlin of WEAF, Squires of WMCA, Granland of WHN, Haupt of WEAF, Cross of WJZ, and Morgan of WGBS.

introduction when going on the air, "Good evening, ladies and gentlemen of the radio audience," helped to establish WEAF in the hearts of millions, as did the friendly and appealing quality of his "Good night, all." These two McNamee "signatures" were so well known that envelopes bearing them, and followed by the single address "New York," were delivered at once to the WEAF studio.

Mr. Heywood Broun, the famous columnist, once paid this tribute to Mr. McNamee's contribution to broadcasting:[4]

> After listening to others, and then to Graham McNamee of our local WEAF, I felt terribly proud to be a New Yorker. And not to be provincial, McNamee justified the whole activity of radio broadcasting. A thing may be a marvelous invention and still dull as ditch water. It will be that unless it allows the play of personality. A machine amounts to nothing much unless a man can ride. Graham McNamee has been able to take a new medium of expression and through it transmit himself—to give out vividly a sense of movement and of feeling. Of such is the kingdom of art.

More than a decade after Mr. McNamee and WEAF had departed from Bell System headquarters, the company engaged him as narrator for an anniversary program for the Telephone Pioneers of America, so that memories of his former Bell System service might be brought back to the listeners.[5]

Anonymous Announcers

While on the subject of WEAF's announcers it is appropriate to quote a communication to the station dated May 1, 1923, and referring either to Mr. Randall or to Mr. Llufrio. It came from Mr. R. F. Outcault, the artist who was so well known for his cartoon character "Buster Brown," and evidenced the interest of radio listeners in the personalities behind the voices at WEAF that addressed them so regularly. His plea for the abandonment of the anonymity of radio announcements was written in verse, and decorated by sketches of his cartoon creations:

[4] From Heywood Broun's foreword to *You're on the Air.*

[5] Some 40,000 members of the organization at dozens of local chapter meetings heard the program from loud-speakers as brought by telephone wires from New York.

Dear Station W-E-A-F,
We're glad we're not D-E-A-F,
Because just think what we have heard!
The show last night was sure a bird,
And we would like to say to each
Performer: "You are just a peach."
Miss Gordon always fills the bill,
Miss Thomas' songs will always thrill,
And those two fellows, Jones and Hare,
Well, all we'll say is, They are *there!*
From start to finish not a one
In his own line could be outdone.
We wish that you would tell them so;
We want each artist there to know
How much they filled the air last night
With genuine and pure delight.
And we sat in among the rest
And knew each number was the best.
Now listen, man, just who is "you"
That tells us what and tells us who?
Next time you talk tell us your name
And get *yourself* a lot of fame.

It was true, of course, that with WEAF's enormous following there was a lot of "fame" possible for announcers if they could identify themselves, and when WEAF permitted such identification the station seemed to acquire an even greater popularity.

Sponsored Programs and Restrictions on Advertising

Readers of this narrative, who were WEAF listeners in 1923, will at once understand Mr. Outcault's reference to Billy Jones and Ernest Hare. They were well-known vaudeville personalities who had been presenting a program of songs and patter as a sustaining feature—the pioneer comedian team of radio. Network broadcasting today is making a household word of the names of such entertainers, but it is doubtful if any of them have a warmer place in the affection of the radio audience than had Mr. Jones and Mr. Hare in the days when comedy was new among broadcast offerings. Their popularity as the "Happiness Boys" when the Happiness Candy Stores, in December, 1923, began to "sponsor" their entertainment was enormous.

Many other early sponsored programs developed from such sustaining features. Professional entertainers seeking new engagements found no better way of maintaining their standing in the entertainment world than by appearing on WEAF's broadcasts, and amateurs seeking to enter professional ranks flocked to the studios for auditions. From this reservoir of talent came WEAF's sustaining programs, for features which had secured extensive popular acclaim were thus available for business concerns that had in mind a test of the radio approach to the public.

The station's rules pertaining to radio advertising, however, were rigid and deterred many from experimenting with it. Nothing that could be termed "direct" advertising, as has already been explained, was permitted. Samples of merchandise could not be offered, and even the color of a can or other container for the purpose of store identification could not be mentioned by a broadcaster. Sales arguments like those in the "commercials" that are common today were considered offensive to listeners and, therefore, antagonistic to the station's experimental policy of building a following by the broadcasting of the best possible programs available and the avoidance of offense. Consequently, it was largely through the gift of entertainment that the station's facilities began to be used for the promotion of public good will. This situation led to the practice of labeling early sponsored programs so as to identify the sponsor or his product, the "Happiness Boys," for example, being so named because the Happiness Candy Stores sponsored their entertainment.

Similarly, public good will was sought for Cliquot Club Ginger Ale by broadcasting the music of the "Cliquot Club Eskimos," a program that pioneered in "sound effects" because it began and ended with the realistic yelping of Eskimo dogs and the jingling of sleigh bells to suggest the coolness of winter.[6] The program of an orchestra featured as the "Ipana Troubadours" reminded listeners that there was a toothpaste of that name. The "Gold Dust Twins," who were to become familiar to an ever growing radio audience as "Goldy" and "Dusty," entertained in behalf of a like-named cleans-

[6] At first the sleigh bells were heard as background for the opening announcement. When the orchestra leader, Mr. Harry Rieser, later wrote some introductory music incorporating the bells, he created the first musical "theme" in radio to identify a program.

ing powder. The "Silvertown Cord" orchestra was sponsored by the manufacturers of the Silvertown Cord automobile tire, and the singing of an anonymous soloist announced as the tenor with the "silver mask" further accented the tire's trade name.[7] There was a "Lucky Strike" orchestra as far back as July, 1923. Another orchestra, led by Miss Anna Byrnes, whose earlier broadcasting for Browning King, Inc., made her the first feminine conductor in radio, was announced as "B. Fischer & Company's Astor Coffee Dance Orchestra."

An especially popular program of the period was that of the "A. & P. Gypsies." An interesting coincidence led to the sponsorship of this orchestra. The group of players had occasionally provided WEAF sustaining programs, and when made idle by a disastrous fire at a local restaurant where they were regularly employed, they sought permission to use one of the WEAF studios for rehearsals. One day when they were thus rehearsing, the sales manager of the Atlantic and Pacific Stores, who was considering the possibility of using broadcasting to obtain public good will for his stores, was being shown through the station's premises. Through the loud-speakers in the reception room he heard music being played in an appealing and distinctive gypsy style and through the glass partition separating the reception room and the larger studio he could see the musicians themselves. At the end of the rehearsal the orchestra was engaged on the spot to provide the "A. & P. Gypsies" program that long delighted WEAF listeners.

The idea of "Cliquot Club Eskimos" also developed from WEAF studio performances. The ginger ale, with a parka-hooded Eskimo pictured on the label, was being advertised as a "sparkling" beverage. Coincidentally, Mr. Harry Rieser, an expert banjoist, was becoming widely known for the arresting and sparkling style of his playing on WEAF sustaining programs. The conception of a sponsored program of music predominantly banjo-like in character, to be rendered by an orchestra identified as "Cliquot Club Eskimos" in order to associate a "sparkling" program with a "sparkling" product, was Mr. George Podeyn's. When he presented the idea personally to the ginger ale concern's president, the latter adopted it with enthusiasm,

[7] The singer was Mr. Joseph M. White.

saying: "My advertising agency doesn't believe much in radio, so we'll go ahead without consulting it." Mr. Podeyn wisely insisted that the agency sign the contract, nevertheless, knowing that if it had a financial stake in the undertaking because of the regular agency commission, its interest in the broadcasting medium would be awakened.

The incident is related here because it illustrates how contemporary disbelief in the radio medium, which in some advertising circles was especially marked, had to be met by WEAF's sales ambassadors.

Other Station Rules

The restrictions against "direct" advertising were supplemented by other station rules designed to protect the public against unwelcome presentations. No broadcaster could use the station's facilities for public talks without agreeing to the following conditions:

> Within a reasonable time before using the station the applicant shall submit to the Company orally, or if requested in writing, a statement describing in detail the matter intended to be broadcast, and agrees to broadcast in a manner satisfactory to the Company only such matter which is thus submitted.

This, of course, was censorship only in the sense that it prevented the "ad libbing" which access to a microphone is likely to encourage. Further safeguarding the radio audience was the provision that "the applicant agrees not to broadcast any matter . . . which in the opinion of the Company is in any way detrimental to the public interest and the Company reserves the right to reject any matter the broadcasting of which would violate this covenant."

It seems that the station's management sometimes had considerable difficulty in deciding just what was "detrimental to the public interest." It is recalled that a vacuum cleaner manufacturer was not allowed to use the clever line, "Sweep no more, my lady," for fear that offense might be taken by some who loved the original line beginning "Weep no more," in the song about "My Old Kentucky Home." And the first sponsored program in behalf of a toothpaste was held up for several weeks while a radio-time salesman and the manager of the station argued about the appropriateness of mentioning on the air so personal a matter as toothpaste. The contrast between this "squeamishness," as a member of WEAF's original staff has termed it, and today's frank references to intimately personal subjects is certainly marked; and there is much evidence that the restraint insisted upon at WEAF would appeal to listeners now.

This restraint, of course, was entirely due to the telephone instinct to avoid giving offense which imposed on Manager Harkness and Program Director Ross a responsibility more complex than that borne by other program-makers. WEAF was operated by an institution already in intimate contact with the public through its telephone service, a service founded on courtesy and consideration. On that account the station's management was watchful that these same attributes should mark the broadcasting service also, since in the public mind the company itself was, in effect, the "sponsor" of every program not otherwise identified. Nor could the station forget that its reputation was a matter of deep concern to telephone employees everywhere whose combined efforts gave Bell System service its character, and who naturally expected the same character to be expressed in the operation of any System broadcasting undertaking.

It was because of an habitual concern for institutional "character" that telephone people in general were disposed to judge WEAF program material by standards of public relations as well as of entertainment. At headquarters especially, as WEAF's popularity grew, there were always various opinions as to the type of broadcasting station that would most truly represent the company and the System. Even President Thayer was heard to inquire, after a prize-fight broadcast, whether the company could be criticized for presenting such an event!

This critical interest on the part of System officials and employees lasted throughout the period of the American Company's operation of the station. When Mr. Gifford, after becoming President, was asked why he wanted to end the broadcasting activity his reply was "Well, the principal reason, of course, was that our experiment had succeeded and we didn't belong in the entertainment business; and besides that," he added reminiscently, "whenever I wanted to consult my top executives they were apt to be downstairs in the studio, 'monitoring' the programs."

As for prize-fight broadcasts, there were bagfuls of fan mail to show that Mr. Thayer need not have worried. One unique letter to the station, from a lady with a Spanish name, read in part as follows:

> I should say I did enjoy your description of the fight. I have seldom been so excited except at bull fights. Do give us some more. I am enclosing a self-addressed envelope so that you please tell if it is permissible here for women to go alone to these box fights. I am almost 50 and have never seen one and want to very much but I know nobody to go with. You tell me please which is a good fight and where to get the tickets. I hope you do not think it revolting, my wishing to see one of these typical American fights.

Religion—Charity—Politics

The reader's attention might be called, at this point, to a problem confronting WEAF's management as a direct result of the station's popularity—that of dealing with requests for the use of the station's facilities by religious, charitable, and political groups.

The problem received a special emphasis, after the start of Dr. Cadman's Y.M.C.A. broadcasts, in the desire of individuals and churches to broadcast religious services. Because of the heavy expense for wires and equipment it was impossible to meet all the requests, and to accede to only a few would expose the station to criticism on the ground of discrimination. This difficulty was explained to central organizations representing Protestant, Catholic, and Jewish groups, and arrangements were eventually made whereby all requests could be referred to them, thus relieving the station of the necessity of decision. The New York Federation of Churches cooperated in meeting the demand for Protestant services by selecting not only ministers but even music and musicians. Catholic services did not lend themselves to broadcasting, but high dignitaries of the Church later appeared before WEAF's microphone on special occasions and the singing of a Catholic boy choir became a very popular program feature. The Jewish group did not desire time on Sunday, but followed on weekdays the Federation's practice for providing religious programs.

Similar dealings with headquarters organizations helped to obviate misunderstanding on the part of those engaged in charitable and political activities. There were approximately 2,000 organizations and individuals in New York interested in charitable works and many wanted to use WEAF for the promotion of their special projects and for soliciting funds.

To escape any suspicion of discrimination the use of the station was restricted to the Red Cross, Boy Scout, Salvation Army, and other organizations with activities that were nationwide rather than local. As for the political field, arrangements were made, as will be described later, so that the national committees of the two major parties would approve or disapprove, during the 1924 presidential campaign, of all political requests for the station's use, and the station was then able to hold to a policy of "first come, first served."

A sidelight on WEAF's earnest effort to be scrupulously fair to its audience is the station's permission to the National Socialist Party to broadcast without expense during the 1924 campaign when the party reported that it had no funds with which to meet the station's regular charge for time on the air.

Advertisers Cautious

In this modern day of universal broadcasting, when large advertisers spend huge amounts both for radio time and for program features, it may be difficult to realize fully the degree of business resistance to WEAF's toll broadcasting idea. In the face of this resistance, which was inevitable because the broadcasting medium was so new, it was not easy for the station's representatives to persuade business concerns themselves to test the station's facilities. Because of the prohibition against the "direct" commercial approach, local advertisers were especially difficult to convince.

As for the national advertisers, such as manufacturers of foods or household supplies, their campaigns for 1923, involving the use of magazines, newspapers, and billboards, had been determined the previous year. Their future plans were undetermined and would be based largely on the recommendations of the advertising agencies which prepared their advertisements and placed them in the media selected. These professional advisers were naturally conservative in their attitude toward broadcasting since there was so little definite experience to guide them. Furthermore there was, for a time, no financial inducement to jog this conservatism and stimulate tests of the new medium. Newspapers and magazines customarily paid advertising agencies a standard commission on billings for space that they bought, and the WEAF management was hesitant about conforming to this practice. There was conservatism at telephone headquarters as well as in agency offices, for the station was a service experiment in an unfamiliar field. It was several months before commissions were allowed to agencies in order to establish broadcasting definitely as an advertising medium and to encourage their interest and participation in the experiment.

Advertising Agencies

The W. H. Rankin Company, as has been said before, was the first advertising agency to use WEAF's facilities, though in behalf of itself and not of a client. The first agency to study broadcasting seriously and to organize a radio service department was N. W. Ayer and Son, the Philadelphia organization that had functioned as the American Company's advertising agent since the company inaugurated, in 1907, its series of institutional advertisements designed to inform the public of the Bell System's problems, policies, and objectives.[8]

Mr. J. M. Mathes of the Ayer organization was in close touch with the company's broadcasting experiment. He had caught the vision of a broadcasting service from frequent talks with Vice-president Gifford and Advertising Manager Ellsworth. By persuading one of its clients, the National Carbon Company, makers of Eveready batteries, that radio was a natural medium for it because batteries were needed for radio receiving sets, the Ayer organization became the pioneer advertising agency to advocate broadcasting as a developer of consumer and dealer interest.

The influence on radio of the National Carbon's "Eveready Hour" is part of advertising history. The program itself as gradually de-

[8] The motive in instituting this series is stated in the opening paragraph of the first advertisement: "A perfect understanding by the public of the management and full scope of the Bell Telephone System can have but one effect, and that a most desirable one—a marked betterment of the service."

veloped by the Ayer staff, headed by Mr. Paul Stacy, was the most ambitious project of the day—a full hour of entertainment and information that was a radical departure from the ordinary "sponsorship" of a dance orchestra, for example. It was a venture that, considering current conditions, was extremely imaginative and courageous. Until network broadcasting made possible the delivery of the Eveready Hour to distant stations, the entertainers were sent to those stations for personal appearances before their microphones. The fact that battery sales increased wherever they appeared proved the commercial possibilities of broadcasting a program simultaneously from several stations, and Mr. Mathes and his associates deserve recognition as pioneers in developing these possibilities.

"Hard Sledding"

As the experiment proceeded during 1923, the station's sales representatives, Messrs. McClelland, Podeyn, and Smith, and Mr. William Ensign, who joined the group in the autumn, had disheartening experiences in their efforts to arouse real consideration for broadcasting as a medium for creating consumer demand or for aiding in the distribution of merchandise to dealers. One of their most serious handicaps was the lack of factual information about the radio audience. Until adequate statistical and economic data had been assembled by the station, to form the pioneer guide to radio advertisers, these men when preaching the gospel of toll broadcasting were armed only with their enthusiasm, and with some time on the air to sell. Both Mr. Podeyn and Mr. Ensign used the same phrase when asked in 1944 about their labors at WEAF two decades earlier, "It was mighty hard sledding!" Yet, as a result of the "hard sledding," some 250 firms and individuals had made commercial broadcasts by the end of 1923, and practically all of WEAF's time on the air was sold for Thursday, Friday, and Saturday evening hours.

The Broadcasting Department therefore had reasons for feelings of encouragement as it reviewed the experience and accomplishments of 17 months of experimental operation, even though the station's income for 1923 was more than $100,000 under the expense of operation. There was no question of the station's popularity. The skill of its technicians had won for it an enviable record of technical

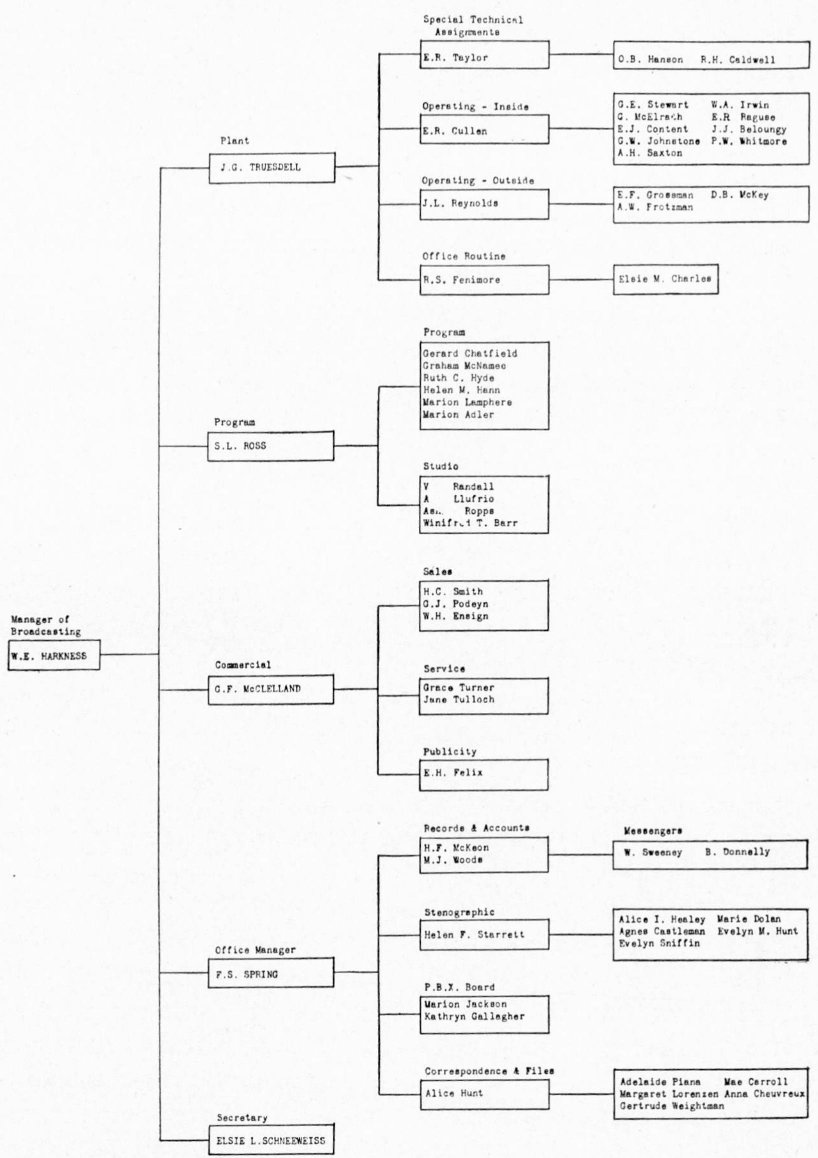

CHART II

The WEAF Organization, October 15, 1923

CARDINAL'S RESIDENCE
452 MADISON AVENUE
NEW YORK

May 5th, 1925.

Mr. H. B. Thayer,
Chairman of the Board of Directors,
American Telephone and Telegraph Co.,
195 Broadway,
New York, N. Y.

My dear Mr. Thayer:-

With each successive day I feel more keenly my debt of gratitude to the American Telephone and Telegraph Company and to your own good self.

Your kind courtesy in placing at our disposal your tremendous resources has made it possible for us to bring to countless thousands our message of Charity.

May I ask you to kindly convey to your associates my deep appreciation for the personal sacrifices they made to be present on that occasion, although it deprived them of the one day given to them to be with their families.

With kindest personal regards and a blessing on those who are near and dear to you, I am,

Faithfully yours in Christ,

P. Card. Hayes

Archbishop of New York.

A letter of appreciation from Cardinal Hayes to Mr. Thayer, May 5, 1925.

performance, and it was recognized everywhere as outstanding in the quality and variety of its programs. Some 20,000 communications to the station in December, 1923, as contrasted with 5,000 received in the first month of the year, were a measure of WEAF's importance to the radio audience, as was also the unusual response to a questionnaire sent to 25,000 listeners, 45 per cent of whom at once returned complete and detailed replies.

The Fourth Floor at Headquarters

As a result of the broadcasting activities that had begun at 195 Broadway in April, 1923, the fourth floor had acquired, by the end of the year, an atmosphere strangely in contrast with that of the rest of the tall building which was the headquarters of the Bell System.

The floors above, where over 3,000 men and women spent their working lives, were peopled by those who studied the problems and details of improving and extending telephone service; by D&R scientists who planned the further development of the telephone art; by forecasters who estimated the nation's growth for which the telephone enterprise had to prepare; by engineers who faced the building problems developing from the public needs of the future. There, too, the headquarters departments of the Western Electric Company hummed with the activities reflecting the great and growing responsibilities of manufacture and supply.

But the fourth floor had sights and sounds and a pervading spirit that gave it the character of another world. Muffled speech and music greeted the ear as one walked along its halls. Its occupants were technicians, announcers, supervisors, clerks, absorbed in duties unrelated to those of their neighbors in the building. Its visitors were orchestra men assembling for rehearsal or for broadcast, eager and ambitious students hurrying for auditions, artists and speakers gathering to stand before America's most famous microphone. It was a world that thought of dancing and singing and laughter, where "Gypsies" and "Troubadours" lived, where "Happiness Boys" joked, where stories were told to children. The fourth floor was the glamorous, romantic world of WEAF, accepted by millions as but a world of entertainment. It was, nevertheless, a communications world as well, for it served as the testing terrain of a communications service idea—and the word had gone forth, "There's no reason to do anything about broadcasting at all, unless we do it right."

The present chronicler would find it a pleasant experience to recreate for the reader this world of WEAF by describing notable broadcasts and by incorporating in this record the personal recollections of those who guided the station's destiny at "195" through three exciting years.

Were there space to do this, there would be stories illustrating the troubles which came to a management that was guiding an experimental plow in a field where no furrow had ever before been turned—an incident, for example, like President Coolidge's displeasure over some remarks of Mr. H. V. Kaltenborn, the "dean of radio commentators." According to the reminiscence of an Operation B staff member:[9]

> Kaltenborn's broadcast was a "commercial" for the Brooklyn *Eagle,* and we piped his talk to Washington as a feature for WCAP's program. It was pretty outspoken and the President didn't like it, but we couldn't do a thing about it except cut Kaltenborn off from WCAP, the WEAF broadcast being on a regular contract. It shows how easily the station could be blamed for something it couldn't control.

Memories of broadcasting triumphs, program emergencies, studio mishaps, and department life in general would show WEAF's resourceful people at work. There would be anecdotes galore of the most vivid figures in the American panorama of entertainment. Well-remembered studio scenes might be pictured as when a cardinal broadcast, and WEAF, recalls a station hostess, "was so solemn and quiet, with people kneeling as he spoke." And in contrast there might be other studio scenes when great personages, seized by the dreaded "mike fright," had to be helped by the station staff through the ordeal of their first broadcasts. "I can never sing here!" exclaimed the great Irish singer, John McCormack, as he entered the studio with its padded ceilings and heavily draped walls for his

[9] Mr. Kaltenborn was associate editor of the Brooklyn *Daily Eagle*. His distinguished radio career began on October 23, 1923, with the first broadcast from WEAF of a series of current events talks. His interesting booklet, "Twenty Year Club of Pioneers in Radio Broadcasting," lists the many who were associated with WEAF while it was operated by the American Company.

radio debut—a triumphant one, indeed, though a studio announcer had to grip his hand in encouragement as he sang. "I'd rather face 50 audiences," said Miss Ethel Barrymore, after her first experience.

In reception room, control-room, mailroom, executive office—everywhere in the WEAF establishment were occurrences that have special retrospective interest for every WEAF pioneer. There is a strong temptation to lighten this record by assembling these recollections, for they are all of historical value and are packed with human interest. It is necessary to pass them over, however, in order not to interrupt a narrative aiming to trace in broad outline, against a background of new and challenging problems, the progress toward the development of a nationwide broadcasting service.

CHAPTER XI

EARLY NETWORK EXPERIMENTS

THE FIRST NETWORK BROADCAST

THE establishment of a broadcasting station in New York was the first step, as the reader will remember, in exploring the concept of a broadcasting service through regional stations tied together by long-distance lines for simultaneous broadcasting. With the Broadcasting Department well organized to study the problems and expenses of local operations, an investigation of the main idea was begun toward the end of 1922.

While the investigation proceeded, an opportunity arose for the first network experiment. This was the annual banquet of the Massachusetts State Bankers Association, held at the Copley Plaza Hotel in Boston in January, 1923, with Mr. A. H. Griswold of the A. T. & T. Co. on the speaker's program for an address, "Some Phases of Radio Telephony." Following his address the guests were entertained, through a public-address system installed in the banquet hall, by a program broadcast from WNAC, the Boston station owned by the Shepard Stores.[1] The program, however, did not originate in the WNAC studios, but came by wire from WEAF in New York, where it was also being broadcast. The account of the event given to readers of *Radio Digest Illustrated* merits inclusion in this record because of its technical references and also because it shows how the correspondent's imagination had been stimulated by the demonstration:[2]

[1] WNAC is today the "key" station of the "Yankee Network."

[2] Vol. iv, no. 4 (Jan., 1923), p. 81.

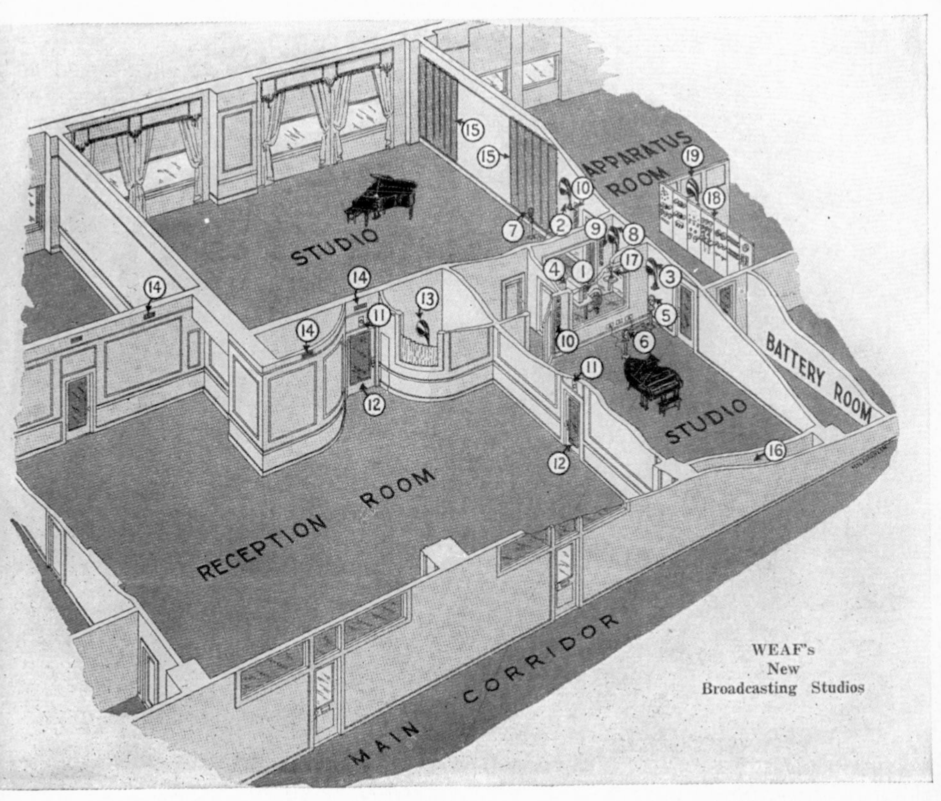

Schematic diagram of WEAF studios at 195 Broadway, 1923.

1. Announcer's microphone.
2, 3. Loud-speakers in the studios.
4. Announcer's control panel.
5, 6, 7. Microphones in studios.
8. Announcer's loud-speaker.
9, 10. Signal lights.
11. Door signal lights showing when studio was on the air.
12. Special door knobs to prevent interruption.
13. Loud-speaker for reception room.
14. Ventilation system.
15. Curtains for acoustic effects.
16. Sound-proof wall.
17. Announcer's telephone for communication with engineers.
18. Equipment panels.
19. Loud-speaker for monitoring engineers.

SEE TOLL PLANT CHAIN

Plans Follow $25,000 Test of Simultaneous Broadcasting Service

* * * * *

American Telephone and Telegraph to Establish First Station in Boston— Two Plants Send Same Program at One Time During Tryout

(By F. N. Hollingsworth, Special Correspondent)

New York—An experiment in Radiophone broadcasting, the first of its kind ever attempted, has resulted successfully—so successfully, in fact, that the world's greatest telephone corporation is about to launch the establishment of a chain of Radio test laboratories and Radio toll stations that will extend from the Atlantic to the Pacific coasts, both north and south in two lines. This experiment, preparations for which covered several months, was that of simultaneously broadcasting from a New York station on a 400-meter wave length and from a Boston station on a 360-meter wave length. The results are declared by experts to have been flawless.

WEAF-WNAC PROGRAM THREE HOURS LONG

The New York station was WEAF, of the American Telephone & Telegraph Company at 14 Walker Street, New York city, and the Boston station was WNAC, of the Shepard Stores, on Winter Street, Boston. The program was three hours long, and comprised a number of orchestral selections, saxophone and cello solos, contralto and baritone vocalists, and most unusual of all, a bird mimic, whose imitations of bird songs and notes were as clearly and flawlessly heard as though he were in the same room with the listeners.

From the New York station was run a long distance telephone circuit of approximately 300 miles, equipped at intervals with repeaters or amplifiers and special filters, which equalized the circuits so that the sound came into the Boston station as clearly as it entered at the New York end. To equalize a telephone circuit means that whatever goes into it at one end comes out exactly the same at the other end, or wherever it might be tapped.

If the lines had not been equalized, the high notes of the saxophone or the low tones of the piano might have been the only ones heard distinctly at the Boston end when broadcast.

PROBLEM DELICATE; FOUR CIRCUITS USED

From a technical standpoint, the control of a broadcasting station 300 miles from New York by means of telephone lines is a most delicate problem. Four circuits were used to stage this feat. The first was the "regular" circuit, which carried the broadcast program. The second was an emergency circuit, which could be plugged in should the regular one fail through storm or other interference. The third was a local circuit, used in Boston, for a big side issue program, which will be touched upon later in this article. The fourth was the "order circuit," by which the telephone and Radio engineers in New York and Boston kept in touch with each other and noted progress of the experiment. There were fifteen experts handling the matter at the Boston end.

Four of these experts were stationed at the Copley-Plaza hotel, about a mile from Station WNAC. Here, in the big ballroom, was installed a "public address system," consisting of four huge loud speaker horns with 50-watt tubes as power amplifiers. A bankers' convention was being held there at the time, and this evening program was rendered to them by combined Radio and telephone as a special entertainment.

100,000 RADIOPHANS LISTEN IN

Owing to the care exercised in adjusting the filters and repeaters, there was no distortion; every note coming over as clear as the original. At least a hundred thousand Radiophans, throughout New England and along the Atlantic seaboard, listened in on this remarkable program. Station WNAC has records of being heard as far south as Porto Rico, and Commerce, Texas, as far east as the Azores, and as far west as Montana. Therefore one can imagine the possibilities of this combined broadcasting.

The expense of the test was $25,000, but telephone officials say it would have been well worth double that to get the results they obtained.

A. T. & T. CO. PLAN FIRST LINK

Within a very short time it is expected that the American Telephone & Telegraph Company will establish in Boston their own test laboratory and Radio toll station. With the New York station it will constitute the first link in a chain that will be established very soon west, north and south along lines in big cities to the Pacific Coast.

Nothing definite had been decided until the big test of January 4, but immediately thereafter word came from New York that the Boston station will be established within a few months. The project will not stop in Boston, however, but the chain will be gradually pushed westward. Already hundreds of letters and telegrams have been received at Station WNAC telling of picking up the New York concert, which was duly announced as a simultaneous broadcast, in the usual matter-of-fact way that the Shepard station has. The letters also mentioned the broadcast's remarkable clearness.

WHAT SYSTEM HOLDS FOR FUTURE

In time, say experts, the country will be covered with Radio toll stations, so that a big concert in New York, or the inaugural address of a President, or the speech of some silver-tongued orator may be broadcast by contract to any part of the country. Arrangements can then be made for loud speakers installed in some big auditorium where the audience can sit and listen to an evening's program without ever seeing the participants. San Francisco will be able to hear the Metropolitan opera, by contract with the company itself and the telephone company with its Radio toll stations as the intermediary and transmitting agents.

Political parties can have the greatest campaign orators in the country speak to a hundred audiences simultaneously, at perhaps no more expenditure than would be involved in their traveling expenses, and at a great saving of their time and nervous energy.

Circuits for First Networks "Made to Order"

Some additional technical background for the test just described should be provided at this point, in order to register the effect of broadcasting's growth on the operating practices of the Long Lines organization.

The circuits used for the WNAC test were part of the wire network that had been engineered for the transmission of speech only and installed for normal wire communication service. In order to utilize such circuits for a broadcast it was necessary to make them nonavailable for telephone purposes by disconnection from switchboards. And since in most cases involving open wire the wires were composited for telegraph operation, the composite sets had to be removed in order to permit the circuits to transmit the low frequencies which were required for program purposes although not necessary for message operation. The public-address system development had already established the facts that a frequency band of about 200 to 3,000 cycles was the minimum for the reproduction of speech on loud-speakers that would satisfactorily meet requirements at this time, and that this band had to be extended up to about 5,000 cycles for satisfactory reproduction of music.

Subsequent use of circuits for regular communication, following their temporary segregation for broadcasting purposes, of course made necessary the removal of amplifiers and equalizing equipment, the restoral of telegraph apparatus, more tests, and finally reconnection to switchboards.

After the isolation of circuits for New York-Boston program

transmission to WNAC, and the installation of amplifiers and equalizers as described by the *Radio Digest* writer, the circuits were measured and tested as shown by the contemporary Long Lines plant records:

TESTING

Jan. 2nd—Three circuits, New York to Boston, 7-9 P.M.
3rd—Three circuits, New York to Boston, 5:30-7 P.M.
3rd—Two circuits, New York to Boston, 8-9 P.M.
4th—Three circuits, New York to Boston, 7-8 P.M.

SERVICE

Jan. 4th—Three circuits, New York to Boston, 8-11:10 P.M.

Cross-Talk Hazard

The use of three circuits, as indicated by this old entry, was of course normal insurance against a number of hazards to telephone service. Particularly important was the hazard of cross-talk, which became of increasing concern to telephone engineers as long open wire circuits became more and more necessary in broadcasting activities.

There were two types of cross-talk—from the broadcasting circuits into the message circuits and from the message circuits into the broadcasting circuits. The first type resulted in occasional complaints from telephone subscribers, but was not so potentially dangerous to telephone service as the second type. The real danger was that telephone conversations, which otherwise would have been completely private, would be broadcast inadvertently and without warning to those conversing. Electrical coupling which can produce cross-talk is always present in some degree among neighboring circuits. Cross-talk from such coupling becomes significant only when it is loud enough to be noticeable above background noise. During broadcasting, however, conditions can become critical because amplifiers are used both at the radio station and in radio receivers. Should the gain-control of one of these amplifiers be set too high at a time when static and other noises are low, normally unintelligible cross-talk might become intelligible.

This was one of the reasons why early broadcasting circuits, as in the case of the WNAC experiment, were provided in triplicate—one for the regular transmission, another for emergency use, and a third to serve as an "order" wire, whereby a wire line connected to a radio transmitter could be "monitored" by an operator who, when detecting even faint cross-talk, would switch the program to the emergency circuit.

From "Layout" to "Network"

At first the circuit equipment required for special broadcasts was returned, when removed from circuits, to the Long Lines office which had furnished it. When the need for such "made-to-order" broadcasting circuits increased, the equipment was left in place on the telephone or station premises concerned, so that it could be quickly connected and disconnected, thus permitting the wires to be used for either message or broadcasting service with a minimum of effort and expense in making a change. Later, as the interconnection of broadcasting stations became more routine for the Long Lines operating forces, message circuits were arranged for quick conversion to broadcasting circuits and were designated as such on the circuit maps.

During 1923 a chart was in use by the Long Lines engineers that showed certain circuits specially designated for broadcasting marked by red pencil lines. The engineers referred to the chart as the "red layout." At first the circuits indicated on it were used for message purposes when not required for broadcasting. By 1926, however, the use of these circuits for program purposes had increased to such a point that plans had to be made to reserve them for program purposes exclusively, and to provide substitute message facilities by new construction. When this had been accomplished, the circuits previously identified as the "red layout" became the original "Red Network." Similarly, other colors were used for charted layouts which indicated circuits serving other groups of stations that became identified as "Blue Network," "Purple Network," et cetera. Thus did the crayons of Long Lines draftsmen and engineers, nearly two decades ago, influence radio broadcasting's present-day terminology.

In the routine just outlined can be traced the challenge, during broadcasting's development as a public service, to provide circuits without impairing regular long-distance service. The final answer to the challenge was the investment of millions of dollars in order to make possible the reservation of thousands of miles of specially equipped circuits for the use of broadcasters exclusively.

The First Broadcasting "Chain"

The WEAF-WNAC joint broadcast of January 4, 1923, can hardly be called the birth of network broadcasting since the circuits were in use but a few hours. What was actually the first "chain" of stations was the union throughout the summer of 1923 of WEAF and of WMAF at Round Hills, Massachusetts, which has been referred to on a previous page in connection with the employment of Announcer Graham McNamee.

The records show that for transmitting WEAF programs to Colonel Green's station, open wire circuits were used between New York and Providence, Rhode Island. From Providence to Round Hills non-loaded cable had to be used, and this made necessary the use of modified four-wire message type repeaters as one-way program amplifiers, together with "home-made" equalizers at several points. Equalization of the non-loaded cable required some ingenious engineering but the results were satisfactory to Colonel Green's listeners, and the engineering methods followed were the forerunners of future standard practices. The constant measurements that ensured these results are suggested by the Long Lines engineering report:

> Service to Station WMAF from 195 Broadway studio started July 1st, 1923; hours, 4:30-5:30 P.M., 7:30-10 P.M., daily except Sunday; Sunday, 7:20-10 P.M. Transmission nominally from 100 to 5,000 cycles but down 15 db at 5,000 cycles. Final equalization accomplished by resonant shunt at 2,000 cycles, giving a 1,000 cycle loss of 12 db. Resulting transmission within 3 db between 200 and 3,500 cycles, down 10 at 5,000 cycles, down 8 at 100 cycles.

A Notable Broadcast on June 7, 1923

Before WMAF began to receive WEAF's programs, the Long Lines engineers had undertaken to provide circuits for a broadcasting venture on a larger scale than had ever before been attempted, and its success made June 7, 1923, a red-letter day in radio history. This was because a "chain" of four stations was involved.

The occasion was the annual meeting of the National Electric Light Association which was held in Carnegie Hall, New York City. From 8:55 to 10 P.M. three out-of-town stations broadcast the speech and music coming to them over long-distance telephone wires. They were General Electric's WGY in Schenectady, New

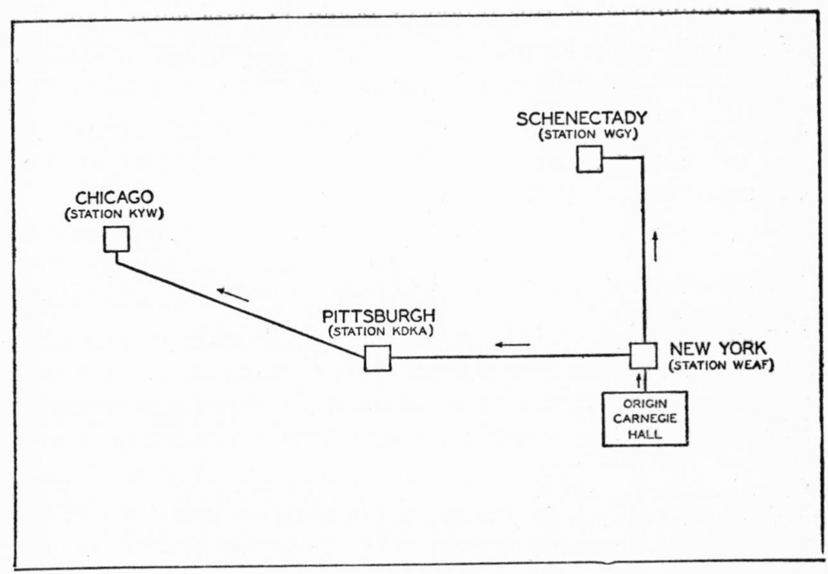

CHART III

One of the First Network Broadcasts, June 7, 1923

York, Westinghouse's KDKA in Pittsburgh, Pennsylvania, and KYW in Chicago, Illinois. Notable features of the program were the address of Mr. Julius H. Barnes, President of the United States Chamber of Commerce, and the singing of Miss Anna Case, of the Metropolitan Opera Company.

This "nationwide broadcast," as it was enthusiastically described in some accounts because of its record coverage, involved many weeks of testing and marked a new accomplishment for telephone engineers in arranging and converting regular long-distance circuits for the transmission of music to distant cities. To one news man it had a tremendous social significance. "The time," he wrote,[3] "is close at hand when farmers at the four corners of the Union may sit in their own houses and hear the President of the United States . . . ."

The President Broadcasts

The fulfillment of this prophecy began 14 days later. June 21, 1923, was an historic day for WEAF and the Long Lines engineers because of the last item on the following program:

4:15 P.M.—Selection on the xylophone by John M. Chaderton, accompanied by Bell Wright.
4:30 P.M.—Selections on the Ukalua by Mario Scandiffio. Program: "Serenade," Schubert; "Sextet" from "Lucia," Donizetti; "Souvenir," Drdla.
4:45 P.M.—Songs by Georgia Lee Morgan, lyric soprano.
7:30 P.M.—Solos by Irving R. Waite, baritone.
8:15 P.M.—Recital by Madame Fely Clentent, mezzo-soprano, accompanied on the piano by Mortimer Browning; violin obligato by Frances Mayer; harp obligato by Arthur Jones.
8:30 P.M.—"The Most Expensive Thing in the World," a talk by William Fellowes Morgan.
9-10 P.M.—Dance music by the Mount Royal orchestra.
10:00 P.M.—Address by the President of the United States broadcast direct from St. Louis, Mo.

The President spoke in the Coliseum at St. Louis, Missouri, with two microphones before him, one to transmit his address over long-distance lines to the WEAF transmitter in New York, and the other giving the program to KSD on the roof of the St. Louis *Post Dispatch,* a station that had begun operations in June, 1922, with a Western Electric transmitter, and is said to have been the first 400-meter station.

The announcement of that famous newspaper on the previous day clearly reflected the wonder and excitement over radio's new rôle in national life:[4]

[3] *Sun and Globe,* June 8, 1923, in an article entitled "Sings Across Oceans of Space."
[4] June 20, 1923.

PRESIDENT HARDING SPEAKING HERE MAY BE HEARD IN EVERY STATE IN THE UNION

Microphones at Coliseum to Carry His Voice Directly Into Post-Dispatch Broadcasting Station—Simultaneous Transmission From New York Station

It appears certain that no human being ever by word of mouth has addressed so vast an audience as will hear President Harding deliver his speech tomorrow night at the Coliseum—thanks to a marvel of science which will be undertaken for the first time. An unprecedented experiment in radio transmission is expected to make the President's words, spoken in conversational accents, audible to listeners in every State in the Union.

The test gains enhanced historical importance from the circumstance that it is the first time a President of the United States has made use of radio to speak to the citizens of the nation on a great political question.

Before the President at the Coliseum will be microphones such as have become familiar to St. Louisans at the Municipal Theater and Odeon. Owing to the use of a loud-speaker similar to that at the Municipal Theater, the orator will not be required to raise his voice. The sound-waves picked up by the microphones will be relayed by wire to KSD, on the roof of the Post-Dispatch, whence they will be, as usual, launched into space by radio.

The novel feature is that the sound-waves received by KSD will also be dispatched, by an all-metal circuit, nearly 1000 miles eastward to Station WEAF, which is operated in New York City by the American Telephone and Telegraph Co., and which will also broadcast the waves by wireless. Owing to the electric current's velocity of 186,000 miles a second, the broadcasting on the Atlantic seaboard and on the bank of the Mississippi River, with 1000 miles of telephone wire intervening, will be for all human purposes simultaneous.

Should a station half way between the two points receive the speech both from St. Louis and New York, he would be unaware of the fact. The difference in time would be 1-196th [*sic;* should be 1-186th] of a second, an interval too minute to create any interference in the ear.

Only a guess can be made as to the number of persons to whom the stations in St. Louis and New York will make the President's address accessible. The Electrical Board of Trade in New York has collected statistics showing that in the vicinity of that city are no less than 2,000,000 people who hear WEAF. The audience of KSD, normally large, is expectedly to be greatly increased because practically all the broadcasting stations in the country, at the request of the St. Louis Chamber of Commerce, have agreed to remain silent as a courtesy to the President of the United States, while KSD is sending out his speech. Newspapers in the 48 States have requested radio listeners to cooperate in the test, in order to determine whether it will be possible for the President to be heard in all of them.

Although the electric current will travel by wire from St. Louis to New York in an unappreciable fragment of a second, the skill of scientific man will enable him to stretch forth his hand three times and manipulate the waves while they are en route. Owing to resistance of the metal, the current would suffer a considerable loss of intensity. Therefore, while racing on its way, it will be stepped up successively by means of proper devices in other cities, and will arrive in New York with an intensity equal to that which it possessed on arriving at KSD.

If this test proves successful, the next step, and one contemplated for the near future, will be some night to link up by land wires as many as 30 of the most powerful broadcasting stations in the United States. Then the President, sitting in his study in the White House, will speak into a microphone with no more volume than if he were conversing with a friend a few feet away. With the process undertaken by KSD and WEAF multiplied by 30, it is hoped that the President's words will be heard by owners even of crystal sets, throughout the country.

The President's Appreciation

The President's St. Louis speech and one on the next night at Kansas City, Missouri, were incidents in a long trip that was to take him from Washington to Alaska. The long-distance line facilities permitting both addresses to be broadcast from WEAF were made available as a courtesy to the President and as a service to WEAF listeners. It was also the Bell System's privilege to equip his train with special facilities for keeping in telephone communication with the National Capital and for addressing gatherings at frequent train stops across the country. The latter facilities involved a public-address system that had been installed in the President's car before the trip began, the effectiveness of which had already been demonstrated to the President at the time of his 1921 inauguration and at the subsequent Armistice Day ceremonies for the Unknown Soldier.

In a telegram from Salt Lake City to President Thayer at Bell System headquarters, President Harding made this acknowledgment of the public-address installation:

I wish to express my great appreciation of the splendid service we have had through the electrical equipment of the Presidential train. I gather that it was more or less experimental from your viewpoint and as the chief beneficiary of it, I desire you to know how vastly it has lessened the burdens of a difficult trip. When opportunity is afforded I wish to make a more adequate acknowledgment than this.

This statement was not the only evidence of the President's appreciation. It was followed by the complimentary invitation to the Bell System engineers detailed to his train that they accompany him to Alaska as his guests:

The President would be very pleased if Messrs. Truesdell, Maloy and Santee of your company could accompany the party to Alaska on the Transport Henderson.[5] Entire party feel deep obligation for their services and would be glad if you care to authorize them to take the trip. Reservations have been made for them subject to your approval.

Just as the President's St. Louis broadcast on June 21 had made radio history, his San Francisco address scheduled for July 31 would have marked another pioneer accomplishment for Long Lines engineers, for circuits were ready to bring his words to Western Electric transmitters at six stations. The broadcast would have been the most ambitious on record at that time, with an estimated audience of between three and five million people served by KPO in San Francisco, WOAW in Omaha, WNAQ in Chicago, WMAF in Round Hills, Mass., WEAF in New York, and WCAP in Washington, the Bell System's second Experimental Station which had been dedicated early in the month. But the speech was never broadcast. His voice was never again to be carried far and wide through the arts of wire and wireless telephony, for after completing his Alaska trip, he died on August 2 in a San Francisco hotel.

New England telephone men gave a fine proof of Bell System watchfulness in the public interest, during the President's last hours, by bringing circuits under difficult conditions to the Vermont homestead of Vice-president Coolidge's father, where Mr. Coolidge was resting, and which was without telephone connection.[6] These tele-

[5] The engineers referred to were J. G. Truesdell of the American Company's Broadcasting Department, J. P. Maloy of the Long Lines Engineering Department, and H. B. Santee of the Western Electric's Loud Speaker Department.

[6] The story is well told in *Telephone Topics* for Sept., 1923: "Service First for President Coolidge," vol. xvii, no. 5, pp. 150-152.

phone men were the first to shake his hand after he had been dramatically sworn into the office of President by his Justice-of-the-Peace father, and his first official act was to talk with Washington. He later wrote to the telephone company's president, "Let me add another word of thanks for the efforts made by your company to extend the service to my father's house. It was an example of efficiency and foresight."

CHAPTER XII

WCAP: A SECOND EXPERIMENTAL STATION

The Establishment of WCAP

IN April, 1923, when the toll broadcasting experiment in New York was well under way and WEAF's new studios were ready for the Broadcasting Department's use, officials at Bell System headquarters believed that the time had come to take the next important step in exploring the idea of a broadcasting service.

This step was the opening of a second Bell System station to which WEAF's sustaining programs could be "piped," thus permitting a broader study of the engineering, commercial, and social considerations involved in the original idea of company-owned stations. The station that was established for this purpose, in Washington, D. C., was WCAP, its call letters including the initials of the Chesapeake and Potomac Telephone Company, the local Bell Company which owned and operated it. The broadcasting circuit between New York and Washington comprised, according to the Long Lines records:

> No. 8 gauge open wire with two short stretches of non-loaded submarine cable, and a few miles of entrance cable at each terminal. At New York the entrance cable is equipped with extra light loading, but at Washington the cable is non-loaded. A 55-A coil is used at either cable as a drainage for noise. A repeater at Newtown Square is normally used for toll traffic, but is patched out when the circuit is used for broadcasting.

Washington was selected as the place for an extension of the broadcasting experiment because the city was near enough to New

York for D&R and Long Lines engineers to study carefully all phases of the technical operation. Another advantage in the location was that the experiment's social and scientific significance would be directly exposed to the observation of all government bodies.

It will be remembered that the cross-licensing agreement of 1920 had been negotiated after the Navy Department had urged such an agreement "for the good of the public," in order that "the market can be freely supplied with tubes." By the spring of 1923 the demand for tubes had already created an enormous business in their manufacture and sale. The main source of supply was the Radio Corporation, which was currently under attack because of alleged monopolistic practices with regard to the distribution of radio equipment. This was disturbing to some members of Congress who considered such practices as being contrary to public interest; this point of view resulted in an investigation by the Federal Trade Commission that will be referred to later in this narrative.

Such control of patents relating to broadcasting as the American Company exercised was being exercised in the public interest, and company officials expected that through the linking of Washington and WEAF, the developing scope and the results of experimental broadcasting in a period of "growing pains" would be clearly demonstrated. The undertaking would show, for example, how large cities need not be deprived of metropolitan radio entertainment even though unlicensed or competing stations were not using telephone wires as adjuncts.[1]

And underlying these specific broadcasting considerations was the American Company's fundamental policy of constant and complete coöperation with every government institution that was concerned with communications.[2] It welcomed regulation by the Interstate Commerce Commission because it believed such regulation to be in

[1] See Mr. Gifford's reference to legislators which is quoted at the beginning of Part III of this record.

[2] An interesting fact in this connection is that following the discontinuance of WCAP as a Bell System station, the original transmitting apparatus was operated and maintained, under an experimental license, for use by the Department of Commerce in connection with aircraft radio exploration by the Bureau of Standards in the promotion of aerial navigation. Later, the equipment was presented to the Department and installed at its experimental station at College Park, Maryland.

the public interest.[3] It was particularly anxious that the Army and Navy Departments, for which the System had done such vital work in World War I, should at all times have first-hand knowledge of all its communication activities and developments. In fact, one of General John J. Carty's most important and most pleasant duties as director of the headquarters Development and Research function was to keep these departments constantly apprised of telephone progress. His "Defense Test" demonstration for the Army in the following year, as will be described on a later page, gave important emphasis to the readiness of the telephone organization and its wire network as a protection to the nation in time of emergency.

WCAP's broadcasting equipment was similar in most respects to that which was giving WEAF such technical distinction but included several new features recommended by the headquarters D&R engineers whose experience and counsel were the constant support of their Washington colleagues. It was housed on the roof of the Washington company's headquarters building at 725 Thirteenth Street, N.W. The antennas, having a span of 184 feet, were suspended between masts of different heights, since one of them was erected on the roof of a building on Twelfth Street that was also occupied by the company.

The station began operations on July 4, 1923, broadcasting on a wave length of 469 meters which it shared with another station. Since its studio was incomplete and a local station identification was therefore not practicable, Washington listeners heard the unusual announcement from New York, "This is Station WEAF, New York City, and WCAP, Washington, D. C., broadcasting a joint program."

And thus, with piano solos played by Miss Winifred Barr in a WEAF studio in New York, WCAP inaugurated the broadcasting activity that won for the station a position of outstanding importance in the life of the Capital City, together with a reputation for technical excellence throughout the country and abroad as well. One listener in Lancashire, England, took the trouble to write:

[3] By Act of Congress the Federal Communications Commission was created in 1934 to take over this responsibility.

I have much pleasure in informing you that I heard your station working in the early hours of Sunday, September 23, 1923. The strength was good. I was using one high frequency and one detector with reaction. Aerial, 100 feet single wire; height, 30 feet. I reckon that I am 5880 English miles from you."

Recollections of WCAP

The operation of WCAP was a function of the company's commercial department, headed by Mr. Walter B. Clarkson, with the station's management the responsibility of the General Commercial Engineer, Mr. Keith McHugh.[4] The station's Director after June, 1924, was Mr. Paul Gascoigne, who today, as District Commercial Manager, has charge of all business relationships arising from the complex and ramified services rendered by the company to government agencies. The program director from the summer of 1924 was William T. Pearson, well known in Washington musical circles as a composer, who had been acting as Manager of Broadcasting while Mr. Gascoigne was serving as Chief Clerk to the company's General Commercial Superintendent. Both men served as announcers with marked competence. Richard Halpenny was the station's notably efficient wire chief.

Washington telephone people have lasting memories of WCAP's pioneer days and of the incidents that made up the station's history. Mr. H. M. Craven, of the company's engineering staff, now retired, who was Supervisor of Broadcasting, has recalled for this recorder the first assembly of the transmitter, which was on the dining-room floor of his own home. He also recalls with much satisfaction his personal training of President Coolidge in "microphone manners."

Other engineers, as well as Mr. Craven, tell of exciting experiences in meeting requirements for public-address systems which became indispensable adjuncts to the broadcasting of Washington public figures. It might be mentioned here that for some time before WCAP's establishment the need for loud-speaker equipment in the area served by the Washington telephone organization was more pronounced than in any other section of the country—a demand

[4] Mr. McHugh is now a Vice-president of the A. T. & T. Co.

Paul Gascoigne says goodbye to the radio audience of WCAP, the second Bell System station, July 30, 1926. At the final broadcast from the station, many well-known entertainers were on hand to take part, some of whom are shown in the picture. From left to right: W. T. Pierson, Program Manager; Mrs. Norrine Norris Dahn, pianist; W. J. McManus, announcer; Gretchen Hood, soprano; Gertrude Kreiselman, pianist; several visitors; O. P. Gascoigne, Business Manager, at the microphone; Harvey Townsend, lyric singer; Helen Marston, studio stenographer; a visitor; Ben Cain, banjoist; and the Hawaiian Melody Boys, Edward Pringle, Charles Baum, Melvin Henderson, and Clinton Rollins. Photo by F. A. Schutz, Washington, D. C.

GENERAL OF THE ARMIES
WASHINGTON

September 13, 1924.

Mr. H. B. Thayer, President,
American Telephone and Telegraph Company,
195 Broadway, New York City.

My dear Mr. Thayer:

May I take this opportunity to express my appreciation to you and through you to the American Telephone and Telegraph Company and its Associated Companies for the generous participation in the Defense Test. In addition to the use of the physical facilities of your great communication system, which have contributed an important part toward the success of this undertaking, the spirit of cooperation evidenced in this matter is, indeed, a symbol of patriotic devotion to the ideals of our country.

In leaving the active service, I send this word of grateful remembrance of the aid furnished me by your signal communication forces in France during the World War.

Sincerely yours,

John J Pershing

A letter from General Pershing, September 13, 1924, acknowledging the participation of the American Telephone and Telegraph Company in the Defense Test Day Program.

which, of course, was brought about by the unusual frequency of public gatherings both in auditoriums and out-of-doors. Often indeed was the telephone "Spirit of Service" invoked by C. & P. engineers in order to have some important installations ready on time for use by the nation's leaders.

There are many memories, too, of program emergencies when local artists failed to appear, and the studio staff had to extemporize entertainment or call upon talented members of the telephone organization. A particular recollection is the frequency with which the call went out, "Get Arthur Lambdin—in a hurry." Probably few who know Mr. Lambdin today as Vice-president and General Manager of the Chesapeake and Potomac Telephone Company of Virginia will identify him as the singer who gave so much enjoyment to WCAP's listeners.

Miss Mary Langley, now Mrs. M. J. Jester, of the Washington telephone business office, was another member of the organization who was often before WCAP's microphone. The program for Christmas Eve, 1924, shows that these two singers, together with Miss Ann Seay and Mr. George Anderson, of the Revenue Accounting and Commercial Departments respectively, were introduced by announcer Gascoigne as the "C. & P. Quartette" for the singing of Christmas carols.

For three full years WCAP gave to the Washington environment a broadcasting service that was conspicuous for its distinction. Washington telephone men, inquiring casually at establishments where they could purchase receiving sets, learned that shortly after the station's opening all radio sets had been sold with a rush. "Your programs relayed from New York," wrote a government official as the station's reputation grew, "have saved the day for radio in Washington." Scores of similar letters, received after the station's opening, testified to the radio hunger that the station's service was to appease. Before the microphone in the station's studio in the Homer Building at 13th and F Streets, N.W., appeared Washington musicians, clergymen, publicists, and scientists, as well as men who were eminent in government and in public life. King Albert of Belgium spoke there in connection with his unveiling of the Ericsson Monument in the city. A memorable occasion was the presence in the studio of President Coolidge's entire Cabinet when each member participated in a tribute to Abraham Lincoln, the program being opened by the President from the White House. The tributes to the station's service, coming in a steady stream from every part of the area it reached, testified to the regard in which it was held. The studio was opened on the evening of February 14, 1924, with a concert by the United States Army Band. The arrangements included a reception room, an office, a small studio for speakers and individual artists, and a large studio for orchestras. Between the two studios was a sound-proof control-room. The station's informal farewell program was given on the evening of July 30, 1926.

WCAP's Rôle in Network Development

WCAP's importance, however, was not only as a purveyor of news and entertainment to local listeners, but also as a practical laboratory for testing the service value of network broadcasting. The station was ready, as has been pointed out here, to broadcast President Harding's speech scheduled for July 31, which the American Company planned to bring via transcontinental circuits to three Atlantic Coast stations among the six in the proposed temporary chain. Soon afterward it became a regular member of a network that made radio history.

This was after the arrangement for summer broadcasts of WEAF programs by WMAF had expired and another station began to radiate them over southern New England. The new station was WJAR, with a Western Electric transmitter, operated by the Outlet Company in Providence, Rhode Island. On the contemporary record of Long Lines jobs one finds the entry:

> Service to WJAR starts Sunday, October 14th; repeat on Fridays and Sundays until further notice; requires transmission frequencies up to 5,000 cycles; in the meantime Outlet Company wants to broadcast World's Series baseball which starts October 10th. Transmission of this will require equalization only up to 3,000 cycles but it seems desirable to equalize up to 5,000 at the start.

Many indeed were the famous broadcasts in which this enterprising Providence station, because of its Long Lines connections, was able to participate, and two of the earliest were historic.

The first of these took place on the eve of Armistice Day, 1923, less than a month after radio news had begun to refer to the WEAF-WCAP-WJAR network. On that day former President Woodrow Wilson, sick and broken from the strain of World War I, spoke in the library of his Washington home where WCAP engineers had installed a microphone. It was the first time in a year that he had addressed any audience outside the city. Wires led from the microphone in the Wilson library to a truck, suitably equipped with amplifying apparatus, standing in the driveway beside the house, and an underground circuit carried the ex-President's voice to WCAP and to the long-distance circuit connecting with the New York and Providence stations. It was a most affecting broadcast, for the speaker's feeble tones, so clearly transmitted, were a startling indication of his broken and failing health.

Three months later there was a still more affecting broadcast from the same three stations when, on February 6, 1924, their listeners heard the ex-President's funeral services. As the New York *Herald* reported the broadcast:[5]

The broadcasting studio of WEAF, the American Telephone and Telegraph Company, at 195 Broadway, presented an aspect yesterday afternoon different from what it did a few weeks ago when the last public message of Woodrow Wilson was thrown on the air for waiting millions. Attention from the small group present then was critical, eager. Yesterday nearly a hundred guests from nearby offices and the press listened with an air of reverence to the last service of organ note, song and prayer as it was being performed for the dead statesman at the Episcopal Cathedral, Washington.

How many millions heard the simple rites—slow strains of Mendelssohn, the fifteenth chapter of the Epistle to the Corinthians, a magnificat, the Apostles' Creed and prayers—it was not possible for the officials to ascertain. But with the Radio Corporation's stations in Washington and New York and others in this vicinity suspending operations from 3 to 5 P.M.: stations WCAP, Washington, WEAF, this city, and WJAR, Providence, each connected by direct telephone wire along the line from Bethlehem Chapel itself, sent out

[5] New York *Herald,* Feb. 7, 1924, p. 1.

the service simultaneously with the increased power of one kilowatt. The tones of the Brahms "Choral" and the words of the Lord's Prayer and "The Strife is O'er" may have been picked up by three or four million receiving sets.

To telephone engineers, listening in WEAF's studio to the impressive ceremonies, came memories of President Wilson's participation in the 1915 dedication of the first transcontinental telephone line when he said, "I want to express my pride that this vital cord should have been stretched across America." And doubtless in the minds of thousands of listeners was the thought so often expressed in later years—that the new radio medium of communication might have powerfully influenced the course of history had it been at the dead President's disposal when in office.

President Coolidge's First Message to Congress

On December 6, 1923, a month after the broadcast from the Wilson library, came one of the most significant joint broadcasts in radio annals, when more people heard the voice of an individual than ever before in the history of the world. The occasion was the message to Congress which President Coolidge delivered in person. The new President had come to his office under tragic circumstances. He was a retiring figure in Washington and generally unknown to the country at large, and there was intense interest in his first important official address. Because of this the American Company and the Southwestern Bell Telephone Company cooperated in making circuits available so that three stations in the latter company's operating area, in addition to the established trinity of WEAF, WCAP, and WJAR, might broadcast the message. They were KSD, the *Post Dispatch* station in St. Louis, Mo., WDAF of the Kansas City, Mo., *Star,* and WFAA operated by the Dallas, Texas, *News and Journal,* all operating with Western Electric transmitters.

The broadcast was an epoch-making event in America's communication history. To the President himself it proved the enormous value of radio as a means of direct and personal communication with the nation.[6] (Four days later President Coolidge broadcast from the White House over WEAF, WCAP, and WJAR.) To a vast public it showed that from broadcasting could come a quick and awakening knowledge of the activities of the government and of great national events. To telephone leaders it was another demonstration of the value of long-distance lines in the development of a national broadcasting service.

"Broadcasting" or "Narrowcasting"

That such a service could best be developed through the use of wires had been the editorial opinion expressed by *Radio Broadcast* after the inauguration of WCAP.[7]

> It is evident to anyone who thinks much about the question that in the final solution of the broadcasting problem a given program must be made to reach as large an audience as possible. As the programs of the broadcasting stations improve, this fact will become increasingly apparent. For example, if an opera is being broadcasted from the Metropolitan Opera House in New York, the artists may be the finest in the world. Why then should people in other sections of the country who enjoy opera, have to listen to some mediocre program from a local station? Of course entirely apart from radio, this is actually the case today. We can't all go to the best opera and so we have to content ourselves with something less expensive and less artistic. But right here lies the great promise of radio—it need cost but little more to broadcast to a million listeners than to a thousand, so that the very best programs should be available to everyone. . . . It seems to us that the future of broadcasting is intimately connected with the establishment of a wire network covering the country and connected to the best broadcasting station in a given locality.

This sensible opinion about wires was not shared at the time by prominent spokesmen for the receiving-set industry, and the contrary view, having some historical interest, should be presented here. In a widely quoted speech made a month before President Coolidge's

[6] Two days after the broadcast Mr. Coolidge wrote to President Thayer as follows: "Reports have come from all over the country of the success which attended the broadcasting of my message to Congress, and I want to take this opportunity of thanking you and the other officials of the company who cooperated so efficiently in assuring the satisfactory results obtained. It was an achievement of which you may well be proud and I should be interested to know in a general way how far the address was clearly heard."

[7] Vol. iii, no. 3 (July, 1923), pp. 187-188.

message had been spread abroad from six stations, one of these spokesmen had advocated the idea of a few "superpower" stations that "preferably" would be joined by radio, and his idea was widely publicized.

It may be that this view was stimulated by experiments in short-wave transmission that had been carried on for some time, or by progress in the manufacture of large vacuum tubes. Whatever the reason, the belief was stressed that such a radio broadcasting system, employing "superpower" stations located at principal entertainment centers, would provide a broadcasting service truly nationwide in scope. The contrasting word "narrowcasting" was used in referring to the broadcasting activities of the time. The impression given was that perhaps the currently active stations represented a transient phenomenon of a rapid radio development, destined to be replaced by a half-dozen or even fewer with 100 or even 200-kilowatt capacity.

Telephone engineers concerned with broadcasting progress were, of course, undisturbed by the discussion resulting from such a proposition. In the first place, the broadcasting art did not have within its technique the facilities required for consummating the "superpower" development being proposed. Five or ten kilowatts of power constituted the technical limitation at the time, and these engineers themselves were even then planning a five-kilowatt transmitter for WEAF because of reception difficulties in its immediate area. In the second place, their criterion of "service"—one that was impelling the continuing improvement of telephone receivers and transmitters, public-address systems and wire transmission—was the *quality* of what was received by the listener. These engineers had more than enough evidence, through their experiments in developing a transatlantic telephone service, of the vulnerability to static of radio transmission over long distances, and the consequent threat to quality.

The year ahead was to show how the local service of many regional stations, receiving programs transmitted to them by wire, could result in what the "broad"-casting exponents believed could best be accomplished, at some distant day, by "superpower" transmission. Thousands of miles of wire circuits were soon to enable local stations to acquaint their listeners with the drama and struggle of an election campaign. The voices of America's political leaders would reach millions of homes in city and country. Citizens were to have, as a new and thrilling experience, immediate knowledge of happenings that were shaping the country's history.

And every special broadcast for which the Long Lines men prepared and watched their circuits would emphasize the importance of the factor that was determining the ultimate place of radio in American life. This factor was the economics of broadcasting, upon which the company's decisions and activities of 1924 were to have a profound and lasting influence.

PART IV

MILESTONES ALONG THE WAY, 1924

CHAPTER XIII

EARLY EPISODES OF 1924

WEAF's Experiment with Increased Power

THERE were 500,000 receiving sets, more or less, in the area served by WEAF, when the station broadcast the famous chimes of New York's Trinity Church on lower Broadway to announce the arrival of the New Year, 1924.

The American Telephone and Telegraph Company's Broadcasting Department had become an organization of sixty, headed by Mr. J. A. Holman as Manager.[1] Before the year had ended the activities of this growing organization were to be reflected in successes of enormous significance in the demonstration and development of radio's function. They were also to bring about gusts and then gales of criticism, to prove that the way of the experimenter is hard when the laboratory is society itself.

Under the conditions of broadcasting's swift advance in public esteem, WEAF's character as an experimental station became completely obscured. On this account, inevitably, there was widespread misunderstanding—in some quarters it was outspoken suspicion—of the company's radio policies. That this situation would naturally generate considerable uncomplimentary news can be shown by reporting some of the early episodes of 1924. The first of these was the station's experiment with increased power.

There were large areas in New York that were not adequately served by WEAF's 500-watt transmitter. The so-called "dead" spots

[1] Mr. Holman succeeded Mr. W. E. Harkness as Manager upon the latter's promotion to Operation B as Assistant Vice-president.

had been determined by a D&R field strength survey, similar to that conducted soon after WBAY began operations, which fully confirmed the complaints of radio listeners and indicated the need for increased power.

In anticipation of this need, there had been initiated in 1923 the development of a 5,000-watt transmitter utilizing the newly developed water-cooled tubes that were being employed in the transatlantic radio telephone development. A model of this new transmitter had been destined for a Signal Corps project which did not materialize and it was this unit which was prepared for actual use toward the end of 1923.

An experimental license with the call letters W2XB was secured, and the first WEAF program utilizing the new equipment was sent out on the eve of New Year 1924. The higher power was to establish the whole course of radio broadcasting toward greater effectiveness in reaching the public, a result which, however, was actually realized only after the lapse of some time and the overcoming of objections and difficulties, as we shall see.

Master-Oscillator, Crystal-Controlled Transmitter

Along in 1924 D.&R. field studies of the effectiveness of the new transmitter showed that areas of weak reception, occasioned by shadows, were sometimes accompanied by a serious degradation of the acoustic quality of the received program. This in turn was traced to a certain effect in the transmitter whereby the modulation of the carrier wave was causing it to be "shimmied" back and forth rapidly in frequency, an unwanted form of frequency modulation. Resort was had to the use of the master-oscillator type of high-frequency input, and this in turn was further stabilized by means of a quartz crystal control. Thus there came into being in 1924, in connection with the high-power equipment, the first crystal-controlled broadcast transmitter, employing a technique that was to set the pace thereafter in broadcast transmission generally.

Four days after it had first gone into service the effectiveness of the 5 K.W. transmitter was reported by the company in the following news bulletin:

The use of the new transmitter has been continued from day to day on an experimental basis in order to determine various factors involved in the use of increased power. Thousands of letters have been received and continue to come in in great numbers commending the use of the new equipment. Except in the case of some single circuit receivers, or receiving sets connected with antennae of too great lengths, radio fans do not experience interference which precludes reception from other local stations.

The new transmitter is unique in that it utilizes water-cooled vacuum tubes similar to those used in the transatlantic telephone experiment several months ago. Essentially it consists of a transmitter similar to the usual 500-watt broadcasting transmitter. The output of this transmitter is supplied to a high power radio frequency amplifier employing two of the water-cooled vacuum tubes.

This is the first broadcasting station of above average power operating near New York, although there are several in operation in various parts of the country including Pittsburgh, Schenectady and Chicago. Eastern radio fans have enjoyed programs from these stations but this is the first time that the exceptionally fine program material available in the East will be audible with consistent volume in the Central West.

The local press naturally gave considerable space to reports of the experiment because of WEAF's local prominence, and a second bulletin was then issued to give further explanation of the experiments which were planned:

Continuing its experiment with high power, WEAF will resume broadcasting its regular program on a gradually increasing scale of power. Beginning on Saturday afternoon, January 5, 1924, the power was reduced to 500 watts. After two or three days transmission on this power the new transmitter will be used on its minimum power of one kilowatt and transmission will be continued with this adjustment for several days until full data as to the results with this power are obtained. Power will then be gradually increased first using two kilowatts and after two days additional testing four kilowatts. . . .

The increase of power WEAF has adopted, is caused by the insistent demand on the part of radio listeners for reception of louder volume. Experiments will be continued until a satisfactory level is determined upon.

At the present time, there are several broadcasting stations all somewhat higher powered than the maximum used with the new transmitter operating on regular schedule. This accounts for the excellent reception in New York, of Chicago, Pittsburgh and Schenectady stations. It is likely that as soon as receiving sets are adapted to the new conditions cause for complaint which may exist at present will be remedied. It may be recalled that when two broadcasting channels of 360 and 400 meters were established last spring and later when four channels were established, radio listeners experienced difficulty but with improvement of sets it was soon found that the new conditions were better than the old.

WEAF HEARD IN BUENOS AIRES

Since experiments were begun with the new transmitter reports from all parts of this country and from other countries have been received of consistent reception of WEAF's program at great distances. Perhaps the most interesting of these is a cablegram received from Buenos Aires, 5,000 miles air line distant from New York. The cablegram advised that WEAF was heard from midnight to 1:30 A.M., December 30 with a consistent volume.

Some Local Opposition to Increased Power

But there were some local listeners who were quick to express their opposition to the change. The receiving sets of the day were not selective, and when they were located near the new transmitter, considerable interference was experienced. Consequently, all local radio stations received letters that were critical of the company's action, and "WEAF Hogs the Air" was the inevitable headline for some newspaper accounts of the situation.

For the telephone engineers, whose efforts to increase WEAF's effectiveness aroused so much transient indignation, it was somewhat solacing to find the experiment's significance recognized in at least one newspaper office. As the Brooklyn *Eagle* editorialized:[2]

Hogging the air is a new expression just coined in response to a new broadcasting situation. Since January 1 Station WEAF of the American Telephone and Telegraph Company has broadcast its daily programs with a current of 1,000 watts instead of the 500 watts used by most other stations. The result has been highly satisfactory—for Station WEAF. Its programs carry much farther and can be heard much more loudly and distinctly.

But—and here's the rub—the programs broadcast by other stations do not reach the simpler and less expensive receiving sets as well as before. Station WEAF cannot be tuned out completely except by sets which have great selectivity. The simple crystal set or the single-circuit set, which, according to some radio experts, should never have been introduced, cannot be adjusted to Station WJZ or Station WHN so as to eliminate all sound from Station WEAF.

The function of a broadcasting station is to make itself efficient. If increased

[2] Jan. 5, 1924, p. 6.

power develops efficiency it ought to be used. The function of a receiving set is to select from the air what the owner wants to hear and bring it in clearly and in sufficient volume. Those who own inferior receiving sets must put up with the handicaps that involves.

Radio fans are apt to forget that they pay nothing for the remarkably fine programs now being broadcast by some of the Eastern stations. If they will compare New York City's programs with those offered farther west they will realize what progress has been made here in the average quality of the offerings which they enjoy without charge. Broadcasting is in its infancy. There must be constant experiment to make it more efficient. The special interests of no group can be permitted to hamper the development of the greatest invention of the age.

From the comment just quoted, and from the popular reaction to an increase to what was but a moderate amount of power from a technical standpoint, the modern student will, of course, detect the general inadequacy of the broadcasting art at the time. The day was not far distant when much greater increases would take place unnoticed.[3]

The Radio Music Fund Committee

Another fundamental inadequacy—a sound basis for broadcasting's support—was accented by an incident that occurred a month after the first expressions of opposition to WEAF's use of increased power. This experience can be called the "Music Fund Committee Episode."

The Radio Music Fund Committee[4] was composed of prominent New York men, well known for their support of musical activities, who believed that radio offered a wide field for stimulating public interest in good music. Since the outstanding artists of the day commanded large fees, the committee planned to raise a fund by popular subscription to obtain their services for radio appearances. WEAF was selected as the appropriate station for these appearances,

[3] It was not until April 19 that WEAF was granted official permission to broadcast regular programs with 1,000-watt power and the station continued on this power until November 19 when 1,500 watts were allowed. In the following year the Department of Commerce permitted power increases in steps of 500 watts and by Sept. 1, 1925, the transmitter's full power of 5,000 watts was utilized.

[4] The original members were Messrs. Clarence H. Mackay, Felix M. Warburg, Frederic A. Julliard, and A. D. Wilt, Jr. Later they were joined by Mr. A. A. Berle, Jr.

and the station agreed to contribute its facilities. Arrangements for engaging musicians were made with a prominent manager of eminent artists and orchestras; the Central Union Trust Company was appointed the depository for contributions, and the plan was announced on February 16.

The committee soon began to receive support for its idea. Besides the contributions of money there were enthusiastic letters from music-lovers, anxious to hear the great artists of the day, very few of whom had ever broadcast. The plan seemed to have a special appeal to people with physical handicaps, one of whom wrote:

> Being a semi-invalid and confined to the house most of the time, I derive a great deal of pleasure and joy out of my radio. God bless the radio, is what I say over and over again. The wonderful lectures and beautiful music we hear help us to forget our physical ailments, and to see a bright lining in many clouds which otherwise would cast a gloom over us. If by contributing our little mite we can obtain better music, I feel we all should be willing to do so. . . . WEAF is by far the best station, and you were wise to choose it for broadcasting your programmes.

But the WEAF management soon realized that in agreeing to be a party to the committee's altruistic efforts it had made a mistake. The prospect of further distinction for WEAF programs brought jealous comment from other local stations. The motive of the plan was obscured by the newspaper reports of interviews with those who controlled the services of artists and of those involved in the use of copyrighted music. The spokesman for one special interest was quoted as saying (in complete disregard of the high business standing of the committee's members):

> The Radio Music Fund is a cleverly devised scheme—a stroke of business genius in fact—which enables the telephone company to get high priced artists to embellish and surround its advertising matter at the expense of the good souls with money to give away.

Also, fears were expressed in many quarters, and duly reported, that the efforts of the Fund Committee would result in a "broadcasting monopoly." Newspaper readers, ignorant of WEAF's experimental function, were made critical by inadequate references to

WEAF's speech-input equipment at American Telephone and Telegraph Company Headquarters, 195 Broadway, New York, 1924.

The world's first 5-kilowatt broadcast transmitter and the first transmitter to be stabilized by crystal control. Started in service by WEAF on the eve of January 1, 1924.

the station's charges for broadcasting service and by such misleading news reports as:

> WJZ operated by the Radio Corporation of America, stated that it could not charge because it was not permitted to do so. At the station an official said that the corporation sold receiving apparatus and considered that it made its profit on those sales. "The cost of maintaining WJZ is charged to the sales department. We would consider we were collecting twice if we charged those who broadcast over our transmitter."

Thus the current news was not the plan itself but the objections to it, and WEAF, as the "middleman" in the controversy, could not debate them, even if given an opportunity. The result, of course, was that the public gained a superficial and distorted conception of the company's position in the matter and of its broadcasting interest in general. As for the plan of the Music Fund Committee, it could not succeed because it was fundamentally unsound, and WEAF was happy indeed when it was abandoned and the contributions returned.

Who Is to Pay for Broadcasting?

This episode is given space here because it so well reveals the psychology of the times when WEAF was exploring the question, "Who is to pay for broadcasting?" The present account has already quoted the views that *Radio Broadcast* expressed on the subject in 1922, when WBAY began experimental operations, and so that publication's comment, two years later, on the Radio Music Fund Committee's objective should also be included:[5]

> So many times we have asked the question "Who is going to pay" that any reasonable attempt at the solution of the question of the cost of broadcasting is very welcome and will be watched by millions of listeners with a great deal of interest. In the very first issue of *Radio Broadcast* an attempt to analyze the possible solutions of this problem was made. One of the possibilities suggested then was that of soliciting contributions from the radio audience. . . . It seemed possible even two years ago, that the public would respond to an appeal for funds in an unexpected degree, and the possibility is even more imminent to-day after the remarkable demonstrations of the way in which

[5] "The March of Radio," *Radio Broadcast,* vol. v, no. 1 (May, 1924), pp. 18-21.

radio broadcasting, properly supported, can instruct and amuse its millions of listeners.

With this idea in mind a committee of New York business men has been formed to try out this scheme of broadcast financing. It seems evident that a station itself could not very well carry out such a scheme because a large part of the public would imagine that their contributions were going to pay dividends for the stockholders of the company rather than for putting out good programs. One or two rumors to this effect would kill completely any scheme managed and controlled by a business concern such as the Radio Corporation or the American Telephone and Telegraph Company.

To convince the public that a bona fide attempt was being made to give them self-supporting radio, the committee which has undertaken the task of introducing this innovation has been wisely made up of prominent financiers, who could not possibly be suspected of any idea of profit-taking, and who have been intimately connected with many other musical ventures. They are men whose names will at once command the respect and confidence of the prospective contributors. This committee has solicited funds from the radio public, calling for contributions of from a dollar up, from all those who are entertained by WEAF, through which the new broadcasting programs are to be sent. This station has been selected, it is said, because of the "excellent quality of its modulation and transmission." All of the funds received from the radio listeners will be directly applied to the securing of artists of the highest caliber. The committee will serve voluntarily and the station, WEAF, has agreed to carry out the programs free of charge. This is no small contribution on the part of the American Telephone and Telegraph Company, in view of the fact that this station commands a fee of $400 per hour for its use for advertising.

There have been favorable comments made about the scheme, and some adverse and discouraging. The manager of a well known station expresses the opinion that the public will not contribute to any extent for a form of amusement which they have a fair chance of getting without paying for it. . . .

Another objection . . . comes from those stations which will not secure the service of these well paid artists. "It looks all right for WEAF," says one manager, "but how about the other 534 stations in the United States?" This bares a very important point in the broadcasting situation: are all these stations entitled to a share of any fund collected from the radio audience at large? Many of them seem to think so, but there is really no justification at all for their stand. How many of us would contribute money to hear a program from a poorly managed, poorly equipped station, such as many of them are today? If these stations put out such a request as has emanated from WEAF it is unlikely that one dollar would be contributed. There are too many stations to-day which feel they have a right to be on the air irrespective of what kind of material they send out. They appear to forget that the ether is the public's and they are on the air not by right but by tacit permission. And the public certainly has a right to send its money in to that station from which it can get the highest return.

Just as every good music lover cannot help but wish success to the Metropolitan Opera, even though this company gets a disproportionately large share of the public's opera money, just so we hope this new scheme will meet with extraordinary success. Even so, it must not be regarded as a final solution to the problem. We expect that it will serve merely as a trustworthy indication of the public's real desire in broadcasting. And it is the good of the general listener, not that of any station or company, which must be of chief importance in determining the method of solving the problem.

Later in the spring this same publication[6] further manifested its interest in the "final solution" of the question of broadcasting's support by asking, in a full-page advertisement, "Who Is to Pay for Broadcasting and How?" and by offering a prize of $500 for a satisfactory answer. Under the heading "What We Want," the announcement stated:

. . . is a workable plan which shall take into account the problems in present radio broadcasting and propose a practical solution. How, for example, are the restrictions now imposed by the music copyright law to be adjusted to the peculiar conditions of broadcasting? How is the complex radio patent situation to be unsnarled so that broadcasting may develop? Should broadcasting stations be allowed to advertise?

These are some of the questions involved and subjects which must receive careful attention in an intelligent answer to the problem which is the title of this contest.

. . . . .

The plan must not be more than 1,500 words long. . . . The plan must be in the mails not later than July 20, 1924.

. . . . .

Judges will be shortly announced and will be men well-known in radio and public affairs.

. . . . .

There are several sources from which the contestant can secure information, in case he does not already know certain of the facts. Among these are the National Association of Broadcasters . . . the American Radio Association . . . the Radio Broadcaster's Society of America . . . the American Society of Composers and Authors, the Westinghouse Electric and Manufacturing Company, the Radio Corporation of America, the General Electric Company, and the various manufacturers, and broadcasting stations.

[6] *Radio Broadcas*, vol. v, no. 1 (May, 1924), p. 69

When this announcement is read in retrospect, the omission of the American Company as a source of information seems strange, but the editor may have felt that his readers already knew of the company's belief in toll broadcasting as the "final solution."

The Federal Trade Commission's "Monopoly" Complaint

The news concerning the Radio Music Fund Committee's proposals and WEAF's new transmitter completely obscured the experimental character of WEAF's operations, and from it the public began to derive unfavorable impressions of the American Telephone and Telegraph Company's relationship with radio development.

A further source of such impressions was a complaint issued on January 27 by the Federal Trade Commission. It charged that eight companies, including the American Company, had "combined and conspired for the purpose of, and with the effect of, restraining competition and creating a monopoly in the manufacture, purchase and sale in interstate commerce of radio devices and apparatus and other electrical devices and apparatus, and in domestic and transoceanic communication and broadcasting."

This charge was the result of an investigation of the Radio Corporation that had been undertaken by the Commission early in 1923, pursuant to a Congressional resolution. The Commission's long report, issued on December 1, had expressed the opinion that "there is no question that the pooling of all the patents pertaining to vacuum tubes has resulted in giving the Radio Corporation and the affiliated companies a monopoly in the manufacture, sale and use thereof. With such a monopoly the Radio Corporation apparently has the power to stifle competition in the manufacture and sale of receiving sets and prevent all radio apparatus from being used for commercial radio and communications purposes."[7]

The inclusion of the American Company in the Commission's complaint was, of course, because of the cross-license agreement of 1920, an agreement negotiated at the request of the government itself, "for the good of the public," in order that the market might "be freely supplied with tubes."[8] President Thayer at once pointed

[7] This last phrase refers to wireless telegraph stations.

[8] Navy Department's letter of Jan., 1920.

this out when newspaper men hastened to telephone headquarters for a statment:[9]

> We have not yet received a copy of the Federal Trade Commission's complaint and only know by the newspapers that one has been filed. We presume that, so far as we are concerned, it rests upon a contract made by us with the General Electric Company dated July 1, 1920. In the first Annual Report after that contract was made (that for 1920), we stated its purpose and scope which, from our point of view, was to clear up a patent situation which might hamper our development. The effect of it has not been to restrain trade but to expand it. We believe that the contract is in the public interest and have been advised that it stands upon a sound legal basis. If there is any doubt about either of those points, we should be glad to have it resolved.

Radio Called a Natural Monopoly

Executives of other companies involved similarly stressed both the legal integrity and the public service value of the agreement, and editorial writers were generally realistic and conservative in their comment on the sensational charge. The New York *Times* editorial of January 30, 1924,[10] opened with the following paragraph:

> The Federal Trade Commission loves a shining mark. That is well. A commission which should infallibly punish the wicked would be a blessing to the good. On the other hand, a commission which pursues the good, is then overruled on its law and contradicted in its allegations of fact, is of doubtful public benefit. Not until the evidence is heard, and the courts pass on the law, can it be said positively that the Radio Trust is in restraint of trade or that the Trade Commission is a nuisance. Is it more likely that the defendants have lower standards of ethics, economics and law than the commission? The defendants maintain that their contractual relations are in the public interest, and that they are advised that these contracts are legal. Their intentions were communicated to the Government, and for a time the Government's representative sat among the directors of the trust. The Trade Commission made a report to Congress on the trust's activities without expressing any adverse opinion. The trust asserts that all its records are open to official inspection, and it abides the result of co-operating with each other to develop the trade.

[9] The complaint was filed for trial before the Commission on Jan. 25, 1924, but no start was made in the taking of testimony until Oct., 1925, twenty months later. There were hearings at various times until Feb., 1928. Ten months after the last hearing the complaint was dismissed.

[10] P. 18.

A concluding paragraph of this *Times* editorial was quoted with approbation by the editor of the *Journal of Electricity,* who wrote for his February 15 issue:[11]

Eight of the most prominent manufacturers of radio apparatus have been summoned before the Federal Trade Commission to answer charges of monopolizing the radio industry. Because these companies have pooled patents in order to combine the good features of each for the benefit of the public and thereby give them the best apparatus obtainable, they are to be made the subject of a sweeping investigation to determine whether or not they are in restraint of trade.

Those companies maintain that their monopoly is based on patents alone, that it is legal and that without it, much of the progress in radio communication during the past two years would have been impossible. As to the legality of their contractual relations we are not in a position to judge. We are morally certain, however, that much of the progress in radio art has been due to their co-ordinated efforts. And if the grant of a patent, which under law gives a monopoly to the patentee for 17 years, is both legal and illegal, the statutes are curious things indeed. If one who controls a patent licenses one or more manufacturers to produce a device, and if these manufacturers are then to be indicted by the Commission as a monopoly in restraint of trade, is not something wrong with the statutes governing either the patent office or the Commission?

To go back to the Federal Trade Commission, the New York Times in a recent editorial offers the following comments:

"The Trade Commission has a record as well as the defendants. It risks no such penalties for mistakes as do the defendants, and therefore makes more of them. The Radio Trust could not survive such errors as the commission makes with impunity. It has issued 1,062 complaints, with the result of final action in only 563. The courts have reviewed 35 cases, finding that in 23 the orders of the commission were wholly void. Only in seven were they valid. On the balance of presumptions the defendants would stand a 3 to 1 chance of being right and commission wrong. In its report for 1923, the commission says that continuous litigation has resulted from appeals from its procedure, with the result of 'developing the law of business practices under the court's rulings.' It would thus seem that the commission is more of an aid to lawyers than to business."

Not until the evidence is heard and the Commission renders a decision and the courts pass on it in appeal, can it be determined whether the radio manufacturers or the Federal Trade Commission is in restraint of trade.

[11] Vol. lii, no. 4, p. 117.

The editorial view of the Brooklyn *Eagle* was that "like the telephone and the telegraph, radio is a natural monopoly," which was also the thesis of the *Financial World*:[12]

> Little apprehension need be shown over the complaint of the Federal Trade Commission alleging that the Radio Corporation, General Electric, American Telephone & Telegraph and other companies have formed a monopoly to control the radio business. This commission has no power to enforce its findings. It only can recommend action. Its complaint, also, is for the moment only an allegation that still remains to be proven.
>
> Yet it is difficult to see where any monopoly exists, for, if we take up any of the large metropolitan newspapers and scan over the multitude of advertisements offering all sorts of radio devices, the radio business as yet is far from being a monopoly which means centered under one control.
>
> As radio is a future form of communication probably it would be better, and far more convenient to the public, if it were centered more under one control. Eventually it must be, as the confusion at present in sending radio messages is one of the problems the business has on its hands. It must be solved so that it may be possible to secure the maximum of efficiency.
>
> Radio fans all over the country can now "butt in" on radio communications, for it is not under any Federal restriction, which is an obstacle, and prevents privacy. The Federal Commission has not complained that the telephone is a noxious monopoly, though it is controlled by a central organization; or the telegraph, whose field of communication is confined to two large companies, since they are natural monopolies.
>
> Radio, in its field, is as much a natural monopoly and its benefit to the public is no less important, if not now, certainly in the future as the telegraph and telephone. Therefore, it should be encouraged and not hindered.

But such tolerant references as these to current radio conditions were in editorial rather than in news columns, and members of the telephone organization everywhere were exposed to much uncomplimentary association of telephone headquarters with the sinister word "monopoly."

The association itself was, of course, proper, since at the time the American Company alone had the legal right to broadcast for hire. The company was, moreover, nearly the only source of high-grade transmitting equipment, the sale of which it was deliberately re-

[12] Editorial in issue of Feb. 9, 1924, vol. xli, no. 6, p. 177: "Radio's Natural Monopoly."

stricting in order to brake a runaway situation. It was normal that fears of such controls should be expressed, for there was no general knowledge of how they came about, nor was there any generally known basis for assuming that they were being exercised in the public interest. The popular assumption is that monopoly or control will be contrary to the interests of society, dictionaries defining the word as "in popular usage, any such control in a given market as enables the one having the control to raise the price of a commodity or service materially above the price fixed by free competition." This being the prevailing conception of monopoly, the public's deduction from current news was that the American Company was bent upon selfish and ruthless exploitation of radio in general and upon anti-social operations at WEAF in particular.

Unfortunately for the American Company's reputation, as it drove its experimental plow through a field strewn with rocks of ignorance and boulders of prejudice, there were dozens of reports that contributed to a misunderstanding of its broadcasting practices and policies. When, for example, the text of a proposed broadcast by one of New York City's medical staff was first submitted by WEAF to a disinterested medical association, according to the custom established by the station as a protection to the public, the action was assailed as a form of censorship involving "freedom of speech" and "freedom of the air."

For another example: a New York clergyman wished to broadcast the meeting of his Sunday Bible class. Since the program time was taken up by the New York Federation of Churches, he could not be accommodated at WEAF; and his idea of purchasing his own broadcasting equipment was discouraged because of the multiplicity of stations in the vicinity. For the reports of such a situation, "Pastor Fights Air Monopoly" and "A. T. & T. Bans Modern Bible Class on Radio" were easy headlines to write.

One who examines the newspaper files of those disturbing days is tempted to give the *non sequitur* prize to a statement of the Radio Trade Association. "This affair," it announced, referring to a course of action that will be considered a few pages further on in this record, "is far more than a patent fight. It looks as though it were a direct blow at the rights of the public to have a choice of radio programs." The new and uncertain status of broadcasting in the social scheme in the spring of 1924 is surely revealed by this vague conception of "rights" being obtained by the mere purchase of a receiving set.

A Memorable Communications Event

All the news in the winter of 1924, however, was not distressing to the Bell System men and women whose loyalty made them resent deeply the current aspersive reports.

On the evening of February 8, 1924, General J. J. Carty, who headed the American Company's Development and Research Department, delivered a notable address on the subject of communications at a meeting of the Bond Club of Chicago. In connection with his talk he conducted an impressive demonstration of the resources of modern telephony, utilizing a telephone circuit extending from San Francisco to Havana, Cuba, a distance of more than five thousand miles. His remarks were broadcast simultaneously from seven radio stations, one of which was in Havana—more stations than had ever before been linked with a transcontinental circuit. Listeners numbered by millions heard General Carty's outline of developments in the telephone art, his roll call of some twenty repeater stations along the line from Havana to the Pacific Coast, the violin music from Havana, and the taps of a San Francisco bugler.

In concluding his address, which was heard by radio throughout the United States, Cuba, and parts of Canada, General Carty made a memorable statement:

> We are only just beginning to appreciate how fundamental are electrical communications in the organization of society. We are as yet unable to appreciate how vital they are to the ultimate welfare of mankind. I believe that some day we will build up a great world telephone system, making necessary to all the nations the use of a common language, or a common understanding of languages, which will join all the people of the earth into one brotherhood.[13] When, by the aid of science and philosophy and religion, man has prepared

[13] Eleven years after General Carty's prophecy of a "world telephone system," President Gifford of the American Company demonstrated telephony's progress by conversing with another official in an adjacent room over a 23,000 mile telephone circuit extending around the world, a technical achievement that justified his statement at the time that "Earth now holds no limits to human speech."

himself to receive the message, we can all believe there will be heard throughout the earth a great voice, coming out of the ether, which will proclaim "Peace on earth, good will towards men." Then will be realized that vision so beautifully described by the poet:

> "Wherein each earth-encircling day shall be
> A Pentecost of speech, and men shall hear,
> Each in his dearest tongue, his neighbor's voice,
> Tho' separate by half the globe."

Before General Carty had left the banquet hall in Chicago, he received a telegram asking, "If you could send to all the world by telephone tonight just one word, what would it be?" His reply was characteristic:

> I am unable to find one word which alone would convey a significant message to the world. If you would but allow me two words, and if you would allow me to choose the language in which these words would be spoken, then, answering your question, I would say, in Latin, "Sursum corda"—"Lift up your hearts." We are looking for a solution of our world difficulties and for the attainment of universal peace. We are looking for this peace through the signing of treaties and the forming of leagues and courts. These things are great and good, and, when the time comes, they will be indispensable. But before they can be converted from symbols of lofty aspiration into terms of practical achievement, there must be a change in the hearts and minds of the people of the world. Anything which delays our recognition of this truth is harmful. Until our hearts are made right, there can be no permanent peace. Until we establish the right state of mind among the people of the world, a treaty of peace—even though signed by all the nations of the earth—is but a truce.

General Carty received several thousand congratulatory telegrams and letters from many parts of the world, not only on account of the technical perfection of the demonstration, but also in acknowledgment of the lofty character of his address. Of the latter a Cleveland paper said editorially what every member of the Bell System knew, with pride, to be a fact, "How is that for vision? He must be a man who can see beyond the end of his nose. He must be one who thinks in other terms than dollars, part of the time, at least. A Corporation with an unchartable future is fortunate indeed to have such a man near its helm."

From the retired Chief Signal Officer of the U. S. Army came this message:

The whole of Washington is discussing with wonder the marvelous achievement which you conducted in Chicago last night in transmitting the human voice and music literally to the whole people of the United States and Cuba as well as far out to sea. This dramatic performance stands today at the pinnacle of achievement of the electrical engineering profession up to the present.

In a radio trade paper appeared this appreciation of the technical progress in communications that had been so dramatically accented:[14]

. . . . Every one . . . must have had his imagination kindled and his admiration of the technical genius of his country enhanced, when, settled in the comfort of his home he heard the speaker say "Hello, Cuba" and the immediate response from Havana, and then a few seconds later "Hello, San Francisco," and immediately back "Hello, General Carty, this is San Francisco talking."

It is a pity that Alexander Graham Bell's death came too soon for him to hear this demonstration of the growth of the art his simple experiments started. He would have heard one man speak to millions, scattered over the length and breadth of our land. Even knowing the step-by-step progress by which this accomplishment has been made possible, it was with difficulty that we kept back the sentiment of that other message so important in the history of communications development: "What hath God wrought." We would also add, What great credit is due to those hundreds and thousands of bright, earnest, young engineers, whose diligent efforts and keen application make possible this almost unbelievable progress!

Thousands of telephone men and women heard this historic broadcast with feelings of intense pride in the accomplishments of their colleagues and of the telephone engineer who was representing them. The present chronicler will not attempt to report how the demonstration awakened listeners everywhere to telephony's service in overcoming the limitations of time and space. Let this be suggested by the following letter from a listener afflicted with blindness:

[14] *Radio Broadcast,* vol. v, no. 1 (May, 1924), pp. 25-26, "Fifty Million People Hear General Carty Speak."

I listened in to a demonstration of broadcasting given by General Carty from Chicago. The whole country was for the first time linked together within the sound of one man's voice. This gave me the thrill of my life. We heard the "Meditation" from "Thais," played on a violin in Havana, and "Home, Sweet Home" played on the chimes in San Francisco. We discovered that it was warmer that night in Denver, Colorado, than in Jacksonville, Florida.

Memory and imagination stirred as I followed the answering voices from sunny, tropical Cuba, through Florida, the Carolinas, and Virginia to Pittsburgh—to busy Chicago, out across the snow-covered prairies to the City of the Latter-Day Saints; up the slopes of the Rockies to Denver—to Nevada, and down to the balmy shores of the Pacific. I reached San Francisco breathless and excited, as if I had been running all the way.

I had crossed the continent so often that I could visualize most of the places on the line. I could hear the roar of traffic on Market Street, San Francisco, and the never ceasing wash of the surf on the Cuban beaches. To me, a prisoner, it was freedom again—the freedom to travel, and meet men and women, and see cities and mountains, and ships at sea silhouetted against the sky as they pass across the horizon.

That the service of the radio telephone, so commonplace a thing in modern life, was new and thrilling only two decades ago, cannot be better shown than through this appreciative expression of one who could understand, though he could not see.

CHAPTER XIV

RESOLVING THE PATENT SITUATION

Resort to Injunction

DURING the winter of 1924 the Bell System's legal advisers took a serious view of the widespread infringement of patent rights relating to broadcasting that has already been described.

The disturbing aspect of the situation was that infringing stations which continued to broadcast without a license under the company's patents were disregarding the fundamental principle of the patent law—the right of a patentee to control the use and application of his inventions during the seventeen-year period established by the law. In the prevailing circumstances a court affirmation of this principle seemed highly desirable, both as a matter of patent protection and as a basis for the negotiations of Bell Companies with infringers in their areas.

Because an injunction restraining an infringing station from broadcasting would create an opportunity for a formal court review, an action was instituted against Station WHN in New York City, outstanding among the infringing stations which had not heeded the company's warning that it was broadcasting illegally. But the objective of obtaining a judicial affirmation of the principle was not realized. The station accepted a license, thus acknowledging the validity of the company's patents, and the precedent made other court proceedings unnecessary.

A later writer on radio developments calls this a "dubious victory," and the reason for his view is to be found in the newspaper files of the period which reflect nationwide publication of misleading statements and unfounded interpretations of the company's motives. It is not necessary, for record purposes, to include here any exhibits of this contemporary newspaper publicity, although they would be interesting evidence of how easily institutional reputation can be affected when such reports get a head start. An adequate historical record can be established by registering only the public statements of both parties.

The initial statement of WHN's management was reported on March 2 as follows:[1]

> According to a letter I [a WHN official] have received from the American Telephone & Telegraph company, they will go after every station using their patents. Broadcasting to them is a commercial proposition and, if carried out as they plan, a monopoly would be established in radio broadcasting. We plan to combat this action because radio is an important blessing to the public and it would be entirely wrong to let one company control the religious and educational entertainment of the nation.
>
> Radio must remain free and an open field for all.
>
> If the American Telephone & Telegraph company wins this fight, it will mean that ultimately it will affect receiving sets and people will not be allowed to build their own sets. It would mean that this company would not only control actual broadcasting, but would also control receiving, as it would force listeners to rent sets, as is the case of the telephone.

This statement, when read today, seems to have been constructed with special skill to arouse popular fears, while ignoring the actual issue. Its absurdity need not be pointed out to anyone who has followed this narrative's exposition of the company's broadcasting venture. Of course, the broad references to monopoly "in radio broadcasting" and to control of "the religious and educational entertainment of the nation" were sensational enough to excite radio listeners everywhere.

The A. T. and T. Company's Public Assurances

An answer to this outburst was sought by the press and one was prepared on the morning of March 7:

[1] Minneapolis *Tribune,* Mar. 2, 1924, from a story captioned "Patent Suit Threatens 484 Radio Stations."

When asked today concerning the suit which the American Telephone and Telegraph Company, operating broadcasting station WEAF has brought against station WHN, for infringement of basic patents involved in radio broadcasting, President H. B. Thayer of the American Telephone and Telegraph Company, said:

"The laws of the United States provide for a reward to those who make meritorious inventions in the shape of control over the right to make, use and sell such inventions during a period of seventeen years from the date when the merit of the invention is recognized by the United States Patent Office through the issue of a patent.

"These rights may be exercised by the inventor or transferred to others.

"Directly and by purchase the Telephone Company has acquired a large number of such patents covering inventions useful in broadcasting by wireless telephony. When the public became interested in entertainment by wireless telephonic broadcasting, the Telephone Company arranged so that these inventions could become available to the public by purchase of apparatus at reasonable prices.

"When it appeared likely that a multitude of broadcasting stations would destroy the value of this entertainment, we established a station and offered our facilities for hire with the hope and expectation that that arrangement would do away with a large number of stations interfering with each other and thus interfering with the enjoyment of the public.

"For the same reason it has refused to license other stations to operate for hire as the cost of a broadcasting station for the purchaser's exclusive use necessarily limits the number installed.

"This whole matter of entertainment of the public by wireless telephony is very new, and regulations necessary for its preservation have not been established but have been under consideration by the only body which can legally provide for their establishment and that is the Congress of the United States. Whenever Congress acts we shall gladly accept its regulations as relieving us of any obligation to protect the public. We have no desire for a monopoly of the air.

"We have referred to patents. Some of our patents which can be used in broadcasting have been infringed—many times unintentionally and some times wantonly. We have offered to license the infringers at reasonable rates.

"The Courts have held that unless the owners of patents protect them and prosecute infringements, the patents lapse; so that, when licenses are not accepted, we must either prosecute infringers or in effect dedicate to the public valuable property.

"The question presented by this suit is a very plain and narrow one. We have brought it because we believe that the defendants are violating our rights. If we are wrong in our belief, the defendants will prevail in the suit and there will be no interference with what they are doing. If we are right in our contention, we shall prevail, and the Court will prevent the defendants from continuing to violate rights established by the laws of the United States. The single and narrow question is, whether the defendants may arbitrarily appropriate valuable rights secured by the laws of the United States?"

Two supplementary statements were also issued by President Thayer in response to press requests for further explanation of the company's position in radio developments. One was dated March 11; it was brief, but singularly "meaty:"

> We intend to develop radio transmission and probably in connection with that development shall continue to broadcast. Whether or not we continue to broadcast for hire, we believe that, in our own interests as well as the interests of the public, others should broadcast and some should broadcast for hire; so that, while we intend to maintain our title to our patent rights, we also intend to make it easy for others to use them. But, until regulation has been established, we shall not encourage the multiplication of broadcasting stations.[2]

Another terse announcement was issued the following day in view of the prevailing misrepresentations of the current situation. Its definite and categorical assertions were:

1. That the American Company has not attempted and does not desire a monopoly of broadcasting;
2. That all broadcasting stations must and should operate under regulation and permits from the Federal Government;
3. That the American Company's policy is to grant rights under its patents for reasonable compensation to all broadcasting stations having proper Federal permission;
4. That the American Company's suit against WHN is brought solely for the purpose of protecting its patents from infringement;
5. That any broadcasting station now infringing the American Company's patents can acquire a license for the life of the patents upon reasonable terms.

[2] In case this concluding sentence seems obscure to the reader, it should be pointed out that there was at the time no actual "regulation." The Department of Commerce issued a license to broadcast to any station applying for one. This licensing procedure was thus nothing more than a routine of registration, and resulted in much interference between stations that were thus permitted to use the same wave length.

Information for the Telephone Forces

Bell operating companies soon reported, however, that these policy representations had not appeared in time to offset the early news reports and that local radio editors and station managers, and telephone employees as well, were confused because of these reports. The companies suggested that the American Company provide them with a review of its radio activities for publication in the periodicals circulating throughout the telephone organizations and for the information of local editors. Accordingly the following summarization was prepared and distributed on March 25:

In view of the conflicting accounts and interpretations of the suits recently instituted by the company to protect its patents affecting radio telephone broadcasting, it will perhaps be helpful to relate the circumstances that resulted in the present patent situation.

Some time before the war the Bell System research laboratories began development of what is now called the vacuum tube, as a long distance wire telephone amplifier or repeater. It was this development that made possible transcontinental telephony. The laboratories of the General Electric Company had also undertaken the development of this apparatus for other purposes. As was inevitable, with two great experimental laboratories engaged in similar research, each company acquired inventions and improvements of mutual usefulness.

PATENT CONSIDERATIONS PUT ASIDE DURING WAR

With the coming of the war and the paramount requirements of the Army and Navy in the field of communications, each company put aside considerations of patent ownership, and there was rapid cooperative development of this apparatus in its application to transmission by wire and wireless.

When the end of the war ended the necessity for this emergency disregard of patent rights, a valuable art had been developed which no one in the business of communications could use without infringing upon the rights of others.

Under such conditions there could be no further manufacturing of certain apparatus nor further development of this art, and the Navy Department of our government requested this company and the General Electric Company to try to relieve the situation for the general welfare.

In response to this request, negotiations were initiated and carried through to an arrangement of cross licenses to which other owners of patents in this field were afterward admitted. For practical operation under this arrangement, it was necessary that the parties to the agreement be given the specific uses of the apparatus in question that were logical to their business.

It was in this way that licenses for certain uses in connection with radio telephony came to us, as our directors reported to the stockholders at the time.

THE COMPANY'S FUNDAMENTAL PURPOSE

This company's prime purpose in operating under these licenses has been such development of the radio art as would be useful in relation to telephone service.

Actuated by this prime purpose, we established an experimental broadcasting station in New York in order to be better able to study not only radio transmission problems, but also public tests in broadcast entertainment, and to furnish advice to our Associated Companies with respect thereto.

By this time there was widespread popular interest in broadcasting, as was evidenced by the growth of the industry furnishing apparatus for radio reception. A realization of the extent of this interest led to a sudden demand for broadcasting stations from individuals and concerns wishing to establish a contact with the public for their own benefit by means of matter transmitted through the ether.

Consideration of many of these applications disclosed that all of the economic factors involved, as well as the high costs of operation and maintenance, had not been fully realized. It was apparent that if there were a free sale of broadcasting apparatus, some purchasers would experience disappointing results. It was also clear that a multitude of stations would create a condition of congestion that would certainly lessen, and might possibly destroy, the value of broadcasting to the public.

From the financial standpoint it would have been profitable to manufacture and install all the broadcasting apparatus sought for. We deemed it a better policy, however, to point out all the factors and risks of the situation, and for those wishing to broadcast, to offer our own station at moderate rates, so far as our allotted limits for broadcasting would permit.

We are confident that by thus assisting in checking tendencies that were putting the future of broadcasting in jeopardy, we have acted only in the best interests of the public.

DEVELOPMENT RELATING TO BROADCASTING

Broadcasting is made possible by inventions that have cost their owners large sums not only in acquiring patents, but also in experimental and development expense. We have recognized the fact that many broadcasters, in making wrongful use of our inventions, have been ignorant of their infringement. We have, therefore, established reasonable license fees, the payment of which, coupled with an agreement to refrain from further infringement, would liquidate any claims for infringement and would give the broadcaster a legal right to the use of the patents during their life. The fees are so moderate as to represent a return far below the customary profits on unpatented electrical apparatus.

BUSINESS PRUDENCE DICTATED PATENT SUITS

With approximately 400 stations in the United States using our inventions without a license from us, it became a matter of ordinary prudence for us to institute legal proceedings that would establish our ownership of patents and our rights as owners. Not to protect them would be sheer neglect of duty.

For an initial suit we decided to select a nearby station so as to minimize the costs to both parties concerned. Pursuant to this plan, we respectfully called to the attention of the owners of a station in New York the nature and extent of their infringement, listing many of the patents involved. Our notification was ignored and suit was brought.

A suit was also brought against another defendant in relation to methods of sending programs of entertainment along wires, which methods we believe infringe upon our patents and which might interfere with operation of neighboring telephone service. Obviously, this suit is also a matter of plain business prudence.

THE COMPANY'S PURPOSES IN THE FIELD OF RADIO BROADCASTING

We have been asked what our future policy will be in connection with radio broadcasting. The art of radio broadcasting is new and changing. Speculation as to the future is difficult and futile. The new problems which are constantly presenting themselves are being given the closest study, but the details of our plans could only develop as the art develops. The general guiding principles are not likely to change. They are: that we keep in and abreast of the development of the art and that we encourage in every way possible such development by others. We shall make it possible, so far as lies with us, for any one to secure broadcasting apparatus at moderate prices and for those broadcasters who are now infringing our patents, to continue their use under reasonable and moderate terms.

For the present we shall continue to operate our own experimental broadcasting station, making its facilities available under reasonable rules, in the public interest, for those who wish to test broadcasting as a medium for attracting the public's notice. Far from desiring the sole responsibility for broadcasting, it is our strong belief that, in the public's interest and in our own interest, nothing should be allowed to interfere with any development of it that may be proved to be beneficial. We heartily favor government control of such activities and the federal legislation that is pending has our cordial support.

A monopoly, either of broadcasting for entertainment of the public or for hire is not desirable from any point of view. There has been no danger and is no danger of such a monopoly.

The WHN Controversy Summarized

The extent to which this WHN controversy was "in the news" is indicated by the progressive references to it that appeared in the well-known "Topics of the Times" column on the editorial page of the New York *Times*. It will help this record to include excerpts from them since they present the episode as surveyed by a disinterested and reflective observer:

March 7, 1924, p. 14:

Beginning a War Over Radio. Extensive use of radio telephony is such a new thing that none of the practical problems involved in its conduct has been solved as yet, and, as a matter of fact, even consideration of them is only beginning. They are highly important problems, however, if for no other reason than that their solution involves the interests of many people, some of the interests being material and financial, and the others those of everybody who can buy or build a "receiving set."

The first skirmish in what looks as if it were going to be a big battle over radio is to be seen in the effort of the American Telephone and Telegraph Company to enjoin broadcasting by station WHN, which is on top of Loew's State Theatre. The injunction is asked on the ground that WHN—and a majority of the other broadcasting stations in the country—are infringing patents owned by the telephone company.

Should the temporary injunction now demanded be granted and later made permanent, it is obvious that all stations against which the same charge can be made and proved must cease operation. They must, that is, if the telephone company's patents are essential to successful or satisfactory operation. Naturally, the cry of attempted monopoly by a great corporation has been raised, and, as the new army of "radio fans" is a huge one, with every soldier in it sure to resent any interference with his joys or any diminution of them, the indications are of lively times ahead.

March 8, 1924, p. 10:

Denies It Seeks a Monopoly. What any lawyer would call a good case has been made out by the spokesman of the American Telephone and Telegraph Company in explaining why it is seeking to enjoin other broadcasting operations than its own and those of broadcasters who recognize its legal rights and pay the tribute it demands. Its asserted object is the protection of its many and important patents from unauthorized use, and there is not a little force in the company's statement that many of the devices now employed in radiotelephony were invented by or for it in its efforts—extremely successful efforts, by the way—to give the American public the best telephone service that is to be found anywhere in the world.

March 11, 1924, p. 18:

Freedom of Patents, Not of Air. As a "slogan," the assertion made by the President of the Radio Trade Association—"the air should be free"—has a fine resonance and may be heard a little later re-echoing from the ceilings of the Senate and the House of Representatives. And of course it is true that the air should be free, or as free as anything can be in this complicated world.

As it happens, however, the controversy between the American Telephone and Telegraph Company and the managers of certain broadcasting stations concerns not the freedom of the air but the freedom of patents, and nobody would get very far, with the laws as they are, in denying the existence of a property right in patents.

Into the merits of this controversy it is not necessary to enter; the courts in time, presumably, will decide them. One cannot but regret, however, that the issue should have been raised on a false line. As the case stands, no question has been presented except that as to whether or not the telephone company owns patents essential to broadcasting. If it does, there is difficulty in seeing what those who want to use those patents can do except pay for the privilege.

April 14, 1924, p. 16:

Quietude After the Storm. Loud cries over the asserted attempt of the big telephone company to "monopolize the air" as regards radio broadcasting no longer are heard. Though Commissioner WHALEN still rumbles occasionally, one by one the alleged victims of a heartless corporation are accepting the terms it offered in the beginning—are paying, that is, the fee it proposed for the use of the patents it owns.

The subsidence of the once noisy quarrel gives to the disinterested the impression that the fee demanded was not excessive, and also that there could be no successful questioning either of the ownership of the patents or of the claim that their use is essential to successful broadcasting. The case therefore seems to have been a rather simple one, and its settlement, so far as it has been settled, one satisfactory to all concerned.

A New Basis for Broadcasting Development

When the widely read *Radio Broadcast* reviewed the American Company's attitude with respect to its patents, its conclusion was, "It is probably fortunate for the broadcasting listeners that this question is at present in the hands of the American Telephone and Telegraph Company." This complimentary opinion was followed, however, by the statement that "WHN, by signing the agreement with the A. T. & T. Co., is not allowed to do any advertising for money," the report further expressing the opinion that this "cannot well be classed as an oppressive measure. . . . We think that the interests of the radio public are being conserved when such stations are prohibited from broadcasting for direct monetary profit . . . advertising by radio is highly questionable even when tried by so excellent a station as WEAF."

This reference to WHN was erroneous for, with that station acknowledging the validity of the American Company's patents, the company was in a position to take radically new steps in order to provide a better basis for broadcasting's development. These steps were impelled by a belief—directly opposed to the opinion just quoted—that the interests of the radio public would be "best conserved" by *not* prohibiting "broadcasting for direct monetary profit."

The basis for development that had originally seemed logical at telephone headquarters was the one under consideration before the experiment in toll broadcasting was under way. If the reader will turn back the pages of this record to the announcement of February 11, 1922, in Chapter v, he will note again:

> This is a new undertaking in the commercial use of radio telephony and if there appears a real field for such service and it can be furnished sufficiently free from interference in the ether from other radio services, it will be followed as circumstances warrant by similar stations erected at important centers throughout the United States by the American Telephone and Telegraph Company. As these additional stations are erected, they can be connected by the toll and long distance wires of the Bell System so that from any central point, the same news, music or other program can be sent out simultaneously through all these stations by wire and wireless with the greatest possible economy and without interference.

This announcement affirmed the company's sense of responsibility at a time when there were but a handful of stations in the country—a responsibility born of the ownership of patents, the ownership of wire lines, and the exclusive right to broadcast for hire.

The same sense of responsibility promoted the offer, when public interest in radio brought about broadcasting operations which infringed the company's patents, to license infringing stations so that they might broadcast legally and with wire adjuncts. But even this offer, though clearing the legal atmosphere during a period of wildcat growth, left the owners of receiving sets dependent upon broadcasting operations which in general meant continued financial loss for the broadcasters. Only a few large enterprises, such as newspapers and department stores, could balance the expense of station maintenance against the good will created by broadcasts of news and entertainment. Toward broadcasting as a public service there was no discernible trend, in the spring of 1924, other than a growing demand and a threatened supply.[3]

The right to broadcast for hire, which was the father of the American Company's 1922 conception of broadcasting service, was therefore the factor that was actually controlling the public's supply of radio programs. Since the company was convinced from the beginning of its broadcasting venture that the supply depended in the long run upon revenues from commercial broadcasting, it could see but one way to resolve its patent problems in the public interest. This was to include the right to broadcast for hire with every broadcasting transmitter sold by the Western Electric Company and with every license issued under its patents—except those issued to colleges, churches, and so forth, for the nominal sum of $1.00—and to make available for purchase by licensed broadcasting stations the speech input equipment necessary for picking up programs at remote points.[4]

Significance of the Decision

Thus, at a time when no one could prophesy as to the future of broadcasting, the patent owner went "all out" to translate "monop-

[3] The estimate of the Broadcasting Department's statistician at the time was that there were about 3,200,000 receiving sets in the United States, 2,500,000 being vacuum-tube sets and the others being crystal sets; that the number of sets using loud-speakers was 800,000, and that the cost of the average set, not including the costs of headsets or loud-speakers, was close to $60. The public's financial stake in broadcasting thus was substantial.

[4] Within a year after the WHN controversy, 250 stations were licensed to broadcast under the American Company's patents and all could broadcast for hire except those from which a nominal license fee of only $1.00 had been required.

oly" into "service" and with two notable results. The first was that the decision "pointed the way," as the author of *Big Business and Radio* correctly states, "to financial salvation for radio stations in general;" and the second was that company-owned stations, as first envisioned for national service, need no longer be the only basis for the development of network broadcasting.

Few outside the telephone organization, however, realized the full import of this radical action, and the economic basis for broadcasting's support long continued to be the moot question in the broadcasting world.

While some believed that the expense of broadcasting entertainment should be met by contributions from listeners, others favored the custom followed by other countries of licensing receiving sets. Secretary of Commerce Herbert Hoover was reported as opposing this idea although, said the report, he "admitted that he could offer no solution for the problem of making broadcasting stations self-supporting except through the sale of their patented devices or by charging for advertisements sent over the radio."

Included in the current debate was the widely quoted view of the chief spokesman for receiving-set manufacturers, who was propagandizing the idea that the multiplicity of radio stations was an unhealthy condition that would soon cure itself through lack of financial support. His solution was the chain of "superpower" stations, already referred to here, to be supported by a tax on the industry, or, in other words, by returns on sales of radio apparatus: "Just as soon as we destroy that freedom and universality of radio and confine it to only those who pay for it—just as soon as we make of broadcasting 'narrowcasting'—we destroy the fundamental of the whole situation." [5]

This conception was of course the diametrical opposite of that which had been the basis of the WEAF experiment. There was much support, however, for the idea that money to meet the ever increasing cost of maintaining a station would have to come from

[5] Mr. David Sarnoff, R.C.A. General Manager, in an address at the convention of the Electrical Supply Jobbers Association, June 4-6, 1924, at Hot Springs, Va. One of Mr. Sarnoff's most forceful presentations of the "superpower" idea was at Secretary Hoover's Third Radio Conference, held in Washington in Oct., 1924, which was the month in which the American Company inaugurated its "Red Network" broadcasting service.

the radio industry. "Naturally, to the business man," commented *Radio Broadcast,* "this seems the logical solution. It is probably the simplest solution of the problem and possibly it will be the final one. A reasonable percentage on the sales profits in tubes, batteries, accessories, etc., will maintain a good many stations, even after the sale of new sets begins to fall off, and this falling off, by the way, is still a long way in the future."[6]

[6] Vol. v, no. 3 (July, 1924), p. 221.

CHAPTER XV

NETWORK BROADCASTING MADE PRACTICAL

Circuit Availability a Fundamental Problem

IN TRACING from the files the development of network broadcasting, one notes with interest the technical and financial considerations that arose when the availability of circuits for simultaneous broadcasting was first being investigated. The initial survey of Long Lines Director Stevenson resulted in the following report to President Thayer on December 16, 1922:

> You asked me the other day regarding the availability of the Long Lines plant to tie together a certain number of broadcasting stations, as indicated on the attached map. I find that the line facilities of the Long Lines are such that it would be possible to tie these stations together for simultaneous broadcasting. It would be necessary, however, to make modifications in circuit arrangements and in the matter of loading of toll entrance cables at a number of points. This work would cost approximately $150,000. It would also be necessary in connection with the proposition of simultaneous broadcasting to install amplifiers of a type not at present used in our regular service in order to provide uniform transmission to all of the points involved. This would cost approximately another $150,000. . . . As for the permanent layout during business hours, this could not be attempted without a very considerable addition to existing line facilities . . . it would involve the addition of approximately 4500 miles of circuit, which on a basis of #8 wire would cost approximately $1,250,000, exclusive of any crossarm work that might be required . . . should the project cover only a few hours an evening, say after 9 P.M. eastern time, it is probable that these stations could be tied together without additional wire facilities or any particular detriment to the service. Of course, any rearrangement of circuits necessary for such a project immediately involves pretty expensive operation costs, particularly if considered as any regular plan. The whole scheme of such a project would mean more or less

regular or permanent organization set-up similar to the requirements for special demonstrations, such as the one given for the Massachusetts Institute of Technology, when a large number of cities were connected simultaneously for intercommunication.

The files for the following year show, in an abundance of other memoranda, how broadcasting experience was stimulating the Broadcasting Department to definite exploration of the idea of a chain of stations for an expanded service. Three separate groups of stations, in fact, were specifically designated by the Broadcasting Department in July, 1923, in a request to Long Lines to estimate "the cost of the necessary lines and facilities in order to provide a three-hour program." Such an inquiry indicated that those at WEAF who were studying the needs of broadcasters were enlarging their field of vision in anticipation of a growing interest in broadcasting on the part of advertisers and their agents.

There was reason for such anticipation. Station WCAP in Washington was receiving WEAF sustaining programs and because of them was rapidly gaining a large and loyal following. More than one advertiser was wondering if the time would come when a station network would be organized so that commercially sponsored programs might go out from WEAF studios over a wide area, to supplement and strengthen advertising messages which were appearing in nationally circulated media.

Every individual broadcasting undertaking was a special problem to the long-distance operating unit, for its facilities had been designed and built for telephone purposes only. The conception of a network for regular service was thus a separate challenge to provide the necessary circuits without impairing the organization's ability to meet the public need for long-distance service. The primary consideration to be investigated in estimating wire costs for a possible network service was therefore a fundamental one—circuit availability.

This problem of availability can be noted in a September, 1923, warning by the Long Lines director that there might be occasions involving the question of "priority in use of Long Lines circuits as an adjunct to radio broadcasting. Last night," reported Mr. Stevenson, "we had a specific case, in which the circuits normally used for connection between WEAF and WCAP in Washington were unavailable on account of induction[1]—the number of circuits available for this type of service is extremely limited; in fact, in this specific case, an available circuit as an emergency proposition meant cutting into the New York-Havana circuit group." [2]

As for the costs of circuits required for the networks that the Broadcasting Department had in mind, this account has already referred to the special effort necessary to segregate, equip, and supervise them. The operating problem, as has been pointed out, involved a special grade of circuit for the transmission of music, as well as wires available as emergency protection for programs during transmission. It was furthermore essential to provide wires for telegraphic supervision, and besides this, the Long Lines plant men had to handle the input apparatus and to monitor the telephone transmission received at the broadcasting end. "If the service is to be high-grade," warned the Long Lines director as he initiated a broad and detailed study of the Broadcasting Department's idea, "it will be expensive."

By the middle of March, 1924, there had been many conferences between Long Lines, D&R, and Operation B groups to consider the technical problems to be encountered in making the Broadcasting Department's idea a practicable one, and to examine into matters of capital outlay. The network being discussed at this time included 22 stations in 16 cities, with wire facilities to be made available in "off-peak" hours for interconnecting the stations between 7:00 P.M. and 11:30 P.M.

That only off-peak hours could be considered at the time is an interesting disclosure of the impact of the idea of network service

[1] Noise picked up from extraneous sources.

[2] Long Lines engineers at the time were planning the new construction required to meet the growing demand for service and were reminded by telephone headquarters, "With the increasing demand for Long Lines facilities for use in connection with radio broadcasting, and also in connection with public-address systems for which the electrical requirements are the same, *we should have in mind the design and installation of future plant* of such a character that it may be used when necessary or desirable for these purposes. Accordingly, in submitting estimates for new plant, also please submit an estimate of the additional cost involved to provide the proposed facilities of the type that will make them available for use in connection with radio broadcasting or public-address systems."

upon the Long Lines normal operating responsibility. The situation also is a reminder that many years previously, when the A. T. & T. and Western Union had been merged for purposes of operating efficiency, President Theodore N. Vail had created the "night-letter" novelty in telegraph service in order to utilize wires when the normal tide of traffic had ebbed.

The Vision of National Broadcasting

The Broadcasting Department reported in the spring of 1924:

> Our experience has shown that there is a real demand for broadcasting for hire. Not only is this true with respect to programs which may be rendered in the studio of the broadcasting station, or at some other location in the same city, but there is also a large potential demand . . . on the part of national advertisers. . . . The best and most economical way to conduct such national broadcasting is to render the program at some convenient city, such as New York, and to simultaneously distribute the program by wire to broadcasting stations in a number of different cities. We have the necessary wire plant and are the only agency equipped to do a creditable job. Such national broadcasting will result in an off-peak or by-product use of the Long Lines plant . . . the cost per job will be materially reduced, and this will make it possible for us to stage events of national importance, such as addresses by the President, in a creditable manner. . . . The details of the proposed plan will involve the negotiation of suitable contracts with selected broadcasting stations . . . the successful operation of this plan will require reasonable sales effort in the sale of national advertising. If we merely wait for the demand to come to us the frequency of use will increase so slowly and the costs would be so high that the Bell System would still be subject to criticism in connection with the charges for the use of our lines for broadcasting events of national importance.

The criticism to which this concluding sentence refers arose from the fact that in the early days of "remote-control" broadcasting, the circuits required so much special attention and were so infrequently used that they were necessarily expensive. Broadcasters did not realize what was involved in segregating, equipping, and supervising wires in order to provide the necessary high-quality circuits and to guard them against any noise and interruption; and, in turn, to guard the regular telephone circuits in the same cable or on the same pole line against inductive effects from the broadcasting circuit.

Wire Costs Misunderstood

This lack of understanding was the reason for an episode early in 1924 that was particularly disturbing to the telephone organization. It happened so long ago that no one will be embarrassed if it is recalled now in order to show how easily unpleasant situations could develop when broadcasting was new.

The broadcasting of President Coolidge's message to Congress from six stations on December 6, 1923, for which the Bell System had provided circuits as a public service, had been acclaimed throughout the nation. The event showed that people everywhere were eagerly interested in hearing other similar official messages through the medium of broadcasting, and it was the American Company's intention to satisfy this interest as often as practicable. Almost overnight the President was established as radio's leading personality and attraction.

Early in the following month, January, 1924, the Rotarian organization in Chicago suddenly announced a broadcast of an address that President Coolidge would make, on February 22, in recognition of the founding of the Rotary Club. Before investigating the availability or cost of the necessary wire circuits, it selected WJAZ in Chicago, and 18 other stations well scattered between the two coasts, as "official" stations for the occasion.

When telephone officials were then approached, they explained the technical limitations to this ambitious undertaking, but offered to broadcast the President's address from the "three-point" experimental network that had recently been established, comprising two Bell System stations, WEAF and WCAP, and WJAR in Providence, Rhode Island. The cost of segregating and equipping and operating regular and emergency circuits, together with a supervisory telegraph circuit, between the White House and a Chicago station was estimated, and Long Lines wire service between Washington and Chicago was offered at that actual cost figure.

About the middle of February a Chicago newspaper offered to pay a portion of this cost, and the company was asked to contribute the balance which the Rotary Club was unwilling to provide. Had the company done this it would of course have exposed itself to a multitude of similar demands from other organizations. Of necessity, therefore, it had to distinguish between Presidential addresses relating to government affairs, such as the December message to Congress, and addresses dealing with non-governmental matters. The decision to maintain this distinction was naturally a difficult one to make at the time, for telephone officials recognized the predicament of the Rotary official who had wired, "There are 1400 Rotary Clubs in United States and Canada whose members are awaiting this address, which absence of Mid-west station will prevent the majority of them from hearing. . . . There is more involved in prestige, good will and publicity than the cost of the service quoted."

The general misconception of the technical situation found expression in WJAZ's astonishing reference to long-distance telephone rates, when broadcasting an explanation of the omission of the President's address from its program:[3]

> We have had so many telephone calls tonight asking us why we were not going to broadcast this address, we think an explanation is due you. . . . Had the proposed plan of the Rotary Club been executed, every owner of even a little crystal set in Cincinnati, Seattle, Buffalo, Pittsburgh, Schenectady, San Antonio, Cleveland, Los Angeles, Louisville, Omaha, Kansas City, Minneapolis, Atlanta, Fort Worth, Portland, Memphis, St. Louis and Chicago would have been able to hear our President clearly. That the Western public has been deprived of the privilege is not due to any lack of effort on the part of the Rotary Club. . . . The American Telephone and Telegraph Company contributed the use of their broadcasting stations located in New York, Providence and Washington. This, however, did not help the Westerners. . . . This great public service corporation told the Rotary Club representative that they wanted . . . $2500 for telephone wires to connect just one Chicago station with the East, yet the normal long distance charge for the use of ordinary telephone wires for calls from Chicago to Washington is only $4.80 for the first three minutes. . . . The original plan was for the President to talk ten minutes. The regular rates, therefore, would have made the cost of these wires $14.40. . . . Our own personal opinion is that this great public service corporation should contribute its wire service to every broadcasting station in the United States desiring to broadcast a presidential address on occasions like this.

[3] The notion persisted for some time that circuits should always be made available for a Presidential broadcast. Mr. Gifford frequently had to answer personal appeals from high quarters by pointing out that such a practice would affect the regular long-distance service upon which the public was depending.

It was most unfortunate that the Rotary plan had been so extensively promoted without prior consultation, for that splendid organization naturally experienced both disappointment and embarrassment.

The telephone organization was likewise embarrassed, not only because of the "profiteering" implication in the news, but also because several hundred telephone employees were enthusiastic Rotarians. The files show that a special bulletin of information was prepared to give these employees—most of whom were not Long Lines personnel—full details of the operations necessary for "made-to-order" service. A section of this bulletin is quoted below because it will give the reader an excellent idea of Long Lines problems prior to the establishment of networks for the use of many broadcasters on what the Long Lines engineers called a "recurring basis:"

> There are given below the various steps and the number of men and the time they would be employed preparing for and transmitting a speech by the President from Washington to a radio broadcasting station in Chicago.

1. Determining the organization circuits and special apparatus required	2 men, 1 day
2. Estimate of costs, preparation of circuit diagrams showing routes and specifying the necessary electrical characteristics	2 men, 1 day
3. A high grade technical man visits the White House to select a suitable location for the control apparatus, to determine the way the wiring can best be run from the control room to the President's study, to locate the microphone in the study and to make any necessary acoustic rearrangements in the study	1 man, 3 days
4. Installation of apparatus at White House	3 men, 1 day
5. Installation of local loops at the White House	2 men, 1 day
6. Installation and test of equalizing equipment on the local loops	1 man, ½ day
7. Installation of local loops at broadcasting station	2 men, 1 day
8. Installation and test of special equipment at broadcasting station	1 man, 1 day
9. Inspection of special equipment at broadcasting station and broadcasting equipment to insure that all is satisfactory	1 man, 1 day
10. Installation and test of equalizers, amplifiers and other equipment at test room at Chicago	3 men, 1 day

11. Transmission tests of local loops at Chicago	1 man, ½ day
12. Preliminary test of entire layout in evening preceding that on which speech is given	
At Washington—1 Morse Operator	
1 Testboard Man	
3 Engineers	
1 Trans. Tester	5 men, 3 hours
At Each of the Seven Repeater Points—1 Man	7 men, 3 hours
At the Chicago Test Room—2 Engineers	
1 Equipment Man	
1 Testboard Man	
1 Morse Operator	
1 Trans. Tester	6 men, 3 hours
At the Broadcasting Station—1 Engineer	
1 Morse Operator	
1 Installer	3 men, 3 hours
13. Immediately preceding and during the speech the same personnel as given under 12 is required	22 men, 3 hours
14. Removing, packing and shipping special apparatus	3 men, 1 day
15. Removing local loops	4 men, ½ day

This memorandum continued:

> Under existing conditions each job involving the use of our toll plant in connection with important radio broadcasting projects must be handled throughout as a special one. Radio broadcasting has developed rapidly and requests for the use of our toll circuits for this purpose until recently have been infrequent. If it should develop that there is sufficient demand to justify our providing the special equipment required on a permanent basis for certain of the more important routes and organizing and training a personnel to handle work of this sort the costs involved in any particular job will be reduced, but it is certain that they will never be reduced to a point *where the charges will be at all comparable to our regular toll message charges.* The relatively infrequent use of our toll plant for projects of this special nature will always require special treatment and it may be expected that the charges will be substantial if these projects are to bear their proper costs.

That there was some appreciation of the situation in radio circles is shown by the comment of *Radio Broadcast* in its May, 1924, issue:[4]

[4] Vol. v, no. 1 (May, 1924), pp. 23-24.

Before condemning the Telephone Company for its apparently excessive charge for this service it must be considered that the ordinary wire connection will not serve at all for such a purpose. Special lines and repeaters have to be taken out of regular service, have to be put through special tests and adjustments, all extraneous "noises" eliminated and a special staff of men, as well as spare lines, be kept in readiness in case the connection should fail.

However large we may think the bid of $2500 for ten minutes' service may be, all of the related factors are not on the surface, and we feel that the Telephone Company is entitled to the benefit of any doubt there may be, when we consider the fine radio broadcast service they have given the public during the past year. Whatever may be the policy of their financial advisors, we do know the company makes a continual effort to improve broadcasting service. This has been of great benefit to the radio public—a public which so far has paid the Telephone Company nothing at all for the service.

Long Lines and the Broadcasting Department

Perhaps it should be explained at this point that the Long Lines business relationship with the Broadcasting Department was that of servicer and client, since the latter department was in the "customer" category along with press associations and others wishing to contract for the use of long-distance facilities.

As a matter of contrast with modern circuit conditions, it is interesting to note from the records how the long-distance operating unit functioned in broadcasting's early days, when an inquiry was received from this "customer" regarding circuits for special broadcasts. For example, we find the Long Lines General Plant Manager,[5] writing as follows to the Long Lines Engineer:[6]

> The broadcasting department has asked for charges covering the use of facilities, testing and operating, required in transmitting a program to a proposed broadcasting station in Bridgeport, Conn. Will you please advise whether the proper type of facilities for furnishing this service are available between New York and Bridgeport, and also whether any construction work or installation of amplifiers would be required.

The engineering report in reply to this question should be given here because it confirms the references on previous pages to the

[5] Mr. T. G. Miller, later one of the American Company's Vice-presidents.

[6] Mr. J. J. Pilliod, now the American Company's Assistant Chief Engineer.

made-to-order character of the early Long Lines wire service for broadcasts:

Our study of the situation shows, as outlined in the attached notes and sketches, that by certain layout rearrangements and daily patches at Bedford Test Station, Hartford, and Derby, Conn., facilities for furnishing broadcasting service to Bridgeport can be made available. The facility situation between Providence and Round Hills is covered in detail in our letter of March 29, 1924.

In arranging this layout, two plans have been considered. The layout under Plan #1 is based on using non-loaded #8 gauge wires 7-8 on the New York Midland Line between New York and Hartford for one of the circuits to Providence, but as we understand that some noise has been experienced at times between Stepney and Hartford, making it necessary to use facilities on another route, we have worked up a second layout as shown in Plan #2, which avoids the use of facilities on the Midland Line between Stepney and Hartford. This plan should be used provided further investigation shows that the conditions between Stepney and Hartford may continue to interfere with the broadcasting service. Should it be necessary to use the layout under Plan #2, an equalizer and an amplifier will be required at Melrose. This equipment is in addition to an equalizer which will be required at Bridgeport under either plan. No construction work except the unloading of wires 5-6 on the Main Line between Stepney and Pole 3236, Plan #2, will be required.

The above layout arrangement is based on releasing these facilities for broadcasting service during the evening period 7:30 to 10:30. Should these facilities be required for service during any other period, further consideration should be given with regard to their release.

The details and intricacies of Long Lines operation at the time, when some important broadcasting responsibility had been undertaken, will be apparent from the following typical notification from the General Plant Manager to key men especially concerned in local and distant Long Lines offices:

January 31, 1924

This telegram concerns the Long Lines service in connection with broadcasting the AIEE program on February 5th, from the Philadelphia Metropolitan Opera House; Gimbel Brothers Station (WIP), Philadelphia; Station WEAF, New York; Station WGY, Schenectady; Station WCAP, Washington; Station KDKA, Pittsburgh; per SCS Order G-7606.

For this service the following telephone facilities will be required:

Pairs 257 and 260 Cable C, Philadelphia to New York, with 4-Wire repeaters at Philadelphia, Princeton and New York.

No. 2 Chicago-New York circuit between New York and Pittsburgh.

No. 2 Boston-Pittsburgh circuit between Newtown Square and Pittsburgh.

No. 3 Harrisburg-Philadelphia circuit between Newtown Square and Philadelphia.

Nos. 7 and 25 New York-Washington circuits between New York and Washington.

Sides of 33-36 group, New York-Buffalo line, New York to Lansingburg.

Sides of 27-30 group, Troy-Elmira line, Lansingburg to Schenectady.

For this service the following Morse facilities will be required:

0194 program co-ordinating circuits with Morse calls and drops as follows:

New York (BY) radio station WEAF
Philadelphia (KF) control room
Philadelphia (RF) radio station WIP (not to be connected unless asked for later)
Pittsburgh (RW) radio station KDKA
Washington (CA) radio station WCAP
Schenectady (GY) radio station WGY

The above circuit to be operated metallic Morse New York, Philadelphia, Harrisburg, Bedford, and Pittsburgh; leg Philadelphia to Washington and New York to Lansingburg half duplex. Single, Lansingburg to Schenectady.

0764 telephone repeater test wire calls as follows: New York (NR), Princeton (PN), Philadelphia (PA), Philadelphia control room in Opera House (KF), Newtown Square (NS), Harrisburg (HB), Brushton (GX), Washington testroom (W), Lansingburg testroom (R).

This circuit to be operated half duplex upset New York and Philadelphia with Princeton in series on regular day assignment of 764 or similar facilities, any available facilities half duplex or metallic Morse Philadelphia to Washington and leg Philadelphia to Pittsburgh via Harrisburg, loop Newtown Square in from Philadelphia. Leg Lansingburg on from New York half duplex.

These telephone and Morse circuits shall be established for rehearsals on Sunday, February 3rd, between 8:00 P.M. and 11:00 P.M., E.T., and again on Monday, February 4th, between 5 P.M. and 9 P.M. E.T.

On Tuesday, February 5th, the night of the demonstration, the circuits will be taken at 5:00 P.M., E.T., lined up and held until good night.

During the periods of rehearsals and demonstration, telephone repeater attendants required at repeater stations en route, and transmission man required at New York, Pittsburgh and Philadelphia. All expense incurred to be charged to Job A-78, Account 708-0002.

For this service provide a New York-Philadelphia order wire between Room 224, 24 Walker Street, N.Y., and the telephone repeater room at Philadelphia and control room of Philadelphia Opera House on dates of rehearsals and demonstration. For this purpose use any New York-Philadelphia circuit.

All points concerned advised. (RSS)

While referring to the engineering and operating problems which the early network experiments brought to the Long Lines organization, another document from the June, 1924, files might be quoted. It is a significant one in that it anticipates the provision of cable circuits for the WEAF-WCAP-WJAR network, established in 1923, so that the network would be less exposed to the hazard of storms; besides, it reveals, in engineering language, how meager were the facilities that could be spared for broadcasting at the time, as contrasted with those that were later provided by special construction for the exclusive use of broadcasters:

This memorandum lists the circuits and equipment which would be required in order to provide circuits in cable between New York and Providence, and also between New York and Washington, for use in transmitting programs to the broadcasting stations in these cities.

General

At the present time the circuits between New York and Providence and New York and Washington used for broadcasting purposes are non-loaded 165 circuits with a small amount of intermediate cable. The circuit to Providence is equipped with two intermediate amplifiers and equalizers. Both of the circuits are so equalized that they are capable of transmitting programs from Station WEAF. Extra-light loaded H-44-25 #19 gauge cable conductors which are used for extra-light loaded four-wire circuits, if equipped with suitable repeaters or amplifiers, can be made to transmit the average program from WEAF with about the same degree of satisfaction to the listener as the present circuits. This means that where extra-light loaded four-wire cable circuits are available, the side transmitting in the proper direction can be used for the transmission of the average broadcasting program if proper repeaters or amplifiers are used. This estimate, therefore, has been worked up on the basis of using #19 gauge H-44-25 conductors and amplifiers or repeaters as indicated below:

Cable Facilities

1. New York to Philadelphia
   There are at the present time 6 quads of H-44-25 #19 gauge four-wire conductors between New York and Philadelphia. One of these quads could be released for use in broadcasting.
2. Philadelphia to Washington
   There are at the present time no extra-light loaded conductors between Philadelphia and Washington and it would be necessary to load existing spare #19 gauge non-loaded conductors in this section.

3. New York to Providence
   There is no H-44-25 loading between New York and Providence. There is, however, one spare non-loaded quad from New York to Providence which could be loaded and used for broadcasting.

Amplifiers

A special amplifier or repeater having characteristics somewhat similar to the present #17-A amplifier would be required at each of the repeater points along both of the cable routes and also at both terminating stations. These amplifiers would be equipped with equalizers to properly equalize for the repeater section from which they receive. Recent tests made on 44-A-1 repeaters indicate that these repeaters can be made suitable for this service. It is estimated that the approximate cost of the amplifiers or repeaters installed would be about $700 each. The following list gives the points at which amplification would be required:

New York to Washington	*New York to Providence*
Princeton	Stamford
Philadelphia	New Haven
Elkton	Hartford
Baltimore	Providence
Washington	

Summary and Costs

The cable distance between New York and Washington is 223 miles, and the distance between New York and Providence is 187 miles. The total distance over which additional loading would be required is 323 miles, since the 87-mile section between New York and Philadelphia is already loaded. The estimated cost of one quad of extra-light loading on the basis of loading a single quad is approximately $110.00 per mile. . . . Present plans call for extra-light loading 6 quads in the New York-Hartford section during 1925 and about 12 quads in the Philadelphia-Washington section during 1927, but no extra-light loading is projected for the Hartford-Providence section. If the required service dates would permit, the loading between New York-Hartford might be combined with the proposed loading, with a reduction in loading cost between these points. But it is assumed that service will be required before 1925 and the estimated costs, as summarized on the attached sheet, are based on loading a single quad especially for this service.

Development of the Network

By April, 1924, the Long Lines engineers had determined several intercity wire routes along which circuits might be operated in off-peak hours as a network for chain broadcasting, and had estimated the cost of new circuit equipment required for the satisfactory transmission of musical programs. On the eighth of the month the Broadcasting Department summarized developments in a formal notification to the Long Lines director:

> In accordance with various conferences between Mr. Elam Miller and various members of your department it is proposed to set up a wire network of Long Lines circuits to interconnect some twenty-two radio broadcasting stations in some seventeen cities, as shown on the attached map, providing special equipment and a suitable operating personnel where necessary to the end that the circuits will be capable of transmitting, satisfactorily, music of about the grade of the Capitol Theatre program. Local loops to connect the broadcasting stations with the toll testboards are to be equalized and retained on a yearly basis. . . . The proposition was submitted to Mr. Thayer and Mr. Gifford and their approval obtained to proceed. . . . We are working out the details of a plan by which we expect to provide a reasonable frequency of use of the network.

The details which required working out were many and complex, for only the technical problems affecting a trial of the network idea had been studied. The commercial problems involved were of a pioneering character that called for prolonged investigation and analysis. The Broadcasting Department could not offer a network service to broadcasters until it had organized a chain of stations that would accept sponsored programs, and to organize such a chain it first had to develop a financial, as well as technical, basis for its operation.

It was in formulating such proposals that Messrs. Miller, Rich, Armstrong, Spence, and Buckard of Operation B performed yeoman service. There was little definite knowledge at the time regarding what might be called the "radio market," that is, the character and buying habits of the local radio audiences. Advertisers and their agents required specific information regarding the number and the economic status of listeners in local areas before deciding whether or not to invest in a radio advertising effort.

The only known cost factor of a network service, as Operation B began the studies upon which a business proposal could be based, was the cost to the Broadcasting Department of distributing programs by wire. Even WEAF studio costs for a network service had to be approximated because of the expectation of greatly increased artist expense for the "super" programs being planned as sustaining features. The costs of picking up programs outside the studio likewise had to be averaged in the first calculations.

The files of the day reveal what a mass of statistical data was collected in the summer of 1924 in order that prospective advertisers might be given concrete information about audiences that could be approached through various groups of stations and at different hours, the matter of Eastern and Central time being one of the considerations. The methods of investigation and analysis established for these early studies made possible later the compendium, *The Use of Radio Advertising as a Publicity Medium,* which became famous in advertising circles because of its detailed and precise information for the buyers of time on the air.

The network plan that crystallized after weeks of exploration by Operation B—exploration that can be followed from the many analyses in the files that are all headed "Use of Long Distance Circuits for National Broadcasting"—can thus be summarized: that WEAF, as the network's key station, should transmit simultaneously to groups of distant stations its own outstanding sustaining programs, as well as other programs which national advertisers might sponsor; that the distant stations should be paid by the Broadcasting Department, on an hourly basis, for the time employed in broadcasting the sponsored programs for which the department itself was paid; that these distant stations should themselves pay, on an hourly basis, for the sustaining or non-commercial features of the evening's transmission from New York. Negotiations with some prospective sponsors had already justified the expectation that the local station's revenue from the commercial program features would offset the cost of the sustaining features.

Thus, the pioneering conception of a national broadcasting service was to make available to the national advertiser a new medium for reaching great market areas at a charge based upon "coverage"—analogous to the circulation of a printed medium. In conjunction with licenses to broadcast for hire, it resolved the American Company's purpose to apply to public service its developments with respect to radio broadcasting, thus removing any need for other Bell System stations, but, of course, creating the responsibility of constructing whatever new wire facilities would become necessary with the idea's general adoption. Just as the responsibility of patent ownership, in 1922, had led to the establishment of WEAF for experimental commercial broadcasting, the responsibility of circuit ownership led to the establishment, in 1924, of facilities for experimental network broadcasting.

Early Conservatism

It was, of course, the hope of the Broadcasting Department that its plan would appeal to the stations which had the best local reputation for technical and program excellence. The expectation for the stations, as already explained, was that revenue and expense would probably balance, the net result being enhanced station prestige because of the quality and variety of the program material transmitted from New York. According to the files for July, 1924, the following 21 stations, 18 of which were equipped with Western Electric transmitters, were considered especially desirable because of coverage and reliable technical performance:

Area	*Wave Length*	*Call*	*Power*	*Owner*
Boston	244	WTAT	500	Edison Electric Company
Providence	360	WJAR	500	Outlet Company
Buffalo	319	WGR	750	Federal Tel. & Tel. Co.
Philadelphia	395	WFI	500	Strawbridge & Clothier Co.
"	395	WDAR	500	Lit Brothers
Washington	469	WCAP	500	C. & P. Telephone Co.
Pittsburgh	462	WCAE	500	Kaufman-Baer Co.
Cleveland	390	WJAX	500	Union Trust Co.
"	390	WTAM	500	Willard Battery Co.
Detroit	517	WCX	500	Detroit Free Press
"	517	WWJ	500	Detroit News
Cincinnati	309	WLW	500	Crossley Mfg. Co.
"	309	WSAI	500	U. S. Playing Card Co.
Chicago	360	WGN	1000	Chicago Tribune
Davenport	484	WOC	500	Palmer School
St. Louis	546	KSD	500	Post Dispatch
Minneapolis	417	WLAG	500	Cutting and Washington
Kansas City	411	WDAF	500	Kansas City Star
" "	411	WHB	500	Sweeney School
Dallas	476	WFAA	500	News and Journal
Fort Worth	476	WBAP	500	Wortham-Carter

It seems, however, that the network proposal, like most pioneering concepts, met with varying degrees of endorsement when the Broadcasting Department began to present it to the stations which it considered most suitable for the purpose. Nearly all were being operated for the fundamental purpose of winning good will for their ownership, and one fundamental consideration therefore was whether good will would be adversely affected by the broadcasting of "indirect" advertising. For stations operated by newspapers there was the further question of the effect upon local advertising revenues if radio publicity should be given to national or "foreign" advertisers.[7]

It was not until October, 1924, that circuits and stations were ready for a test of the idea of simultaneous commercial broadcasting under the off-peak hour plan. The pioneer group comprised six stations only—WEEI in Boston, WGR in Buffalo, WJAR in Providence, WCAE in Pittsburgh, WEAF in New York, and WCAP in Washington. These six stations have an outstanding place in broadcasting history for they were the original stations on the "red network,"[8] the expansion of which will be described on a later page.

The General Broadcasting Situation

A review, at this point, of broadcasting developments in the United States may help to show the radio soil in which the network idea was planted.

By May 1, 1924, according to government bulletins, over a thousand licenses to broadcast had been issued, and 576 of them were still in force, although many of the stations holding them were not in active operation. In fact, over 10 per cent of the stations licensed by the government had never operated at all, and more than 30 per cent of those that had discontinued broadcasting had done so because of the expense of operation. Of the 576 licenses in force, 371

[7] The listing of entertainers rather than of sponsors in today's daily program news is a continuance of the practice established by newspapers in the early days of network broadcasting because of the supposed opposition of local merchants to direct references to other radio advertisers.

[8] This was not the first chain broadcasting of commercial programs since the original network comprising WJAR and the two Bell System stations had already been so used.

were held by radio and electric companies, 60 by educational institutions, 27 by churches and Y.M.C.A.'s, and 19 by newspapers and publishers.

The Western Electric Company had sold station transmitting equipment to the following:

	Owner	*Business*	*Call*
CALIFORNIA			
Los Angeles	Earle C. Anthony, Inc.	Automobile	KFI
" "	Echo Park Evangelistic Assn.	Religious	KFSG
" "	Times-Mirror Company	Newspaper	KHJ
" "	Express Pub. Company	Newspaper	*
Oakland	Tribune Publishing Co.	Newspaper	KLX
San Francisco	Hale Brothers	Dept. Store	KPO
DISTRICT OF COLUMBIA			
Washington	Chesapeake & Potomac Tel. Co.	Communications	WCAP
GEORGIA			
Atlanta	Atlanta Journal	Newspaper	WSB
ILLINOIS			
Chicago	Sears Roebuck Company	Dept. Store	WLS
"	Daily News	Newspaper	WMAQ
"	Calumet Baking Powder Co.	Chemical	*
Mooseheart	Loyal Order of Moose	Fraternal	*
Zion City	Zion Institution & Industries	Religious	WCBD
IOWA			
Davenport	Palmer School of Chiropractic	Educational	WOC
Des Moines	Bankers Life Ins. Co.	Insurance	WHO
Iowa City	Iowa State University	Educational	WHAA
KENTUCKY			
Louisville	Courier Journal	Newspaper	WHAS

* Indicates not yet in operation.

MASSACHUSETTS			
Boston	Shepard Stores	Dept. Store	WNAC
“	Edison Elec. Illum. Co.	Public Service	WTAT
“	Tremont Temple	Religious	*
“	Round Hills Radio Corp. (This station had both 100-watt and 500-watt equipment)	Educational	WMAF
Worcester	Sherer Dept. Store	Dept. Store	WDEH
MICHIGAN			
Detroit	Detroit Police Dept.	Municipal	KOP
“	Detroit Free Press	Newspaper	WCX
“	Detroit News	Newspaper	WWJ
Lansing	Reo Motor Car Company	Automobile	*
MINNESOTA			
Minneapolis	Minneapolis Subscribers	Radio	WLAG
MISSOURI			
Jefferson City	State Marketing Bureau	Government	WOS
Kansas City	Kansas City Star	Newspaper	WDAF
“ “	Sweeney Auto School	Educational	WHB
St. Louis	Post Dispatch	Newspaper	XSD
“ “	Principia School	Educational	*
NEBRASKA			
Omaha	Woodmen of the World	Fraternal	WOAW
NEW JERSEY			
Newark	L. Bamberger & Co.	Dept. Store	WOR
NEW YORK			
New York	Western Electric Co.	Manufacturing	WBAY
“ “	American Tel. & Tel. Co.	Communications	WEAF
“ “	Police Department	Municipal	WLAW
“ “	Gimbel Brothers	Dept. Store	*
Richmond Hill	A. H. Grebe Company	Radio & Elec.	*
Rochester	Democrat and Chronicle Eastman School of Music	Newspaper	WHAM
Troy	Rensselaer Polytechnic Inst.	Educational	WBAZ

* Indicates not yet in operation.

OHIO			
Cincinnati	Crossley Manuf. Co.	Radio & Elec.	WLW
"	U. S. Playing Card Co.	Manuf.	WSAI
Cleveland	Union Trust Co.	Bank	WJAX
OREGON			
Portland	Oregonian Pub. Co.	Newspaper	KGW
PENNSYLVANIA			
Philadelphia	Lit Brothers	Dept. Store	WDAR
"	Gimbel Brothers	Dept. Store	WIP
"	John Wanamaker	Dept. Store	WOO
Pittsburgh	Kaufman and Baer Co.	Dept. Store	WCAE
RHODE ISLAND			
Providence	The Outlet Company	Dept. Store	WJAR
"	Dates W. Flint	Automobile	*
TENNESSEE			
Memphis	Commercial Appeal	Newspaper	WMC
TEXAS			
Beaumont	Magnolia Petroleum Co.	Oil	*
Dallas	Dallas News	Newspaper	WFAA
Fort Worth	Star Telegram	Newspaper	WBAP
Houston	Will Horowitz, Jr.	Oil	*
"	Humble Oil Co.	Oil	*
UTAH			
Salt Lake City	Nathaniel Baldwin	Religious	*

* Indicates not yet in operation.

There were 10 stations owned by the so-called "Radio Group" as follows: by the Westinghouse Company in Pittsburgh, Cleveland, Chicago, Springfield, Mass., and Hastings, Neb.; by the Radio Corporation in New York City and Washington, D. C.; by the General Electric Company in Schenectady, N. Y., and Oakland, Calif., with one under construction in Denver.

Western Electric equipped stations totaling 59 were operating at the time. All but five of these were operating 500-watt transmitters and none had been discontinued.

Of all the 576 stations for which government licenses were in force on May 1, 1924, less than 2 per cent had a power of 1,000 watts. The percentage operating 500-watt transmitters was 17, more than 23 per cent were 100-watt stations, and nearly 50 per cent had less than 100-watts antenna input. Thirty-one of the active stations whose broadcasting had constituted an infringement of the American Company's patent rights had obtained licenses from the company and the number was rapidly increasing as licenses, including the right to broadcast for hire, were offered to stations still infringing.

There were probably about seventy-five stations in the United States, as the Broadcasting Department and Long Lines engineers prepared for the off-peak hour experiment, which were capable of real service to the public. Since newspaper-owned stations were among the most important, a brief reference to the radio experience of newspapers may perhaps provide some interesting background for the beginnings of network broadcasting.

Newspapers as Broadcasters

The public interest in broadcasting that mounted during 1922 was observed by the press in general with mingled suspicion and curiosity, for it raised such questions as whether continued growth would make broadcasting a serious competitor, and whether the operation of stations by newspapers themselves could help to increase circulation.

By 1923 several important newspaper enterprises included the operation of stations that had won radio audiences of substantial size because of the character and quality of their programs. The pioneer of all was the Detroit *News,* which began broadcasting as a public service several weeks before Pittsburgh's KDKA sent out election returns on the night of November 2, 1920. By 1922, when its radio department had 11 members, its radio outlook was thus expressed by its radio editor:[9]

> . . . we immediately give rein to our imaginations and begin to speculate upon the future development of radio and its ultimate possibilities and appli-

[9] *WWJ—The Detroit News—History of Radiophone Broadcasting by the Earliest and Foremost of Newspaper Stations.* Published by the Radio Staff of the Detroit *News.* A measure of this newspaper's continued effort to utilize radio as a public service is in the contrast between its low-powered station of 1920 and one of 5,000 watts a dozen years later.

cations. The prospect staggers us, because we realize that all the time we are merely standing upon the threshold of a world of wonders and that we are dealing with an element which only exists as yet in theory but which is supposed to be the basic element of which all created things are composed and to which all created things may be, by some unknown process, again converted.

The editor of *Radio Broadcast* was arguing in December, 1923, that the broadcasting of news from newspaper stations would increase newspaper circulation. He wrote:[10]

The few newspapers which have installed broadcasting stations have not, up to the present time, used them in a way which we believe will become customary a few years hence.

. . . . The front page is what sells the newspapers and the headlines are the selling agents.

Now, if this is so, why should not an enterprising newspaper take ten minutes a day in the evening when most people are at home, to put the important news items of the day on the air. They don't because, so the skeptics say, if the people already have the news via radio they won't bother to read a paper. This is certainly not so. . . .

. . . . This use of radio, putting real news on the air, is as yet practically untouched, although it is probably one of radio's most promising fields.

By the middle of 1924 the broadcasting newspapers had had experience enough to dispute the theory that radio news would sell papers. The general verdict was that circulation had not been stimulated. Broadcasting's value in developing good will for a newspaper, however, had many advocates. The radio editor of the Detroit *News,* as quoted in *Radio Broadcast,*[11] justified the heavy expense of a good broadcasting station by affirming:

"Our paper and our call letters, WWJ, have become known in every state in the Union and in countries within 4,500 miles of Detroit through our broadcasting service.

"Goodwill is about the only return we expect from our station. The circulation department tells us positively that they list no increases in circulation due to our efforts in radio. The advertising department is of the same opinion. The Detroit *News* maintains its broadcasting station as a part of its public service."

[10] Vol. iv, no. 2 (Dec., 1923), p. 99.

[11] Vol. iv, no. 4 (Feb., 1924), p. 346, in "What Broadcasting Does for a Newspaper," by Winfield Barton.

The same service point of view was expressed at the time by the radio editor of the *Daily News* in Chicago, as quoted in *Radio Broadcast:*[12]

"The creation of good will, that intangible, yet nevertheless invaluable asset for quasi-public institutions, such as newspapers, results from our broadcasting. Dollars may not directly follow from the pleasures experienced by listeners to programs broadcasted by newspapers, but the feeling of friendliness is there, and the friendship of the masses makes strength for the newspaper.

* * * * * *

"The radio broadcasting station of the newspaper pours inoffensively its name into the willing ears of thousands of listeners. The various departments of the paper become known to great numbers who had never given a thought to the variety of newspaper service before. The automobile editor, giving his talks on motor trails, local traffic regulations, and helpful hints on safety in driving, interests that group among his listeners who own motor cars. And those who are interested in automobile tours, safe driving, and the problems of the motorist will turn to their radio-friend's column for information when they buy the paper. The broadcasting of football, baseball, and other sporting returns emphasizes the sporting department. So, in giving service to the public, the newspaper builds up its clientele.

"Some of these reasons for the newspaper entering the broadcasting field may not seem especially 'practical.' But newspapers do not gain their strength from being too 'practical' or cold-bloodedly commercial in their relations with the public. The newspaper must be willing to serve."

That the public service of a newspaper station, referred to in these opinions, could be enormously enhanced by the broadcasting of events of national interest, was already the experience of those that had been enabled, because of the Bell System's provision of wire circuits, to give their listeners the addresses of President Harding in June and of President Coolidge in December, 1923.

The Special Challenge of an Election Year

It was during preparations for a start of the network experiment that another important responsibility came to the Broadcasting Department and the Long Lines engineers in the broadcasting requirements for the political campaigns of 1924.

While the department was considering the idea of broadcasting,

[12] *Ibid.*, p. 344.

as a public service, the high lights of the 1924 Republican and Democratic national conventions, the possibility that long circuits might be in considerable demand came to its attention through an early inquiry from a newspaper in Chicago, the city which was first considered as the place for the Republican meeting. This newspaper had secured an option on the exclusive privilege of broadcasting the convention proceedings from its own station, and its primary interest at the time was in serving the public in the surrounding area; but

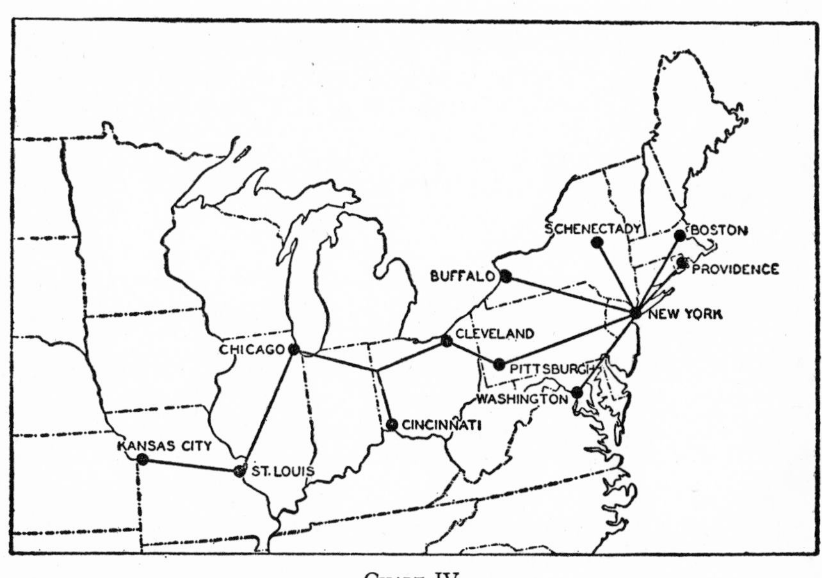

CHART IV

Bell System Wire Circuits Connected Radio Stations in Twelve Cities for Broadcasting from the Republican National Convention in 1924

it also was investigating the possibility of distributing the program by telephone wires to stations in other cities.

The files of the period show in an interesting way the various steps which led to the actual convention broadcasts. These steps were prefaced by a report to the Chicago station that even if wire facilities were available, which was doubtful, it would be necessary to deal with the Republican National Committee because of the national importance of the event. Then began consultations with the national committees of both major parties to ascertain their probable needs and to work out a plan of meeting them without interference with telephone service to the public.

By the end of April the Long Lines engineers reported the probability of making circuits available to connect several cities with Cleveland, the location that had been finally selected for the Republican convention. They also reported that because of the lack of equipment and trained personnel it would be technically practicable to serve only twelve cities. The Republican Committee was asked to take the responsibility of selecting twelve cities from a list of eighteen with which connections were possible and was given a list of the stations that were licensed to broadcast under Bell System patents. The Committee itself then arranged with the stations for the sharing of service charges for the wire facilities involved, the Bell System contributing the facilities of its stations WEAF and WCAP, together with the memorable services of Graham McNamee as announcer. The same procedure was followed with regard to the Democratic convention.

The major political conventions were held in June and July of 1924, the Republican Party delegates meeting in Cleveland, Ohio, June 10 to 12, and the Democratic convention occupying New York's Madison Square Garden from June 24 to July 9 in the most protracted convention in America's political history. The Republican nominees were Mr. Calvin Coolidge and Mr. Charles G. Dawes. The Democratic convention, after its historic deadlock, named Mr. John W. Davis on the 103d ballot, with Governor Charles W. Bryan as his running mate.

Broadcasting brought the proceedings of both conventions—the speeches, the cheers, the colorful descriptions of convention scenes and personalities—to the ears of millions who never before had heard a broadcast by "remote control." [13]

[13] The stations broadcasting the Republican convention proceedings were:

WEAF—New York, N. Y.
WCAP—Washington, D. C.
WNAC—Boston, Mass.
WJAR—Providence, R. I.
WJZ—New York, N. Y.
WGY—Schenectady, N. Y.
WRC—Washington, D. C.
WGR—Buffalo, N. Y.
KDKA—Pittsburgh, Pa.
WJAX—Cleveland, Ohio
WTAM—Cleveland, Ohio
WLW—Cincinnati, Ohio
WGN—Chicago, Ill.
WLS—Chicago, Ill.
KSD—St. Louis, Mo.
WDAF—Kansas City, Mo.

Writers on radio's development quite properly accent the history-making aspect of this simultaneous broadcasting from many stations in a dozen cities. It was, of course, a notable event in radio history as regards both the size of the radio audience and the technical accomplishments of the Long Lines forces. But to identify these convention broadcasts as notable only because of the record-breaking hook-ups involved is to overlook their significance as milestones in progress toward broadcasting's economic stability. Such a significance can be ascribed to them because of the fact that the broadcasting stations themselves shared in the expense of the wire network that was temporarily set aside for the service. In so doing they were accepting the principle which based the idea of serving a chain of stations by delivering programs during Long Lines off-peak hours, and their experience showed how local station prestige could be increased and new listeners gained because of program material brought by wires from a distant source.

Telephoto Demonstrations

A mention of election-year communications accomplishments should include a brief reference to the Bell System's demonstrations, during the major political conventions, of progress in the transmission of pictures by wire.

World-wide interest had been aroused by a demonstration on May 19 of the apparatus which had been developed by laboratory specialists employing vacuum tubes, electrical filters, light valves, photoelectric cells, and accurate synchronizing methods.[14] With sending apparatus installed in Cleveland and receiving apparatus installed in New York, some pictures were transmitted by wire which were reproduced in New York papers on the following day.

The gathering of Republican delegates in Cleveland afforded opportunity for a further demonstration, and many convention pictures reached the New York papers with a speed that was astonish-

For the Democratic convention the list was the same except for the omission of WJZ and WGY (which were served by Western Union Telegraph wires) and the addition of WDBH, Worcester, Mass.; WMAF, South Dartmouth, Mass.; WSB, Atlanta, Ga.; WMAQ, Chicago, Ill.

[14] The development can be traced from a number of articles published in the *Bell System Technical Journal*.

ing at the time. A flashlight picture of the assembled delegates, for example, was made at 12:20 P.M. on June 10, and at 1:35 it was put on the wire. Five minutes later it was in New York and at 2:56 a large number of negatives were ready for distribution.

In order to give the same unusual publicity to the Democratic convention, arrangements were made to transmit convention pictures from New York to Chicago. The sending apparatus was installed in an office building not far from Madison Square Garden, with the receiving apparatus located in a Chicago telephone building, and many convention scenes were photographed and transmitted over long-distance wires for the use of the Chicago press.

The delay in nominating the Democratic candidate was the cause of a little-known episode. There was a dearth of pictures of news value because of the long proceedings, and such novelties as handwriting specimens, pen and ink sketches, music, and convention programs were used as photographic subjects. It was in a further search for photographic material that the idea was born of transmitting fingerprints. New York's famous fingerprint expert, Deputy Police Commissioner Faurot, was invited to the transmitting room, and plans were made to send to the Chicago police department a telephotograph of a fingerprint selected by the Commissioner and known to be in the Chicago police files. It was wired to Chicago, with technical descriptions of the other nine fingerprints, and two minutes after being developed and received it was identified as the print of a well-known pickpocket.

Following this interesting demonstration the transmitting apparatus was transferred from New York to San Francisco and the receiving equipment in Chicago was moved to Long Lines headquarters in New York for tests of transcontinental picture transmission. These were begun in October, 1924, and were conducted in the early morning hours, from 4 A.M. to 10 A.M., in order not to interfere with the normal use of the circuits.

In April of the following year, with the use of improved apparatus a limited service was inaugurated for the transmission of pictures over long-distance circuits between New York, Chicago, and San Francisco, following successful demonstrations in March. One of these demonstrations was the transmission from Washington of nine news pictures of President Coolidge's inauguration, prints being distributed to newspapers in those cities. The service was gradually extended to include other cities, but there was insufficient demand to justify its maintenance; it was discontinued in 1933, much of the original apparatus being donated to technical schools and museums. An entirely new system, designed by the telephone laboratories, was manufactured by the Western Electric Company for the Associated Press to operate on a nationwide network of specially designed Bell System telephoto wire circuits.

There is interest in this evolution because the historical pattern is the same as for network broadcasting, i.e., the initial promotion of a service idea until its economics were determined, and then the development and provision of necessary wire facilities for its further commercial application.

One of the exhibits in the American Telephone Historical Library in New York is the letter (reproduced in facsimile opposite page 271) which President Coolidge sent to President H. D. Pillsbury, of the Pacific Telephone and Telegraph Company, acknowledging photographs of inauguration scenes as received in San Francisco over long-distance wires:

> This group of photographs . . . is, of course, one of the products of present-day advancement in science and the mechanic arts that are so numerous and continuous that we hardly have time to realize them as they come to our attention.
>
> * * * * * *
>
> I shall preserve these pictures as a memento of peculiar historic and scientific value, and in thanking you for your thoughtfulness in sending them to me, I wish to add appreciation of the wonderful service which was rendered in the nation-wide distribution of the Inaugural Address.

Campaigning with Public-Address Systems

Telephone engineers both active and retired have vivid memories of the problems connected with the 1924 campaign, which was distinguished by the first extensive use of broadcasting for political purposes. For the broadcasting of notification ceremonies, speeches of acceptance, important mass meetings, and addresses by candidates, federal officials, State governors, and others there was the constant challenge to provide not only circuits but also loud-speaking equipment for outdoor meetings.

A new feature in the campaigning was the speaking by candidates from Pullman cars equipped with public-address apparatus which was operated and maintained by Bell System experts. The Democratic candidate for President, Mr. John W. Davis, was the first to use such a car. On his first campaign tour, which covered some 5,000 miles, he made 46 speeches from his private car, and in subsequent trips, which covered 12,000 miles, he depended to a large degree on the equipment which was so useful in saving his voice and his energy. Mr. Dawes, the Republican Vice-presidential candidate, also used the loud-speaking equipment extensively, his audiences varying from a few hundred to five thousand or more.

One incident of the campaign is especially well remembered by the telephone men involved because it led to an important equipment change. The Democratic campaign opened with the acceptance speech of Mr. Davis, which was delivered on August 11 at his home city of Clarksburg, West Virginia, 13 stations being included in the broadcasting network. Engineers in the control-room in New York at once detected a curiously muffled quality in the transmission from Clarksburg, and over the order wire there went at once a request for an explanation from the engineers of the Chesapeake and Potomac Telephone Company who had installed the pickup equipment. These "trouble shooters" soon discovered the cause. There was a violent storm in progress, and though Mr. Davis himself was protected from it, the microphone was exposed to the driving rain which spread a film of water over the wire mesh protecting the transmitter, thus interfering with its normal efficiency in picking up the speaker's tones. The practical result of this experience was a new design for the microphone housing.

Coöperation with Political Committees

On the day following the acceptance speech of Mr. Davis one newspaper[15] gave special prominence to its report on the Broadcasting Department's problem in dealing with the several com-

[15] New York *Herald Tribune,* Aug. 12, 1924, p. 12, col. 2 (one-star edition).

mittees seeking the use of circuits for campaign broadcasting. The account presents that specific situation, as well as current conditions in general, in so readable a form that it is inserted here in full:

Officials of the American Telephone and Telegraph Company regard with some dismay the present confusion of authority in the issuance of requests for the broadcasting of political speeches, and served warning yesterday, when questions arose as to the stations to be connected by land telephone wires for the transmission of the Davis speech of acceptance from Clarksburg, W. Va., that such requests must come from a major party's national committee.

Up to late in the afternoon it was not known what broadcasting stations were to be linked up by telephone for the Democratic notification ceremony. The company regards it as its prime duty to supply telephone service to subscribers, and when beset, as it may be in the heat of the campaign, with numerous conflicting requests for broadcasting it may have to deny some of them.

Regular Service Placed First

At present requests are made by the national committees of the three major parties, by state and county committees of all parties, by a Senatorial campaign committee and by Congressional campaign committees. It is the hope of officials of the American Telephone and Telegraph Company that these various committees will achieve some measure of co-operation before the campaign grows too hot.

"Our business is the supplying of telephonic communication to all the people," said W. E. Harkness, assistant vice-president of the Bell company, who has charge of its broadcasting interests. "Our plant and lines are designed for this purpose, and their use for the connection of broadcasting stations with a central point of transmission is but an incident which cannot be permitted to interfere with our regular service. Therefore, it becomes apparent that our wire lines, repeater facilities and trained personnel necessarily are limited and must be arranged for some time in advance of their actual use.

"We are ready to supply our part of the broadcasting service impartially to all political parties at a price which will probably be a little below its actual cost to us, but we must have enough time in advance to make our proper arrangements. Also, we require the authority of the national committee of whatever party is requesting the use of our lines. Up to the limit of our facilities which, in the past, has been the connection of from fifteen to eighteen broadcasting stations, we are perfectly willing to co-operate. But it behooves the national committees of the various parties to get together and arrange a program which will not include conflicting days and hours. The responsibility for the successful use of radio broadcasting in the approaching campaign rests entirely with these committees."

Expense Must Be Shared

Some of the broadcasting stations have expressed a willingness to pay their proportion of the land-wire service charge, while others think that they should receive this free, in view of the fact that they give their station facilities free for the broadcasting of political speeches. It is certain, however, that only those stations which are willing to share the expense will get wire service, and this number is bound to be limited by the number of circuits which the Bell company can spare from its regular traffic demands.

One complete wire circuit and sometimes two must be given over for the connection of each broadcasting station. From three to six hours, aside from the actual transmission period of the speech, are required for adjusting the lines and for testing its capabilities. Often another lengthy test is necessary just before the scheduled transmission occurs.

Isolated broadcasting stations, from which political speeches will be put on the air for local hearing, will not require land-wire connections. But, in order to retain the interest of their audiences, the programs must include many other items beside the political features. They must provide, as usual, a "balanced program," or the political element will lose its attraction and force, and, therefore miss its purpose.

Fans who tune in on station WEAF at 9 P.M. daylight saving time on Thursday will hear the notification speech in Washington by Frank W. Mondell, permanent chairman of the Republican National Convention, which is scheduled to last about ten minutes, and the acceptance speech of one hour by President Coolidge. Preliminary announcements are to be made by Graham McNamee. Under the direction of Captain William H. Santelmann, the United States Marine Band will play a musical program between speeches. Arrangements for radiocasting these proceedings are in charge of the American Telephone and Telegraph Company.

A "Long Lines Election" Year

The 1924 campaign was called a "radio election" because broadcasting for the first time was a potent instrumentality of the campaign managers, and because millions for the first time simultaneously listened to the political debates and to the broadcasting of voting results on the night of November 4.

It might also have been called, with considerable propriety, a "Long Lines election," because of the responsibilities that were assumed and carried through by the telephone forces in providing wires and equipment called for on a constantly increasing scale to serve an eagerly listening nation. When President Coolidge was the guest speaker at the convention of the United States Chamber of Commerce on October 23, radio history was made by creating a network of 22 stations for broadcasting the occasion. On election eve there were 27 stations broadcasting his final campaign address, with Denver, Seattle, Portland, Los Angeles, Oakland, and San Francisco on the line. If America's radio listeners in this exciting year hailed nationwide broadcasting as a wonderful experience, the Long Lines men best knew what made it so.

President Coolidge's Inaugural Broadcast

The broadcast on March 4, 1925, which the President termed a "wonderful service," was of tremendous interest to the entire country since it was the first inaugural broadcast in America's history. WEAF and 21 other stations brought the ceremonies and the President's address to an audience of millions, keenly conscious of the new part being played by radio in national life. Educational institutions everywhere were reported as noting the broadcast's historical significance. WEAF's mail following the broadcast told of loud-speakers installed in schools so that the entire student body, together with parents and other guests, might listen. In many areas rural school children were transported to a location where there was a loud-speaker for the new and thrilling experience of hearing the voice of the President of the United States.

CHAPTER XVI

THE ARMY TESTS THE BELL SYSTEM

A Day's Program in 1924

THE radio program of WEAF for Defense "Test" Day, September 12, 1924, ended with a special broadcast which was as inspiring to men and women of the Bell System as it was reassuring to the nation's military heads, because it illustrated one of the far-reaching services that telephone lines could render in case of national emergency.

Perhaps it will awaken memories of WEAF's programs of 20 years ago, with their interesting mixture of sustaining and sponsored offerings, to reproduce the entire program announcement for the day:

PROGRAM—FRIDAY SEPTEMBER 12, 1924
STATION WEAF—AMERICAN TELEPHONE AND TELEGRAPH COMPANY

(492 Meters 610 Kilocycles) (Daylight Saving Time)
195 Broadway, New York City

11:00 A.M.	Helen Morris, Soprano.
11:10 A.M.	Health Talk under the auspices of the Association for the Prevention and Relief of Heart Disease, by Dr. Wm. St. Lawrence.
11:25 A.M.	"The Flower Garden's Big Opportunity" by Leonard Barron, Editor of *Garden Magazine and Home Builder*.
11:50 A.M.	Consolidated Market and Weather Reports by the United States Department of Agriculture and the New York State Department of Farms and Markets, together with American Agriculturist.

4:00-5:00 P.M. "Women's Club Program."

- 4:00 P.M. John Burnham, Concert Pianist. Program: "The Harmonious Blacksmith" (Handel); First Movement "Sonata" (Beethoven); "By the Brook" (Boisdefre).
- 4:10 P.M. Talk by Mr. Arthur J. Westermayr.
- 4:25 P.M. John Burnham, Concert Pianist. Program: "Fantaisie Impromptu" (Chopin); "Waltz" (Chopin).
- 4:35 P.M. "When Every Voter Votes" the second in a series of lectures on "Getting Out the Vote" by Mrs. Raymond Brown, Managing Director of Woman's Citizen, speaking under the auspices of the New York League of Women Voters.
- 4:50 P.M. John Burnham, Pianist. Program: "Impromptu" and "Gavotte Antique" (compositions by Mr. Burnham).

6:00 P.M. Dinner Music from the Rose Room of the Hotel Waldorf-Astoria, New York City, Joseph Knecht, Directing. Program: "Marche Lorraine" (Ganne); Selection "Les Huguenots" (Meyerbeer); "Arlésienne" (Bizet); "Caprice Viennois" (Kreisler); Entr'acte and Valse from "Coppelia" (Delibes); "Habanera" (Chabrier); "Lob der Frauen" (Strauss); "Madame Sherry" (Hoshna).

7:30 P.M. "Sir Hobgoblin Broadcasts a Get-up-Time Story" by Blanche Elizabeth Wade, the G. R. Kinney and Company Story Teller.

7:45 P.M. Harry Jentes, Jazz Pianist.

7:55 P.M. Rosella Sheiner, 10-year-old Violinist.

8:05 P.M. Isabel Duff "Scotty" Wood, Soprano, Program of Scotch Songs.

8:20 P.M. Harry Jentes, Jazz Pianist.

8:35 P.M. Joseph White, Tenor, accompanied by Winifred T. Barr.

8:50 P.M. Rosella Sheiner, 10-year-old Violinist.

9:00-10:00 P.M. B. Fischer and Company's "Astor Coffee" Dance Orchestra.

10:00 P.M. Joseph White, Tenor.

10:15-11:00 P.M. Special Radio Program on National Defense Test Day direct from the War Department Building, Washington, D. C., Speeches by General J. J. Carty, Hon. John W. Weeks, Secretary of War, and General John J. Pershing, General of the Armies of the United States and Chief of Staff, in order named.

The "Defense Test" Ceremony

The forty-five-minute ceremony which concluded the program on September 12 was a record-breaking event in national broadcasting. Some 19,000 miles of circuit, the Bell System's contribution to Defense Test Day, had their focus in the national capital and were operated as a single unit, enabling the generals in charge of Defense Test activities at four widely separated Army corps centers to communicate with Army headquarters in Washington where sat Secretary of War Weeks, Chief of Staff General John J. Pershing, Chief Signal Officer General Saltzman, and General John J. Carty of the American Telephone and Telegraph Company. Furthermore, the 19,000-mile network was tapped in 18 cities to permit the proceedings to be broadcast from that number of stations extending all the way from Boston to San Francisco, and from Minneapolis to Atlanta and Dallas. This use of the circuits, as a contemporary writer reported, "virtually reduced the nation to the dimensions of a small chamber for the time being."[1]

The broadcast was of particular interest to telephone people because it presented a complicated operating problem to the Long Lines organization, as a brief description of the ceremonies will make clear.

After the radio audiences of 18 stations had heard the introductory remarks of Secretary Weeks, General Saltzman, and General Pershing, General Carty graphically described the extent of the facilities required to provide nationwide telephone service, and then said:

> To illustrate in a practical manner the functions of communication, I will now call over the long-distance wire a number of cities and towns extending from the Atlantic seacoast westward to the Pacific, placing all of them in direct wire communication with this room at Washington. Tonight the radio stations are connected with these wires, so that the radio listeners may hear the conversations taking place over them. In the event of a national emergency, such messages would not be heard by the radio listeners, but would only reach the individuals for whom they were intended.

[1] The participating stations were: WCAP, Washington; WEAF, New York; WOO, Philadelphia; WJAR, Providence; WNAC, Boston; WGY, Schenectady; WGR, Buffalo; KDKA, Pittsburgh; WLW, Cincinnati; WGN, Chicago; WLAG, Minneapolis; KSD, St. Louis; WDAF, Kansas City; WOAW, Omaha; KLZ, Denver; KGO, Oakland; WSB, Atlanta; WFAA, Dallas.

General Carty then "called the roll of the continent," the radio audience hearing the immediate answers from telephone men at fourteen stations on the transcontinental line. Following this roll call he called the four corps headquarters in New York, Chicago, Omaha, and San Francisco, after which General Pershing received direct reports of the day's activities from each of the four generals in command.

Two-Way Transmission

Since these conversations involved two-way transmission over part of the network, the Long Lines engineers undertook an operation that was exceedingly complex in comparison with the one-way transmission of a common program to several stations. To permit two-way transmission, the main circuit of the network connecting Washington and San Francisco, which also passed through the Army corps centers, was operated on the "four-wire" principle, one pair being used for transmission in one direction and one pair for the other direction. Probably no radio listeners who were not telephone technicians realized that they heard the various speakers by way of Washington. For example, when the Army corps commander in San Francisco spoke into his transmitter, his words were carried to Washington and then back to Oakland, California, before passing to the antenna of Oakland's KGO.

There was added interest in the conversations which were broadcast because the occasion was General Pershing's last opportunity to speak directly with his fellow-officers as their commanding general —his official retirement as General of the Armies of the United States, because of his having reached the age limit, was scheduled for noon of the next day.

General Saltzman's introductory remarks to the radio audience contained the following appreciative references:

> The Department desires me to express its appreciation to the American Telephone and Telegraph Company, and its associated Bell Companies, for all that they have done to make this possible tonight. . . . And this is not the first time that the American Telephone and Telegraph Company has rendered great aid to the Army on a defense day. The very first day of the World War, this company organized an office of the Signal Corps of our Army. Ten complete

battalions of signal troops were recruited from the Bell companies, which were promptly sent to France, and commenced the building of a great communication system for General Pershing's Army.

In closing the ceremonies the General described them as "an epoch-making event in the history of communications."

The event was indeed epoch-making, for it was the first attempt at nationwide broadcasting enabling one person to address the nation at large. *Radio Broadcast* commented:[2]

> When Washington made his farewell to that handful of officers and men gathered at Rocky Point, New Jersey, in 1783, his voice was heard by that scattering few only. But now, the retiring General of our Army speaks to the Nation . . . . History was made during that hour when General Pershing as their commanding officer bade farewell to these Generals with whom he had long been associated. . . . it will remain in the memory of some of us as about the most impressive hour ever lived through.

Among the appreciative letters received by the American Company following "Defense Test Day," there are two which it particularly treasures. Both are dated September 13 and are from General Pershing himself; the one to Long Lines Director Stevenson in tribute to the technical accomplishment read:

> It was a great pleasure to me last night to witness the remarkable operation of the transcontinental line system of your Company. From an organization standpoint I can appreciate the great amount of foresight, care and skill that had to be mobilized to assure such a communication achievement. What you contributed was the culminating factor in the great success of Defense Test Day.
>
> I cannot begin to express to you and to the able technical personnel under you my deep appreciation of this most wonderful accomplishment. Will you kindly extend my very sincere thanks and cordial good wishes to them all.

For the General to be so impressed by Long Lines' "foresight, care and skill," he must have been aware of the preparations for the broadcast and doubtless learned of them from General Carty. Circuits to be used in case of emergency between Washington and all broadcasting stations were provided in addition to those selected for

[2] Vol. vi, no. 1 (Nov., 1924), p. 35, "Pershing's Farewell Address."

the broadcasting service. All the telephone circuits arranged for the event were paralleled by an elaborate network of telegraph circuits. The total number of miles of wire involved in both the regular and emergency layout included 39,000 miles for telephone purposes and 11,000 miles for telegraph.

Furthermore, a considerable amount of equipment was specially installed at each of the five points from which the Army Corps Commanders were to talk. After the whole network had been set up, extensive tests took place to make sure that everything was in satisfactory shape. A small army of technical men such as special repeater attendants, test-board men, telegraph operators, and telephone engineers were needed at these five "talking points" and at repeater stations along all the routes. Altogether about 250 of these specialists were actively engaged in the service, and many linemen were at their stations ready to go into action at the first signs of trouble along the lines.

Such details as these are evidence of the effort involved in simultaneous broadcasting in the days when circuit arrangements were made to order.

The other letter from General Pershing (reproduced opposite page 175) was to the American Company's President, Mr. Thayer:

> May I take this opportunity to express my appreciation to you and through you to the American Telephone and Telegraph Company and its Associated Companies for the generous participation in the Defense Test. In addition to the use of the physical facilities of your great communication system, which have contributed an important part toward the success of this undertaking, the spirit of coöperation evidenced in this matter is, indeed, a symbol of patriotic devotion to the ideals of our country.
>
> In leaving the active service, I send this word of grateful remembrance of the aid furnished me by your signal communication forces in France during the World War.

PART V

THE TRAIL IS BLAZED, 1925-1926

CHAPTER XVII

NETWORK EXPANSION

Proving the Possibilities of the Network

IN LAUNCHING its network project in October, 1924, the American Company's Broadcasting Department undertook a triple responsibility: (1) to provide participating stations with at least a three-hour program of sustaining and commercial features; (2) to provide advertisers with a broadcasting service which would enable them to seek contacts with consumers in market areas of their selection at the hours of their choice; (3) to assume the expense of the specially equipped circuits released by Long Lines for the transmission of programs to the cities where the station outlets were located.

At first it was easier to find broadcasters who were willing to pay for the distribution of sponsored programs by wire than it was to convince stations that they ran little or no risk in participating in the experiment. The technical basis of the project was, of course, the employment and skilled operation of long-distance circuits for the transmission to local stations of programs of a quality and variety otherwise unavailable to them. The business basis, as has been pointed out, was that the local stations would obtain these programs at no cost, since the charges for sustaining features would probably be offset by revenues from the sponsored features, with station prestige accruing from the distinctive entertainment thus offered to local listeners.

But the general proposal did not immediately appeal, according to the record, to a number of the stations which the Broadcasting Department considered most desirable as outlets. Some of them, in fact, did not give serious consideration to the network idea until there was a demonstration of its potential benefit that made radio history. This was the appearance before WEAF's microphone, on January 1, 1925, of Mr. John McCormack, the famous Irish tenor, and Miss Lucrezia Bori, of the Metropolitan Opera Company. This was the first in a series of broadcasts by great figures in the musical world who had not been heard previously over the air because of the fear that broadcasting might adversely affect the sale of their recordings for the Victor Talking Machine Company.

It was WEAF's Mr. George McClelland, arguing that radio would give these artists a popularity which would stimulate the sale of their records, who persuaded the Victor Company to permit them to broadcast experimentally, and WEAF coöperated in the experiment by waiving all charges for a series of ten one-hour concerts. Then WEAF's Broadcasting Department arranged for the broadcasting of the concerts through thirteen other stations, as a promotional measure for the network plan. Each concert was, of course, a musical treat such as radio had never before provided. Some sixty thousand letters were received from radio listeners after the first concert to prove their interest in the superior programs that the wires could bring to their communities, and the enthusiasm increased with each succeeding broadcast in the series. Letters like the following one from a Canadian listener showed the eagerness with which music-lovers awaited the quality programs that were demonstrating the entertainment possibilities inherent in the network idea:

Ruthven, Essex County,
Ontario, Canada.
February 13, 1925.

Having until this year spent all my life in the cities of England and Canada with periodic visits to the U. S. to indulge my love of music, *and am now located on a tobacco plantation "far removed from the haunts of men,"* I cannot adequately express my delight whilst listening in on Thursday night to the Victor Hour Artists.

Madame Renee Chemet afforded a rare treat to all lovers of the violin, whilst Emilio de Gogorza revealed splendid interpretation in his selections. The orchestra, as was to be expected from such talented performers, acquitted themselves to the admiration of all privileged to hear them.

I feel that radio listeners owe a great debt of gratitude to your station for the most inspiring programmes presented and I should fail in my mission this morning if I did not say how indebted we all are to the exceptional interest the gentleman who announces the various items takes in rendering information relative to the numbers presented.

It is a little matter to you perhaps to receive this note of appreciation, but I assure you WEAF is a constantly recurring source of pleasure. May you have much success in your most laudable effort is the earnest wish of at least one listener who eagerly tunes in since Feb. 1 to feast on the good things provided by your generous treatment. The rural life takes on added interest to a life-long city man now in retirement.

And besides showing how network programs could help in building prestige for the stations broadcasting them, the ten concerts set all fears at rest concerning broadcasting's effect on commercial enterprises concerned with recorded or printed music. All Victor dealers experienced an accelerated demand for recordings by every artist who broadcast during the series. There was particular significance in the demand for the song "All Alone,"[1] which Mr. McCormack sang at the first concert. Although this song had been recorded, the record had neither been announced nor catalogued; immediately after the song's radio presentation, however, the record was specifically demanded by thousands, and sheet-music sales exceeding 150,000 copies were quickly reported.

Sponsored Programs on the Network

Programs of unusual interest and quality like those of the Victor recording artists helped to attract station outlets for the network experiment, but the success of the project rested primarily on the offerings of the pioneer advertisers and the public's response to them. A tribute should be paid to the early users of the network for their faith and courage in exploring the new medium as a means of making themselves and their products better known, for their ventures were viewed with much skepticism in many quarters.

Radio's usefulness to advertisers had been a topic of debate ever since the establishment of WEAF for toll broadcasting, some of the disparaging discussion being doubtless inspired by fears of the radio as a competing medium. But much of the opinion also reflected sincere beliefs that the technique of "indirect" advertising, as evi-

[1] Copyright by Irving Berlin, 1924, and featured in his "Music Box Revue."

denced in the sponsorship of entertainment, would not result in returns commensurate with the expense involved.

In this connection it is of interest to record the verdict on radio advertising that was reached at the 1925 meeting of the American Newspaper Publishers Association. While warning the members that "advertising by radio means a split in advertising appropriations and hence less money for other mediums of advertising," the chairman of the Association's special radio committee submitted the following analysis of radio advertising in general:[2]

> Since the removal of the government ban on broadcasting from the higher grade stations, advertising programs are becoming more and more dominant. The quality of advertising programs is usually good, but the same argument used in news for the printed page rather than impermanent ether waves may be used in the case of advertising. The direct result of radio advertising is still as intangible as the results from the experiment of broadcasting itself. . . . Broadcast advertising, whether direct or indirect, is expensive. One Chicago station charges $120 an hour for broadcasting programs presented by advertisers. The charge for broadcasting programs through a chain of seven stations is $1,500 an hour. None of these experiments by broadcasters has been claimed to be profitable.
>
> . . . . Broadcast advertising if it becomes more specific in its nature is likely to create a reaction on the listeners which will be unfavorable rather than a help to the advertiser. Radio fans are beginning to resent the dissemination of the lower forms of radio advertising through the ether lanes. Only programs of the highest calibre can survive the turning of a radio fan's dials. Such programs mean great expense within the reach of few national advertisers. . . . As soon as the advertiser finds out that he is not getting a response from his broadcasts he will reject that medium as quickly as he will refuse to buy advertising in other mediums which do not produce results.

The conclusion of the radio committee's report was "radio has not proved itself to be an advertising medium."

But this dictum was disputed by some concerns which had already discovered through their broadcasting experiments at WEAF that sponsored programs of entertainment were useful supplements of other advertising efforts, and which were awaiting a broader field for a test of radio's power to stimulate curiosity and interest among both

[2] Quoted from the account of A. E. Haase in *Printers' Ink*, Apr. 30, 1925, p. 76. See footnote 6 on page 118 of this volume.

consumers and dealers. The makers of Eveready Batteries, for example, had been sending entertainers from one broadcasting station to another; they had local evidences of an awakened interest in the batteries, and were anxious to test chain broadcasting. Their advertising agency, N. W. Ayer and Son, was the first advertising organization to coöperate actively with the American Company's Broadcasting Department in inducing a client to adopt the new medium for a thorough test of its effectiveness. On October 6, 1924, with WGR of Buffalo linked to the network connecting the two Bell System stations and WJAR in Providence, there was launched the famous "Eveready Hour" that brought varied and appealing entertainment to more and more listeners as the network outlets increased in number.

Before many weeks this pioneer network program was being transmitted every Tuesday night, from 9 to 10 o'clock, to nine stations. On Monday evenings during the same hours the playing of the A. & P. Gypsies was delighting the listening audiences of six stations; on Tuesday evenings from 8:30 to 9:00 the wires brought the unique programs of the Gold Dust Twins to eight stations; the music of the Goodrich Silver Town Orchestra and of the Silver Masked Tenor was a Thursday transmission from WEAF to ten stations from 10 to 11 P.M.

From the example set by these and other pioneer network broadcasters stems the development of network broadcasting. One of them, according to a summary in the files dated May, 1925, was committed to an annual expenditure of $61,000 for station time and $47,000 for artists. Another concern is listed as sponsor for programs costing $64,000 for station time and $9,000 for artists. A third had appropriated $60,000 in order to broadcast through nine stations. The famous Atwater-Kent program, inaugurated October 4, 1925, which brought to WEAF's microphone and thence to the antennas of eleven stations the voices of the world's most eminent musicians, represented a total annual cost of nearly $120,000.

Such experimental expenditures, though small when compared with the huge sums employed today in sponsoring radio entertainment, represented great faith in what were being termed the "intangible" results of sponsored entertainment, for the only commercial publicity which the advertisers obtained was through the opening and closing announcements with which sponsorship was identified. Here for the record is a typical set of these announcements which will seem exceedingly conservative and "indirect" to radio listeners familiar with the announcement practices of the present time:

Opening:

Relax and smile, for Goldy and Dusty, the Gold Dust Twins, are *here* to send their *songs there,* and "brighten the corner where you are." The Gold Dust Corporation, manufacturer of Gold Dust Powder, engages the facilities of station WEAF, New York, WJAR, Providence, WCAE, Pittsburgh, WGR, Buffalo, WEEI, Boston, WFI, Philadelphia, and WEAR, Cleveland, so that the listeners-in may have the opportunity to chuckle and laugh with Goldy and Dusty. Let those Gold Dust Twins into your hearts and homes tonight, and you'll never regret it, for they *do* brighten the dull spots.

Closing:

Perhaps you open your hearts and homes to them each week—Goldy and Dusty, the Gold Dust Twins, who come to "brighten the corner where you are," and perhaps you have written them of your pleasure, or perhaps you have delayed. Won't you then do it tonight? Notes of encouragement from the audiences of WEAF, New York; WJAR, Providence; WCAE, Pittsburgh; WGR, Buffalo; WEEI, Boston; WFI, Philadelphia; and WEAR, Cleveland, serve to brighten these dusky entertainers. Address the Gold Dust Twins, care of Station WEAF, 195 Broadway, New York City, or to the station through which this program has reached you.

The reader will probably notice the newness of chain broadcasting and the conservatism of the Broadcasting Department, both reflected in such announcements as those just quoted. One interesting detail is the mention of all stations by the key-station announcer. This practice represented the only way of identifying participating stations, since the network was set up for continuous operation and the technique permitting interruptions for local station identification had not been developed.

Another detail is the frank request for letters of "encouragement." Fortunately for the development of network broadcasting, these "applause letters" were numerous enough to constitute definite evidence of public good will toward the concerns providing the programs. The following sample, selected at random from the files and referring to the Gold Dust program, shows the manner in which many listeners in the early days of network broadcasting were moved to respond:

Keota, Iowa,
January 4, 1926.

My dear Radio Friends—

Now, you ask us to write if your programs please us—and did you never stop to think that would keep us writing nearly every day in the week? And really it is hard to truly say which is best—we always know that WEAF has something good. Your way of getting the programs to us is the best ever. Why! really, one night we had a hard time making ourselves believe we were not in Canada, or some place where the Eskimos are.

But let me paint a picture for you:

A *scene in the rural district of snow-clad Iowa—a farm* house with Mother and Father sitting by the hard-coal burner; both are very gray-haired and often hungry for good music and good lectures. The children are grown and gone, the roads bad and it isn't easy for us to hitch old dobbin to the sleigh or phaeton any more and then listen! Somebody says "Radio," and here is where you will find us, on Tuesday nights waiting for Goldy and Dusty to brighten the corner where we are, and they have never failed (especially last Tuesday night). Then again Friday night we were all excited when they sang "Hear dem bells"—many a time have we sung the same song.

Your program Friday night was wonderful and best wishes to you for the year 1926 if that is a good start—we will always be on the air waiting for WEAF, so tell the Goldie Dustie Twins to do their best for us—and good night.

(Sgd.) Mrs. . . . .

To the announcer: Anytime you are motoring in our part of the world, just drop in for a friendly visit with us—3 miles west of West Chester, ¼ mile north (on Primary No. 2). We are always glad to have friends stop for a visit in the house at the side of the road.

The Problems of Growth

In developing its pioneer broadcasting service for advertisers, the Broadcasting Department of course encountered many special problems that increased in complexity as the station outlets and sponsors grew in number. It was frequently exceedingly difficult to adapt the network operation to the desires of advertisers and to the preferences of stations that wished to reserve some station time for local broadcasting responsibilities. Such stations received the full three-hour program for three nights each week, paying a nominal charge for the sustaining features and receiving a nominal recompense for broadcasting the commercial programs, the two tending to counterbalance. On the other nights of the week sponsored programs only were transmitted, and since they seldom filled more than half of the evening's broadcasting period, time was available for scheduling local broadcasts. On the other hand there were evenings when the Broadcasting Department was committed to provide a full evening's program to the entire network but when only a few of the stations were involved in a commercial broadcast. Because of the impossibility of transmitting two programs simultaneously, the local stations not receiving the commercial programs furnished their own artists at the Broadcasting Department's expense.

The special situations that were created as more stations joined the network and new users ventured to test the medium were a constant challenge to station executives to develop and administer suitable accounting and business practices, and to the station's engineers as well.

By the spring of 1925 there were 13 stations in 12 cities participating in the network experiment which included the WEAF-WCAP-WJAR combination. Two were in Philadelphia but of course were not used simultaneously, the choice being determined by the station schedules:

Minneapolis, Minn.	Washburn Crosby Co.	WCCO
Davenport, Ia.	Palmer School	WOC
Detroit, Mich.	Detroit News	WWJ
Cincinnati, Ohio	U. S. Playing Card Co.	WSAI
Cleveland, Ohio	Goodyear Rubber Co.	WEAR
Buffalo, N. Y.	Federal Tel. Mfg. Co.	WGR
Pittsburgh, Pa.	Kaufman Baer Co.	WCAE
Boston, Mass.	Edison Elec. Illum. Co.	WEEI
Philadelphia, Pa.	John Wanamaker	WOO
Philadelphia, Pa.	Strawbridge & Clothier	WFI
Providence, R. I.	The Outlet Co.	WJAR
Washington, D. C.	C. & P. Tel. Co.	WCAP
New York, N. Y.	A. T. & T. Co.	WEAF

Even though only twelve cities were linked together at the time, the "coverage" of the network stations was impressive to advertisers who were weighing the usefulness of the radio medium as a means of identifying themselves and their products in the public mind. The twelve territories in the aggregate included 42 per cent of the country's population, 57 per cent of the urban population, 27 per cent of the rural population, 58 per cent of the estimated incomes of over $10,000, 59 per cent of the wage earners—and 48 per cent of the radio receiving sets.

An interesting memorandum in the May, 1925, files shows how actively the Broadcasting Department was negotiating for more station outlets and how these negotiations affected the plans of the Long Lines engineers for setting aside circuits:

> There were 18 cities in the network plan discussed with us in September, 1924, but as yet there have been no network contracts made with broadcasting stations in Atlanta, Dallas, Fort Worth, Kansas City and St. Louis. It appears that these cities should be dropped from the circuit network for the present, although they may again be included at some other date—Worcester and Hartford have been added.

The "Red Layout" of circuits to which this May report further refers shows that long-distance routes were actually ready for the transmission of programs from New York to 14 cities, with wire service available to the Broadcasting Department during the following hours:

	Week Days	Saturdays	Sundays and Holidays
NewYork to Chicago and stations east of Chicago	6 P.M.-11:30 P.M.	3 P.M.-11:30 P.M.	8 A.M.-11:30 P.M.
New York to all other stations	7 P.M.-11:30 P.M.	4 P.M.-11:30 P.M.	8 A.M.-11:30 P.M.

Long Lines Construction

It is apparent from this schedule that the Broadcasting Department had more need for circuits than at the beginning of its network venture. The circuits could be obtained because the off-peak period on Saturdays began in the middle of the afternoon and, as compared with the use of Long Distance on week days, all of Sunday was an off-peak period.

Circuits for broadcasting purposes had of course been planned ever since the Long Lines management had been warned, in 1923, "With the increasing demand for Long Lines facilities for use in connection with radio broadcasting and also in connection with public-address systems for which the electrical requirements are the same, we should have in mind the design and installation of future plant of such a character as can be used when necessary or desirable for the purposes."

As a result of this foresight many construction and manufacturing projects were immediately launched, one of the most imaginative being the design of new telephone cables containing special broadcasting wires.

It was not long before the Long Lines engineers had provided an effective wire system for transmitting the wide range of frequencies inherent in music, with cable circuits equipped with special loading coils approximately every half-mile. Special amplifying or repeating apparatus was needed about every fifty miles on these cable circuits, and about every two hundred miles on the open-wire circuits. This system of program transmission circuit routes was constantly refined and extended to meet the needs of broadcasters, until today more than 90,000 miles of Long Lines circuits are reserved exclusively to serve them. More than 65,000 miles of these circuits are in the full-time networks. The remainder are used to provide one-time or recurring programs and as standby protection circuits for instant use in cases of trouble.

During the spring of 1925 the circuit situation was challenging, but much construction was under way to relieve it. One of the transcontinental lines, extending from Denver to El Paso and thence to Los Angeles, was continued eastward to Dallas and New Orleans, thus giving the southeasterly section of the country a more direct telephone route to the Pacific Coast. Work was also started on a third transcontinental line extending west from Minneapolis to Portland and Seattle. The additional open wire circuits provided by these projects were soon to have a most important relationship to network broadcasting's development as a national service. The year was also marked by the completion of a most ambitious undertaking, a storm-protected cable between New York and Chicago.

Organizational Responsibility

Network broadcasting as now known and enjoyed utilizes many separate networks, each consisting in general of basic long-distance trunk circuits, with branches reaching stations in various cities and towns to be served by the same programs. These networks range in size from small local networks connecting a few stations, possibly all within one State, up to the great national networks which connect hundreds of stations in cities and towns in all parts of the country. Including the 90,000 miles of Long Lines circuits just mentioned, the total mileage of Bell System program circuits reserved full-time for program purposes amounts to about 135,000. Approximately 95,000 miles of these circuits make up the full-time networks. The remaining 45,000 miles handle the very substantial but fluctuating load of part-time service and provide standby protection for the working circuits.[3]

There is of course no popular realization of the extent of the distributing system required to bring to local stations the programs to which radio listeners are now accustomed. Quite unsuspected, also, is the organizational accomplishment that coördinates these far-flung transmission facilities and includes under the simple term "maintenance" the effort that makes possible nationwide broadcasts under normal conditions or under emergency storm situations.

This reference is not particularly to the technique of transmission —to the operations in hundreds of repeater stations where circuits are monitored and vacuum tubes guarded to ensure the faithful transmission of a whisper over thousands of miles of wire; or to the supervision at vital control points where the touch of a button can

[3] As of Aug. 1, 1944, there were 867 commercial stations in the United States, of which 655 were served every day with sustaining and commercial programs. A review of engineering requirements for program transmission to meet the needs of radio broadcasters for nationwide wire networks was presented at the A.I.E.E. Winter Convention in Jan., 1941, by Messrs. F. A. Cowan and I. E. Latimer of the A. T. & T. Company and Mr. R. G. McCurdy of the Bell Telephone Laboratories. See *Electrical Engineering* (Transactions Section) and *Bell System Technical Journal* for Apr., 1941.

arrange new station groups to conform with ever changing network schedules. Transmission quality and operating efficiency are modern service requisites, and to provide them to broadcasters is a normal business obligation. The reference is rather to unusual demands upon organizational efficiency, as when, for example, there is a sudden decision by the President to speak to the nation.

At times there are broadcasts which, to the initiated, are striking demonstrations of Long Lines' service responsibility and operating efficiency. Both were splendidly illustrated on "D" day, June 6, 1944, when at 7:32 A.M. in Britain an army colonel began to read an historic announcement:

> Under the command of General Eisenhower, Allied naval forces, supported by strong air forces, began landing Allied armies this morning on the Northern Coast of France.

Transatlantic telephone channels, "according to plan," brought this historic message, and the stream of news that followed, across the ocean to broadcasting networks, press associations, and government agencies. Telephone wires carried to some 640 American broadcasting stations the tidings that all America awaited. Long Lines on D Day emphatically gave proof of the "foresight, care and skill" which had so impressed General Pershing on Defense Test Day, two decades earlier.[4]

Gratification and Doubts

During the early months of the network operation the Broadcasting Department was naturally spurred on by the knowledge of successful accomplishment. Its income was at last greater than its expense, and its prospect was one of continuing financial success. The operating profit for 1925 was estimated at $150,000, a gratifying figure indeed when contrasted with the operating loss of more than $100,000 for each of the two preceding years.

And there was the special satisfaction of having proved the economic soundness of the network idea. The outlet stations were receiving, from their broadcasting of sponsored network programs,

[4] See page 252.

revenues which were a substantial aid in meeting their operating costs. Their audiences were being regaled with a radio fare of a quality and variety that only the network plan could make possible. The network advertisers were receiving, from their investment in good will, increased sales and prestige as well as dealer interest and coöperation. Many of these advertisers, in fact, were inquiring when further network expansion would include stations in the Far West, so that a truly national audience might be obtained for sponsored entertainment and commercial messages.

All concerned were thus benefited, and in this fact lay the economic soundness of the network project. But the project's success had to be based on the value of network service to the public, and the evidence of this value was a stream of intensely personal, naïve, excited, and uninhibited reports of pleasure received from the broadcasts.

Letters deluged WEAF, and its network advertisers, to tell of happiness brought by network programs to old and young, to the sick and blind, to remote villages and snowbound farms. A large collection of these messages remains in the files, and it is an illuminating experience to read them today, when all America tunes to favored wave lengths as a matter of course—to mark the gratitude expressed then for the miracle of radio itself, and for the uplift given to workaday lives by those who spoke or sang or played before WEAF's microphones. They range from the testimonials of the cultured to the equally genuine praise of the unlettered—from the scrawled thanks of a boy for harmonica music to the formally phrased acknowledgments of societies and other listener groups. In their personal tributes to artists, their appreciation of orchestras, their thanks for news or humor or the comforts of religion, they reveal how thrilling an experience it was, less than twenty years ago, to own a receiving set.

For the present record the following letter, which bore 215 signatures, is a useful example of this enthusiasm for network programs because it contains a direct reference both to a local station outlet and to a commercial broadcaster. It thus is real evidence of how network broadcasting was operating for the benefit of advertisers, station owners, and public alike:

Radio Station WEAF,
195 Broadway,
New York, N. Y.

Philadelphia, March 30, 1925

Gentlemen:

The undersigned, employees of the Office of Superintendent Car Service, Pennsylvania Railroad System, Philadelphia, desire to express their appreciation of the wonderful manner in which they are being entertained on certain nights each week by the broadcasting from Station WEAF through WFI.

While all of the music, vocal and instrumental, is being sent in a highly efficient and pleasing way, we particularly wish to commend the broadcasting of the singing of old opera numbers by the National Carbon Company artists on Tuesday night. The comfort and ease with which we received the music of these opera numbers was made possible only in the expert handling of your instrument, and we want to express our gratitude for your efforts in furnishing us such wonderful entertainment and hope that you will be so situated that this delightful evening's entertainment may be repeated.

We feel that you are particularly fortunate in securing the services of such able announcers who are assisting so materially in the broadcasting from your station, and their contributions to the entertainments are very excellent indeed.

This letter is therefore written in the hope that it will encourage you in your work of making it possible, not only to the undersigned, but to the country at large, to receive the best of music in the comfort of our own homes.

This particular communication well reflects the psychology of the period, so gratifying to the Broadcasting Department because of tributes to WEAF programs, but so disturbing to American Company officials because of the expressed expectation that the company would ultimately provide these programs "to the country at large."

A quick glance at the situation will explain this seeming paradox. The Broadcasting Department was, of course, perfectly organized to undertake the commercial development of a national service. It had discovered and established the pattern for such a service, it thoroughly understood the service possibilities which further Long Lines construction would afford, and its experience with an experimental network was a complete guarantee that it could operate a larger one with conspicuous financial success. It was an extremely competent organization, and some of its members would have welcomed an opportunity to undertake the larger responsibility.

Mr. Gifford, who had become President of the American Company in January, 1925, and his official staff appreciated this under-

President Walter S. Gifford of the American Telephone and Telegraph Company opens regular two-way telephone service between America and England, January 7, 1927. Photo by Rosenfeld.

THE WHITE HOUSE
WASHINGTON

March 11, 1925.

My dear Mr. Pillsbury:

This group of photographs of Inauguration scenes, which you have been good enough to send to me, is, of course, one of the products of present-day advancement in science and the mechanic arts that are so numerous and continuous that we hardly have time to realize them as they come to our attention.

A few months ago, the idea of a photograph being transmitted by electricity and produced in such perfection would have been ridiculed by most people. A few years ago, the notion of bringing them back from the Pacific to the Atlantic Coast by air-mail would have been equally preposterous. It would be hard to find a finer illustration of the wonders which in this age of marvels are happening every day.

I shall preserve these pictures as a memento of peculiar historic and scientific value, and in thanking you for your thoughtfulness in sending them to me, I wish to add appreciation of the wonderful service which was rendered in the nation-wide distribution of the Inaugural Address.

Very truly yours,

Calvin Coolidge

Mr. H. D. Pillsbury, President,
The Pacific Telephone and Telegraph Company,
San Francisco, California.

A letter from President Coolidge, March 11, 1925, acknowledging photographs of inauguration scenes, which had been transmitted to San Francisco over long-distance wires.

standable enthusiasm for a successful and profitable activity. They were concerned, nevertheless, over an obvious fact of great importance: that the provision of entertainment was changing the character of the telephone institution in the minds of telephone users, investors, and employees. In this fact they had a basis for believing that continued network expansion and operation under the company's auspices would adversely affect the company's progress and accomplishment in the sphere where its responsibility was paramount.

Incompatibility had, in fact, become evident at the very start of the broadcasting experiment, which had been undertaken with the typical telephone motive of ascertaining the utility of facilities, but had at once involved the company in the rather incongruous activity of providing programs as well as facilities. The experiment had been instituted, however, with the resolve, as has been shown here, to "do it right," and so had been carried on with thoroughness, despite inevitable misunderstandings of motive and purpose. Yet the effort was a diversion from the company's primary function of developing the telephone art and assisting Bell System operating companies in extending and improving their telephone service. Besides being a foreign activity and a distracting one, it contained within itself the power of generating frictions which impaired the relationships essential for the full attainment of System plans for service and growth. The risk of offense was always present, not only offense to broadcasters because of station regulations established to protect listeners from inaccuracies or lapses from studio standards, but also offense to the listeners themselves because of their individual interests, tastes, and opinions. As a studio executive once said, when explaining a station rule to a broadcaster, "The top floor is always thinking of public relations."

Despite the enthusiasm for broadcasting on the fourth floor, then, the official view at telephone headquarters was that the company required all its energies, and the understanding coöperation of the public as well, to fulfill its primary obligation as custodian of telephone progress; that, in the public interest, the company's further responsibility toward broadcasting was not the business of providing programs but related only to the provision and operation of the circuits whereby programs could be telephoned to the various sections of the country. Indeed the System's attitude with respect to broadcasting can be expressed in two phrases: as an experiment, broadcasting had been necessary; as a business, it was almost certain to be a liability.

This was the feeling, broadly speaking, in the executive offices at 195 Broadway, when the American Company, and the companies comprising the "radio group," were suddenly confronted with a new situation involving the cross-licensing agreement of 1920, which will be outlined in later pages of this account.

CHAPTER XVIII

ANOTHER DEFENSE TEST DAY

Success Repeated

WHILE the Broadcasting Department continued its enthusiastic efforts to interest advertisers and broadcasting stations in the network proposition, the War Department in Washington was planning for another Defense Test Day and on June 6, 1925, the Acting Secretary of War wrote to President Gifford to suggest the American Company's coöperation. His letter belongs in this record because of his complimentary reference to the ceremonies of the previous year:

My dear Mr. Gifford:

The War Department is well aware of the fact that the radio broadcasting program on Defense Test Day last year was an outstanding feature of the day, and carried a message concerning preparedness to millions of the people of the country. The generosity of your company on that occasion, as well as on past occasions of national emergency, is deeply appreciated by the War Department.

I would like to invite your opinion as to the practicability of similar broadcasting on Defense Test Day this year, July the fourth.

It is the hope of the Department that in any national broadcasting this year a message can be given to the people of the country from one of our great industrial corporations.

Realizing the degree to which the American Telephone and Telegraph Company and its Associated Companies reach the people of this country in every section, and the fact that you were the Director of the Council of National Defense during the war, the Department would be greatly pleased if you would consent to make a short address from New York in connection with the broadcasting program of Defense Test Day, should such be deemed feasible.[1]

[1] Besides serving as Director of the Council of National Defense, 1916-1918, Mr. Gifford was also Supervising Director of the Committee of Industrial Preparedness of the Naval Con-

Our plans contemplate that the Vice President of the United States, the Secretary of War, the Chief of Staff of the Army and General Pershing will also speak, the former from Chicago, and the latter three from Washington. These plans, so far as the Vice President is concerned, are tentative and dependent on the Vice President's plans.

Yours very truly,
Dwight F. Davis
Acting Secretary of War.

The company, of course, acceded to this request of the government and on the night of July Fourth the record-breaking number of 28 broadcasting stations were joined for the test that again demonstrated the important service which the Bell System could render in case of a national emergency. Seventy thousand miles of wire were employed to bring to these 28 stations the defense addresses from Washington, Chicago, and New York and the two-way conversations which were carried on as in the previous Defense Test programs.

As in the case of the 1924 demonstration, Chief Signal Officer Major General Saltzman was the master of ceremonies in the office of the Secretary of War in Washington. Addresses there were given by General Pershing and by the Army's Chief of Staff, Major General John L. Hines; Vice-president Dawes spoke in Chicago; the New York addresses were by Acting Secretary of War Dwight F. Davis and by President Gifford of the American Telephone and Telegraph Company. A report covering the eastern part of the country was made by General Charles P. Summerall, Commander of the Second Corps Area at New York and by Major General Harry C. Hale, Commander of the Sixth Corps Area at Chicago on the mobilization for Defense Day tests.

To the Bell System men and women in the enormous radio audience the broadcast was especially interesting because it brought to them for the first time the voice of Mr. Gifford as their President. His Defense Day address, so significant in its reference to "fighting industries," was as follows:[2]

sulting Board in 1916, and Secretary of the American Section of the Inter-Allied Munitions Council in Paris from July to Sept., 1918.

[2] See also Mr. Gifford's address, "The American Communications Companies and National Preparedness," before the Army Industrial College, Dec. 10, 1936. A striking example of

High officials of the Government have addressed you. Distinguished soldiers have spoken to you. The task assigned me as a private citizen is to say something to you about the relation of industry to national defense.

Clearly there is one thing we know about modern war. We know that it is not a matter of armies and navies alone; it is even more a matter of the organization and utilization of the Nation's entire population and resources. War today demands not fighting men only but also fighting industries. Today in war the whole nation fights. In any national emergency which may confront this country its industrial organizations and resources must be the backbone of its defense. For every man at the front there must be four or five men at home engaged in producing food and raw materials and in collecting, manufacturing, and distributing them.

Every citizen in this country has back of him the power of all the people. From them, through their Government, he receives protection. In return every individual is under an obligation of loyalty and obedience. He owes allegiance to his Government. At all times he must contribute his due share of service if his Government is to be strong and endure. In time of peace he must obey and support the law. He must do well his private tasks, and he must perform numerous services of a public nature. He must contribute from his means toward the burdens of Government. In times of peril his contributions must be magnified, and he must be prepared even to give his life in order that the Nation may not perish.

Like individuals, business Corporations and industrial enterprises owe allegiance to the Government. They must at all times, in all places, and in all ways, obey the law. They must bear their share of the expenses of government. They must contribute to the general welfare in the discharge of the functions for which they were created. In short, they must be good citizens; and, like individuals, industry must not only do its part in time of peace but also when the life of the Nation is threatened and war comes, it must strain its energies for the common protection.

For the national defense it is essential that we should educate and prepare not only individuals but also our business organizations. They, too, require preliminary education and training. Every firm, every corporation, every factory, every farm, must realize that it has duties in respect to the national defense and should know what they are and what they involve. It will not do to wait until war begins. The result and cost are too great. If the matter is de-

communications preparedness is referred to in the American Company's *Annual Report for the Year 1942:* "Included in the 1942 projects was the completion of the transcontinental cable—a great engineering and construction feat, marking a milestone in telephone history. It was decided to go ahead with this cable over three years ago in anticipation of the possibility of war with Japan. It required the installation of the final long link of cable half way across the continent from Omaha, Nebraska, to Sacramento, California. The cable for this entire distance was laid underground in order to provide maximum protection from the elements, from possible enemy action and from other hazards."

ferred, confusion reigns, life is sacrificed and wealth is squandered. Our whole history carries this lesson. Without such preparation and without such support from individuals and business, no commanding general, however great may be his genius, and no body of men, however brave and well disciplined, can be confident of winning the ultimate victory.

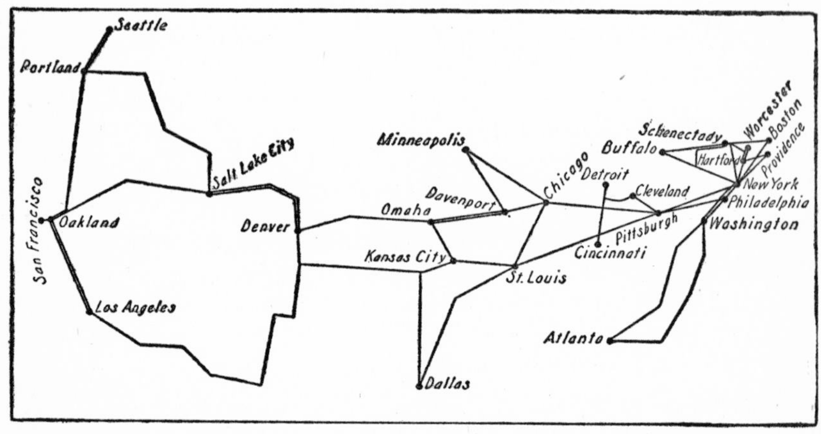

CHART V

Bell System Wire Circuits Connected Radio Stations from Coast to Coast in the National Defense Test Day Program, July 4, 1925

Just as citizens have duties to their governments, so likewise, the government has responsibilities toward its citizens; and this responsibility in respect to the national defense involves leadership. In this field the government must plan and must lead. That our Government is now alive to this high responsibility is made manifest from the very fact that we have this Defense Day.

On this day the Nation stops to consider the problem of safety and to emphasize its seriousness. This day it turns its thought to the need and method of mobilizing man power and material resources. This is not incitement to war. It is not an invitation to war. It is an act of safe citizenship. We intend to lead the sort of national life we have fashioned and we shall not invite interference by weakness. In taking precautions we are merely following the dictates of wisdom and prudence. Properly understood, this day and this preparation are merely insurance against national disaster.

The well-being and opportunity here to enjoy life and the pursuit of happiness are greater than can be found elsewhere in the world. They are beyond the promise held out in any other nation in the world. To safeguard them is our only desire and our solemn duty. We abhor war. We resent its menace. We desire peace. We shall not be the aggressors against any nation. We earnestly hope that some way may be found to prevent the recurrence of war with all its tragedies. But we can not exist in blind confidence. We are not for peace at any price. There is a price too great to pay for peace. We cannot pay the price of self-respect and the direction of our own lives. We pray that war may not come, but if it should come we must be prepared to meet it. Unpreparedness is not protection against war but may be an invitation to war. While steadily planning and striving for peace, let us see that our national household is in order and that we are ready to strike quickly and surely if need be for national freedom and integrity.

Mr. Gifford's personal files, to which this recorder has had access, contain many letters, received after the July Fourth ceremonies, that reflect the excitement caused only a few years ago by a broadcast involving 28 stations. Two letters of congratulation might be added to this record because of their official recognition of the technical accomplishments that contributed to the success of the test. One from Chief of Staff Hines was as follows:

In behalf of the War Department, it is a great pleasure for me to extend to you congratulations on your company's wonderful exhibition of the possibilities of signal communication staged on the night of July 4th in connection with the Defense Test.

The coordination of your long line facilities with the principal broadcasting stations in the United States, was a demonstration of the preparedness to meet a national emergency of the American Telephone and Telegraph Company and its associated companies.

A very important feature of your effort, to the military mind, was the transmitting from San Francisco to New York by wire of a photograph taken in the West, reproduced in the East, and sent by rail to Washington in about twelve hours. It is stirring to realize the advances you have made in the relaying of military information by signal communication, and it is desired that you know that the achievements of your company and yourself as well as the patriotic impulse back of your cooperation with War Department endeavors, are appreciated.

And from General Summerall came this:

I am just in receipt of a letter from an acquaintance of mine of Honolulu who happened to be in San Francisco on the night of July 4th. The following are paragraphs from his letter:

"Last Saturday evening, July 4th, at between 7:00 and 7:30 o'clock here in San Francisco, I had the extreme satisfaction and pleasure of hearing you deliver your report from New York to General Hines in Washington, D. C., over the radio. I felt all the time you were talking that you were right alongside of me. We could hear every word that you said as distinctly as if you were with us, and I felt all the time that I wanted to talk to you. It was a real treat to hear your voice again and to hear your report. General Hines' voice was as clear as could be, as were also those of the Generals from Chicago and Omaha who made reports.

"I had never really enjoyed the radio until that evening; heretofore it has been so jumbled and muddled that I did not get much pleasure out of it, but listening to you on the Fourth of July evening was a real satisfaction and splendid demonstration of what can be done over the radio."

No doubt your organization received many thousands of such communications but I thought this one particularly interesting because of its reflection upon the big undertaking on the evening of July 4th which your institution so successfully turned out. It must be a source of satisfaction to those of you who are contributing so much to the development of radio to know that your efforts are being appreciated.

CHAPTER XIX

THE SALE OF WEAF

AS HAS been indicated on a previous page, it was while radio listeners and broadcasters were showing marked interest in the prospect of a service "to the country at large" that there was an unexpected development with respect to the cross-licensing agreement of 1920.

Since this agreement has not been referred to beyond the early pages of this record, the reader is reminded of the following circumstances so that he can bring the matter into focus:

(1) That the agreement resulted from the Government's suggestion, in January, 1920, that the public interest required the removal of legal inhibitions from postwar vacuum-tube development;

(2) That the agreement's purpose was to establish a basis for developments in the fields normally and historically occupied by the parties concerned;

(3) That when a new field of development was created, by the mounting public interest in radio entertainment, disputes arose as to rights under the agreement;

(4) That because the interpretations of the agreement by the American Company and the Radio Corporation (the selling agent for radio receivers and other apparatus manufactured by the General Electric and Westinghouse Companies) were irreconcilable, Mr. Gifford of the American Company suggested, in September, 1923, a disinterested arbitration to settle the matter.

For the purposes of this review it is not necessary to report the details of the arbitration hearings which began in May, 1924, at the American Telephone and Telegraph Company's offices. It might be remarked, however, that the conflicting interpretations of the agreement involved scientific distinctions which were perhaps too technical for the lay understanding of the referee upon whom both disputants had agreed. A tentative draft of his report was issued in November, 1924. Before the final report was ready, however, the explosion of a legal bombshell dissipated any possibility that the final decision could be accepted as a basis for a *modus operandi.*

The bombshell was in the form of an opinion rendered by one of America's most distinguished legalists that, if the referee's construction was correct, the 1920 agreement itself contained provisions which might be regarded as contrary to law. The American Company and the Radio Corporation therefore resumed the negotiations for which the arbitration had been proposed as a substitute.

New Factors in the Negotiations

These negotiations lasted for many months and related to what had seemed so easily determined in 1920, namely, the exclusive or non-exclusive rights to tube developments that would establish natural and legal fields for institutional operations.

But far more was involved than in 1920, for scientific progress had brought visions of new fields in which the tube function was basic. Tube development in the telephone laboratories was inseparable from the development of communications facilities. Whatever pertained to sound—its creation, amplification, transmission, and reproduction—was of course constantly explored by telephone scientists. Their research accomplishments therefore, which were of such fundamental importance in the improvement of telephone facilities, naturally contributed to progress in many other fields, such as the electrical recording of speech, the synchronizing of sight and sound, and television.[1]

Four years of this telephone research had followed the signing of the 1920 agreement, and there was consequently an entirely new business horizon with respect to tube applications when Vice-president Bloom, of the American Company, and Mr. David Sarnoff,

[1] The first public demonstration by wire and wireless of television as developed by the technical staff of the Bell System took place on Apr. 7, 1927, and television in color was demonstrated at the Bell Telephone Laboratories in 1929. The laboratory developments leading to talking motion pictures are described in many articles in the *Bell System Technical Journal.*

Vice-President and General Manager of the Radio Corporation, began a new series of discussions aimed at the reconciliation of patent rights. Broadcasting developments alone had invested such rights with an extraordinary commercial significance. One reporter of the situation, perhaps having in mind the business possibilities in exploiting the popular craze over broadcasting, has characterized the long discussion between the two principals as a "battle for the control of a mighty industry."[2]

The Objective of Service Integrity

Such a phrase as the one just quoted completely misrepresents the American Company's position in seeking a workable agreement as to fields of activity in which the principals might operate without conflict. The company's primary stake in the "battle" was not the control of the new broadcasting industry, but rather the Bell System's freedom of action in the sphere of its normal and historical commitments. The fruits of telephone research were, of course, also involved. But for President Gifford, for Patent Attorney Folk, and for Vice-president Bloom, who were the principal telephone negotiators, there was a consistent and controlling purpose throughout the give-and-take of negotiation—to protect the System's traditional area of operations from limitation and to protect its own inventions in its own fields.

To this end it was essential to guard against restrictions in the use of whatever apparatus and equipment might be necessary in order to develop and apply telephony, both wire and wireless, as a public communications service. Of fundamental importance, for example, was the freedom to develop and manufacture tubes as amplifying equipment for telephone lines;[3] to continue the development of two-way overseas and ship-to-shore telephony; and to remain un-

[2] The sales of the Radio Corporation, as the marketing agency for the radio products manufactured by the General Electric and Westinghouse Companies, were already at the rate of $50,000,000 a year, an astonishing contrast with the sales totals of less than $23,000,000 in 1923, less than $12,000,000 in 1922 and only about $1,500,000 in 1921. And there were still only 4,000,000 receiving sets in the United States, of which approximately 2,400,000 were manufactured tube sets, the balance comprising home-made tube sets and crystal sets in almost equal proportion.

[3] A count made in Nov., 1944, showed about 1,500,000 vacuum tubes of many types continually in operation in the Bell System, with an annual requirement of about 250,000 for replacements.

hampered with respect to the use of one-way radio transmission for service purposes and with respect to the utilization of carrier current principles. Many other service considerations might be mentioned to suggest how tube rights affected telephonic progress—to suggest, too, the responsibilities carried by the telephone negotiators, who had to protect and ensure the telephone service of the future. Their success in accomplishing this, under such challenging circumstances, was the result of great patience, foresight, and negotiating skill.

As for the right to make, use, and sell radio receiving sets, which was a main point of controversy because the arbitrator was proposing to grant it to the Radio Group exclusively, the company's position was laid down by President Gifford early in the discussions and consistently held to throughout. He wrote to General Electric's President:

> A fundamental difficulty has been with reference to radio broadcast receiving sets. I feel it necessary that we should make and sell a sufficient number to keep us in full touch with all phases of the art. . . . No suggestion that I know of has been made by the Radio Corporation to meet this necessity. . . . The proposal that we make receiving sets of types to be specified by the Radio Corporation, to be sold solely to it, would not meet our basic purpose which is to afford our engineers experience in the development of radio art and science. *The sole benefit to us would be of a financial nature which . . . is not a controlling consideration.*[4]

This is an appropriate communication to include in this record for two reasons: first, it shows how the continuing discussions were marked by proposals and counter-proposals; and second, it supports the outline above of the company's point of view in the so-called "battle for the control of a mighty industry." The point of view is, of course, one that will be best understood by those who are members of the telephone organization. For them the fact need not be stressed that the controlling consideration of a service-minded management would naturally be its ability to function efficiently, and with homogeneous instrumentalities, in the field where the public expected continuous and progressive performance.

[4] Italicized by the present writer. The right to sell in moderate quantities receiving sets involving the patented inventions of the other parties, which the company secured under the agreement that was finally reached, was never largely exercised.

The gradual approach to an agreement regarding tube rights will not be described here at length, since this record deals with a more specific matter—the evolution of the American Company's broadcasting experiment. To carry the account into its final pages, therefore, only the negotiations relating to WEAF and its network need be referred to.

WEAF's Place in Negotiations

These negotiations developed from the arbitrator's announcement that, according to his interpretation of the 1920 agreement, the American Company did *not* have an exclusive right to broadcast for hire—a right which had seemed secured by the 1920 differentiation between "public service" uses and other uses of radio telephone equipment and which had been one of the main impulsions of the "toll broadcasting" venture.

It is not necessary to search the American Company's files in order to recall the ensuing developments, since many pertinent documents are quoted in *Big Business and Radio,* published in 1939.[5] Its author was evidently given free access to the Radio Group's intercompany and interdepartmental correspondence. Therefrom he reports the steps in arriving at what is characterized as "a document that will no doubt figure in radio annals as the most important contract concerning the broadcasting industry that was ever consummated"—a document providing, as this historian further states, for "the purchase of the physical assets and the goodwill of the most efficient broadcasting organization in the world." It appears from this liberally documented volume that the Group's position regarding activities in the broadcasting field, as a factor in the negotiations that were resumed in 1925, was determined by several considerations. One was the high cost of operating the individual Group stations. There is a reference to this matter in a published contemporary report:[6]

> By 1924, the economic situation had become acute. The shoe was beginning to pinch. Obviously, something had to be done. . . .

[5] Issued with the imprint of "The American Historical Company, Inc."

[6] *This Thing Called Broadcasting,* by Alfred N. Goldsmith and Austin C. Lescarboura (N. Y., 1930), p. 148.

WJZ was operating on a budget of over $100,000 per year, without visible or tangible earnings of any kind. Meanwhile, the Westinghouse Company, operating a group of broadcasting stations, was wondering seriously whether there was a way out. Once amply repaid by publicity for its organization, the competition of many other broadcasting stations had reduced the publicity value to the point where it was considered hardly worth the cost.

Such an outlook undoubtedly was a disturbing one when contrasted with the proof, from the WEAF experiment, that a network could be operated profitably and that network programs constituted the most potent stimulus to the sale of receiving sets.

Another consideration also seems to have been before Group councils when weighing the arbitrator's view that "toll" broadcasting was not the American Company's exclusive right. This was the recognition that the "superpower" idea for program transmission, so vehemently argued in 1924, was impractical. "The fact remains," wrote the Group's chief negotiator to one of his colleagues in 1925, "that at this date there does not exist a fully developed and effective substitute for wires to connect local stations. This, together with the possession by the telephone company of a national network of wires, has naturally given WEAF and its associate stations a great advantage in the air over the Radio Corporation and its Associated Companies." [7]

Because of such considerations it appears from the record that a situation developed which had a direct bearing on the course of the negotiations that were under way. One side in the discussion became increasingly interested in expanding its operations in the broadcasting field. The other side in the discussion, having experimentally developed network broadcasting with conspicuous technical and financial success, already considered further operations as alien to its traditional function of developing, maintaining, and operating facilities for the use of others. Thus, as the conditions of the period can be reconstructed from the documents at hand, there

[7] The "advantage" referred to in this communication resulted from the fact that Group stations normally used telegraph circuits for program pickups, and such circuits were of course inferior to telephone circuits for the purpose, having been engineered for dot-dash communication and not for the transmission of speech and music for satisfactory loud-speaker reproduction. The American Company frequently provided Group stations with high-grade telephone circuits, however, so that they might broadcast events of great national importance to their audiences.

developed what was more or less a "demand-and-supply" situation with respect to WEAF's network.

Summary of the Broadcasting Situation

At this point in the record there should be a quick survey of broadcasting conditions as they existed near the close of the year 1925.

The stations operated by the companies comprising the Radio Group were 14 in number, with two others of the "portable" classification, and were located as follows:

Call Letters	*Location*	*Owner*
KGO	Oakland, Calif.	General Electric Company
KOA	Denver, Colo.	" " "
WRC	Washington, D. C.	Radio Corp. of America
KYW	Chicago, Ill.	Westinghouse Elec. & Mfg. Co.
WBZA	Boston, Mass.	" " " "
WBZ	Springfield, Mass.	" " " "
KFKX	Hastings, Neb.	" " " "
WJY	New York, N. Y.	Radio Corp. of America
WJZ	" " "	" " "
WGY	Schenectady, N. Y.	General Electric Co.
KDPM	Cleveland, Ohio	Westinghouse Elec. & Mfg. Co.
KDKA	E. Pittsburgh, Pa.	" " " "
WEBL	Portable Station	Radio Corp. of America
WEBM	" "	" " "

Broadcasting in general had developed along the lines previously described here, the American Company's experimental policy having radically changed the former uncertain outlook.

Of the 1,429 broadcasting licenses issued by the Government since January, 1922, only 562 were classified as "active" in the current bulletin issued by the Department of Commerce. Seven per cent of the licensed stations had never been placed in operation, and over 40 per cent disappeared from government lists, largely for financial reasons, within eighteen months after licenses had been issued. About 65 per cent of the active stations were licensed under the American Company's patents, and nearly 100 stations were broadcasting for hire, the most common rates (exclusive of WEAF and network stations) being $50 and $100 per hour. It is of interest to note from the records that the American Company had granted licenses under its patents to 288 stations which had formerly infringed them—more than twice as many stations as had been manufactured and sold by the Western Electric Company under the same patents.[8]

Over 300 stations, therefore, had the legal right to charge for time on the air, but many of them restricted their operations because of expense and program difficulties. A backward look at such conditions provides a reminder of what it meant to radio listeners for stations, instead of being dependent upon local programs and local revenues for their support, to be supported by the programs and revenues available from the development of the principle of network operation. This principle had been completely demonstrated as sound and constructive by the end of 1925, when WEAF's network had become a prominent factor in the negotiations under way. Seventeen stations, in whose areas were more than 60 per cent of the receiving sets in the United States, were linked for the broadcasting of WEAF's sponsored and sustaining programs.

The operation was a substantial one, for gross annual revenues were in the neighborhood of $750,000. The fourth floor at telephone headquarters was a hive of industry, with a personnel of 94 functioning at many correlated tasks under the leadership of Mr. George McClelland as Manager of Broadcasting. With Mr. Phillips Carlin as Studio Director there were six announcers introducing WEAF's "key station" varied and distinctive programs, and four "hostess" assistants including the well-remembered station pianists, Miss Winifred Barr and Miss Katherine Stewart. Sales Manager George Podeyn had six assistants; Publicity Manager Johnstone needed two for his service to the press; Mr. Mark Woods, responsible for accounts and office routine, headed a force of ten; Miss Adelaide Piana, who supervised WEAF's correspondence clerks, required six assistants for the interesting and important task of analyzing the letters arriving by the thousands every day.

These active operations reflected the fact that WEAF was on the air approximately 245 hours each month, or an average of slightly

[8] At the end of 1925, 113 Western Electric stations had been installed and were in operation, 16 being of 5,000-watts antenna input, 26 of 1,000 watts, 71 of 500 watts, 7 of 100 watts, and 11 of 50 watts.

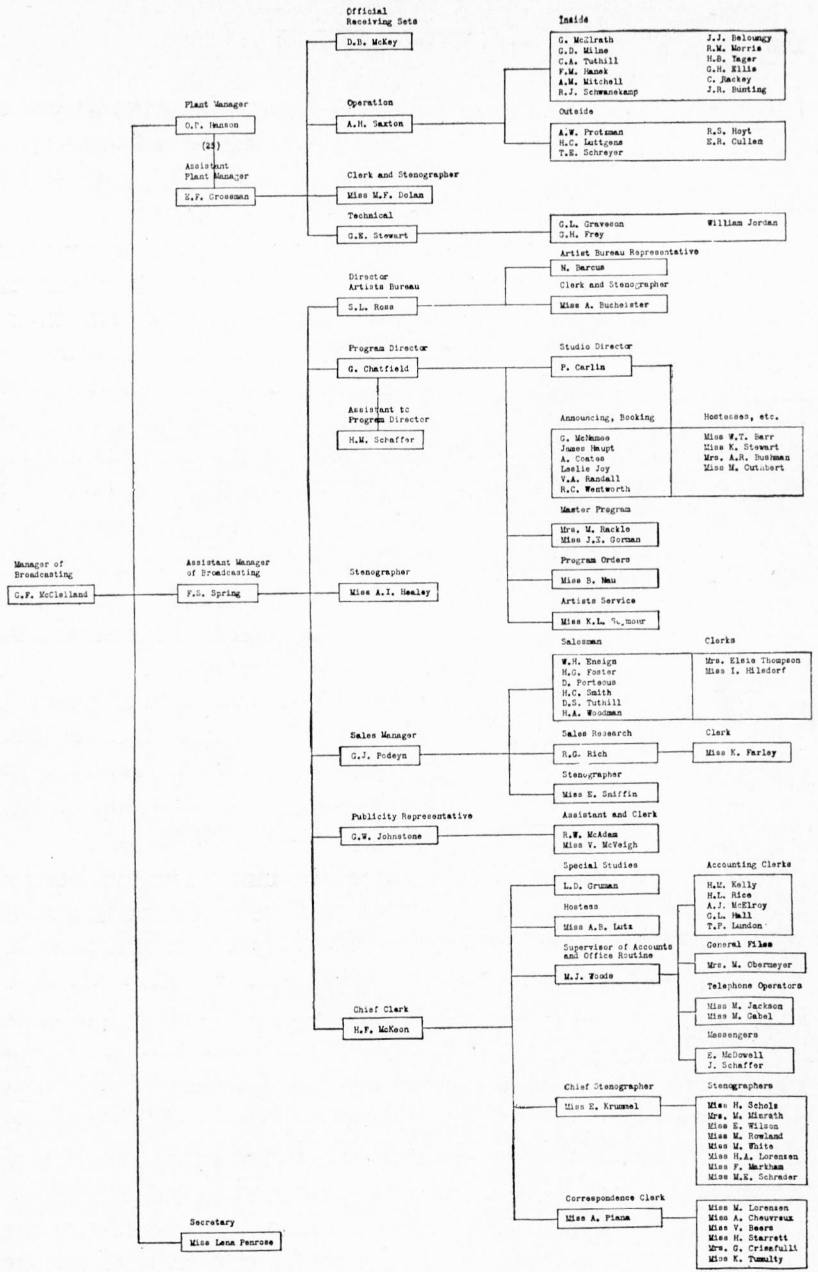

CHART VI

WEAF's Operating Organization in January, 1926

A meeting in the office of Sales Manager Podeyn, WEAF, 1926. Left to right, seated: G. J. Podeyn, H. C. Smith, H. A. Woodman, D. S. Tuthill; standing: R. L. Clark, W. H. Ensign, R. G. Rich, D. Porteous. Photo by Herbert Photos, Inc.

more than eight hours each day. During one month's time more than 450 features, consisting of either individuals or groups, appeared before the station's microphone. Of this average some 300 were classed as "regulars," that is, program features heard at a definite time each week, with the others classed as "occasional." Of the regular features there were 85 of the sponsored "good will publicity" type, and 210 or more of the type known as sustaining programs. In a review of artist personnel at the end of the year it was found that an average total of 1,015 artists entertained WEAF's invisible audience from "195" in one month's time. Another review at the time covered technical operations between January 1 and November 30. During these 11 months, when the station was on the air almost 2,800 hours, delays due to equipment trouble aggregated only 5 hours and time lost between program presentations totaled only 12 hours. Other delays totaling 17 hours were occasioned by SOS calls from vessels in distress.

In the meantime a new activity had come to the fourth floor. As the network programs increased in popularity, there was a constantly expressed desire of clubs, societies, and musical organizations to engage for local appearances the artists who were becoming so well and favorably known through their network broadcasts. The demand for the services of these artists was the result of radio's phenomenal power to popularize new personalities as well as to increase the fame of established figures in the entertainment world.

The demand was one that the public seemed to expect WEAF to meet, and to satisfy it the Broadcasting Department established what was the first formally organized artist's bureau in radio. WEAF's program director, Mr. Samuel Ross, was of course the natural choice for its directorship because of the special qualities and discriminating judgment in dealing with musicians and other artists which he had demonstrated from the beginning of the WEAF experiment. Under Mr. Ross's guidance the Artist's Bureau performed a valuable service both to the public and to the entertainers themselves. Its functioning also helped to keep WEAF's talent reservoir full, since new artists recognized that their selection by Mr. Ross for WEAF appearances would have an important influence on their future careers.

And so the American Company found itself more or less forced into another activity connected with public entertainment, that of managing artists and of securing engagements for them. It was an unavoidable part of the effort necessary to maintain the broadcasting service providing distinctive radio programs upon which seventeen stations and millions of listeners were depending, but it further accented how far afield the broadcasting commitment was leading the Bell System.

From the general background that has just been presented it can be seen why the WEAF network project should occupy an important place on the negotiations agenda.

Negotiations Concluded

The concluding steps in the negotiations involving WEAF can be quickly summarized. In November, 1925, the discussions had reached the point where details of a contract between some Group consolidation and Long Lines relating to the use of a basic network were being considered. By December the Radio Group was studying and analyzing the network's cost and revenue data. A few weeks later an exploratory committee of Group members had proposed a consolidation of the broadcasting activities of both parties under some such name as the American Broadcasting Company. By the spring of 1926 the value of WEAF's physical assets and the "going" value of the network operation were being argued as a basis of sale.

With the general negotiations thus seemingly approaching a climax, the American Company announced on May 11, 1926:

> The radio broadcasting activities heretofore carried on by the radio broadcasting department of the American Telephone and Telegraph Company, under the general designation of WEAF, will be incorporated under the name Broadcasting Company of America.[9] This step has been made desirable by the growth in these activities and by the fact that the problems involved are of a special nature. These problems differ from those of regular telephone operation and can therefore be more effectively handled by a separate organization. This Corporation, owned entirely by the American Telephone and Telegraph

[9] The officers of the Broadcasting Company of America were: President, Mr. J. C. Lynch; Vice-president and General Manager, Mr. W. E. Harkness; Manager of Broadcasting, Mr. G. F. McClelland; Secretary and Treasurer, Mr. F. S. Spring; Auditor, Mr. H. F. McKeon.

Company, will continue the same general policies as those obtaining heretofore in conducting these activities.

Thus, the American Company prepared itself to carry on the network enterprise under another name in case it should become isolated from any final agreement. But this did not happen. On July 7, the various documents were signed that brought the long controversy over tube rights to an end and changed the history of broadcasting in America. Among them was one that gave the Radio Corporation an option to purchase WEAF, its equipment, contracts, good will, et cetera, for the sum of one million dollars. Another was a service contract for making available to Group stations the Bell System's wire network.[10]

Announcing the Sale of WEAF

The American Company's formal announcement of the sale was issued on July 21, together with an assurance to WEAF's loyal staff that the station and the network would continue operations with no change in plan or personnel. The public announcement stated:

Arrangements have been completed for the sale of Broadcasting Station WEAF to the Radio Corporation of America. The actual transfer will take place before the end of the year.

It has always been the purpose of the A. T. and T. Co. not only to improve the known means of telephone service but to seek any new means which would further facilitate electrical communication. This company, therefore, undertook to develop radio broadcasting in order to discover how it could be made most useful in our business.

That the Bell System might be enabled to utilize any new means of communication, the A. T. and T. Co. established a broadcasting station in New York for the purpose of continuing the physical experiments in this art and also to experiment in its commercial possibilities. This station, WEAF, was equipped with the best available apparatus known to the art. It was organized to develop the best possible programs and make a careful analysis and study of the reactions on the part of the public to these programs. It was also designed to determine the place of a commercial station, where broadcasting could be done for hire, in the business and social conditions of the day.

[10] WCAP, the Bell System station in Washington, D. C., which had been dividing time on the 469-meter wave length with RCA's Washington Station WRC, discontinued operations on August 1, the latter station taking over the former's program features and joining the WEAF network.

That experimental station has been very successful in transmitting music and entertainment which would be acceptable to the listeners and it has also been successful in furnishing a medium through which business men could make friends for their businesses by assisting in the entertainment of the public.

The further the experiment was carried the more evident it became that while the technical principle was similar to that of a telephone system, the objective of a broadcasting station was quite different from that of a telephone system. Consequently, it has seemed to us after several years of experimentation, that the broadcasting station which we built up might be more suitably operated by other interests.

If WEAF has helped to point the way to that future it has served a useful purpose. In the hands of the Radio Corporation of America with a concurrent experience in radio broadcasting, the future of the station WEAF should be assured.

It is generally recognized that there is a great future for radio broadcasting and that it has an important and permanent place in our national life.

This is evidenced, if evidence were needed, by the fact that there are 536 broadcasting stations now in operation and that there are some 600 applications for new stations.

And on the evening of July 22, radio listeners heard the following broadcast from WEAF's studios:

The daily press of today is carrying a statement regarding arrangements that have been made for the sale of Broadcasting Station WEAF to the Radio Corporation of America. We want to assure you that WEAF will continue to be operated under its present plan and manned by its present personnel. The same programs will continue to come to you, the voices of the same announcers will continue to introduce these features. The programs will be built and presented by the same people. In short, WEAF remains WEAF with an added interest and endeavor to supply you with those programs which you have received so favorably in the past.

And so pioneer network stations had a new program supplier; Long Lines had a new "customer;" the Broadcasting Department that had made radio history had a new employer.

Of all the newspaper writers who commented on the news of WEAF's transfer, one of the most understanding was the author of the following editorial reference, in the New York *Herald Tribune* of July 23,[11] to the station's past and future:

[11] July 23, 1926, p. 12.

THE RADIO MERGER

The decision of the American Telephone and Telegraph Company to turn its famous broadcasting station, WEAF, over to the Radio Corporation of America, sponsor of the equally successful and popular WJZ, constitutes a logical move on the part of the former company when viewed in the light of its well established policy. The station has never been anything but an experiment on the part of the telephone company. Mr. H. B. Thayer, former president and now chairman of the board of the company, made this clear more than two years ago when he issued an inclusive statement of the latter's position in the radio field. "The company's prime purpose," said Mr. Thayer, "has been such development of the radio art as would be useful in relation to the telephone service. Actuated by this prime purpose, we established an experimental broadcasting station in New York in order to be better able to study not only radio transmission problems but also public taste in broadcasting entertainment and to furnish advice to our associated companies with respect thereto."

The great single purpose of the American Telephone and Telegraph Company is that of providing adequate telephonic communication throughout this country, a task so enormous that it required the addition of approximately $1,000,000 a day to the company's huge and far-flung plant. Not only are unremitting efforts made to meet the demands of further growth of this business, but also to progress in the art of telephony.

From the research department of the company have come such noteworthy developments as transcontinental telephony, the extension of telephone service to great distances in storm-proof cable, the multitude of intricate mechanisms which have made possible the interconnection of millions of telephones and the scientific work which has resulted in the beginnings of transoceanic radio telephony. It was in pursuing the company's studies in the adaptation of the regular telephone plant to extended use in connection with radio broadcasting that WEAF was established. To protect the company's rights to its wave length it was found necessary to keep "on the air," and from this point the telephone company, through its research department, was drawn into the field of popular broadcasting.

The experiment has been highly successful, not only from the standpoint of the company but from that of the public, in whose esteem WEAF has won a high place. It is good news for the millions of friends and admirers of its programs that they are not only to be carried on, but carried on under such capable direction as has been demonstrated by the Radio Corporation in the case of WEAF's eminent contemporary, WJZ.

References to a few more dates will complete this record of WEAF at telephone headquarters. On September 13, announcement was made of the formation within the Radio Group of the

National Broadcasting Company, of which WEAF's Mr. George McClelland became General Manager; on October 29, the Radio Corporation formally conveyed its rights in relation to WEAF to the new organization; on November 1, a check for one million dollars changed hands and a new executive, NBC's President, Mr. M. H. Aylesworth, moved into the fourth-floor offices from which Mr. W. H. Harkness[12] had so long directed "the most efficient broadcasting organization in the world." [13]

And while WEAF's new management was planning gala "christening" ceremonies for December 15 for a "red network" broadcast through 19 stations,[14] the Long Lines engineers were spotting the Group's own stations on long-distance circuit maps. They marked the connecting routes with a blue pencil, and on January 1, 1927, the engineering records received the entry, "Service starts today on the BLUE NETWORK; WJZ key station—WBZ Springfield—WBZA Boston—temporary service to Pittsburgh and Chicago." [15]

Recapitulation

This record has shown, so its compiler hopes, how Bell System headquarters faced the condition of broadcasting's swift development from a scientific novelty by contributing everything that it could—technical experience, patent rights, financial resources, and

[12] Mr. Harkness transferred to the Long Lines organization where he was active in the development of "auxiliary services," such as the transmission of pictures by wire.

[13] WEAF remained at 195 Broadway until August, 1927, when it joined WJZ in NBC's uptown headquarters.

[14] By Sept. 1, 1926, Long Lines service was on a 16-hour basis to 3 cities on the Red Network: New York (WEAF), Washington (WCAP), and Philadelphia (WLIT or WFI). On Oct. 13, four additional cities received 16-hour service: Hartford (WTIC), Worcester (WPAG), Providence (WVAR), and Boston (WEEI). The other cities on the network when NBC took over the operating responsibility had varying hours of service: Pittsburgh (WCAE), Buffalo (WGR), Davenport (WOC), Cleveland (WTAM), Detroit (WWJ), Cincinnati (WSAI), St. Louis (KFD), Minneapolis (WCCO), Chicago (WGN and WLIB), Portland, Maine (WCSH), and Kansas City (WDAF).

[15] As a result of an order of investigation of chain broadcasting instituted by the Federal Communications Commission on March 18, 1938, the Commission on May 2, 1941, adopted a regulation prohibiting the multiple ownership of networks serving substantially the same area. This regulation was suspended for some time to make it possible for NBC to negotiate the sale of the Blue Network. On Oct. 12, 1943, the Commission approved the purchase of the Blue Network from the Radio Corporation of America by Mr. Edward J. Noble, as the chief initial step in the founding of the American Broadcasting Company.

an unwavering spirit of investigation—to assist and guide that development. A four-year test of a service idea has been traced from the establishment of a pioneer experimental station to the passing of an experimental network to other hands; the successive steps of a fundamental and successful exploration have been recounted.

The last of these steps, the organization of a network for experimental toll broadcasting through a chain of stations, was the culminating and decisive one, because it established the economic basis upon which nationwide broadcasting now rests.

Great broadcasting enterprises today operate on the principle that was first tested in the fall of 1924, when programs originating in WEAF's New York studios reached half-a-dozen stations over long-distance wires that were especially equipped to pass wide frequency bands, and were first available for program transmission only in evening off-peak hours.

Today, as was the idea of twenty years ago, these program suppliers offer to regional broadcasting outlets both sustaining and commercial programs, charging these outlets for the former and paying them for the latter. They offer broadcasters a communications service whereby sponsored entertainment and commercial messages may be broadcast over part or all of the nation at a charge based upon cost and value. They provide notable and expensive "key-station" broadcasts, as well as other sustaining features involving pickups of events of national importance, as a public service, and in competition with one another in attracting station listeners and in maintaining the structure of their services. They are the historical successors of the American Company's Broadcasting Department which set the pattern for the future by applying to broadcasting the telephone principle that the cost of communications should be borne by their originators. Because this idea encouraged the commercial presentations that could help to finance local stations, it brought support to broadcasting in general. Because it promised a national audience for advertisers seeking to promote the distribution and sale of merchandise in a nationwide market, broadcasting became a national service.

Each modern network organization now has its own history of

growth and accomplishment. It was generous of one of them, a decade and a half ago, when praise for its endeavors was flowing from everywhere, thus to acknowledge the parentage of its service:[16]

> Broadcasting, then, is the child of the telephone; in America it is certainly the child of the American Telephone & Telegraph Company. The whole structure of commercial chain broadcasting as we know it today has grown out of the pioneer work done prior to 1926. . . .

[16] "Broadcasting: A New Industry," by H. A. Bellows, Vice-president of the Columbia Broadcasting System, in the *Harvard Alumni Bulletin,* Dec. 18, 1930, p. 383.

INDEX